Gwent – its Landscape and Natural History

Gwent – its Landscape and Natural History

as reflected in the diaries

of

COLIN TITCOMBE

Published by the Author

Published by
Mr C. Titcombe, The Brockwells Farm
Caerwent, Newport, Gwent, NP6 4AJ.

ISBN 0 9532756 0 4

*Printed in Wales by
Dinefwr Press
Rawlings Road, Llandybïe
Carmarthenshire, SA18 3YD.*

To my mother

Contents

~

Introduction ... 9
Prehistoric Gwent ... 12
Fungi ... 19
Plants ... 26
Invertebrates ... 37
Fish ... 62
Amphibians and Reptiles ... 68
Birds ... 74
Mammals ... 97
Diary of the Winter 1962/1963 ... 112
Selected Notes from the Diaries ... 120
Wildlife in Gwent's Churches and Churchyards ... 132

Appendix

Glossary ... 138
List of Sites ... 140
Fish from Uskmouth Power Station (Brian Whittaker) ... 144
Churchyards having 'A Good Mix of Plants' ... 145
Churchyards with Exceptional Floral Diversity ... 146
Churchyards having Scarce/Unusual Plants ... 147
Churchyards with Yellow Meadow Ants ... 148
Map (1-4) ... 149
Colour Plates ... between pages 100 and 101
Bibliography ... 153
Acknowledgements ... 156
Species Index (by Chapter) ... 158

Photo Credits

~

The author is responsible for all of the photographs in this book with the exception of the following –

1. The Hall of Thirty in Otterhole Cave near Chepstow. (Photograph by Graham Crisp, Hades Caving Club, Bristol).
2. Columns and straws in Otterhole Cave, near Chepstow. (Photograph by Peter Collings-Wells, Flint Cottage Photography, Great Offley).
3. Hyaena Teeth and Jaw Fragments from Caerwent Quarry Cave. (Photograph supplied by Newport Museum and Art Gallery).
4. Silurian Moth. (Photograph supplied by the British Museum of Natural History, South Kensington, London).

All of these photographs were supplied free of charge, for which generosity I am most grateful.

Introduction

~

Gwent as a county is no more, but to residents of more than a few years' standing it represents a generally accepted area, though not, perhaps, precisely defined.

The area considered here as Gwent, covers what was the old county of Monmouthshire (created 1536), but includes in addition, some parts of the former county of Breconshire. The boundary would therefore be formed in the west by the River Rhymney, moving away north-easterly to encompass the general area of Trefil, then directly east to include Blackrock, Clydach, Llanelly and Gilwern, before rejoining the original Monmouthshire boundary through the Black Mountains, across to Grosmont and down the line of the River Monnow, sweeping wide above Monmouth, and finally running roughly along the River Wye which we can take as the eastern boundary. The southern boundary would seem to be the estuary of the Severn between the river mouths of Wye and Rhymney, but a strip of tidal flat to the mid-section, and including the island of Denny, must here be included as an essential part of Gwent.

Within the confines of this boundary are to be found a variety of distinct habitat types, which are represented by the following areas –

(1) THE COALFIELD.

(2) THE NORTHERN HILLS.

(3) THE USK VALLEY.

(4) THE TRELLECH PLATEAU.

(5) THE WYE VALLEY.

(6) THE GWENT LEVELS.

(7) THE SEVERN ESTUARY INTERTIDAL FLATS AND DENNY ISLAND.

It is the wildlife of these areas which I intend to describe in the following pages, the information being taken largely from a series of diaries spanning the period 1958–1997, but also from memories of the earlier 1950's. As an example, I can recall nights during the summer when, while walking home from the 'Welfare Centre Cinema' (Dinham), we saw what I now recollect as 'dozens' of Glow-worms in the hedgerow to the right of the lane leading from Caerwent Brook to the top of Brockwells Hill.

My Father, a farmer, frequently worked on after dark and it was not unusual for us to be called out to hear the 'night sounds'. Vivid memories come back from those days of the early 1950's, when, on one particular spring evening my mother and myself were summoned to hear the songs of the Nightingales. I remember this, rightly or wrongly, as a complete ring of sound. It was as if they were singing from every brake and woodland around us, and, in reality, probably were. Winter nights bore different sounds – the wails and barks of Foxes, the 'music' of the wild geese or, perhaps in the Autumn, the flutings of Curlew as they passed overhead, to or from the estuary.

My diaries, and therefore the notes now taken from them, reflect my activities in various areas at different periods of my life. My home, during the whole of this time, and still as I write, is Brockwells Farm, Caerwent.

Virtually all of the early records come from the farm and its vicinity, the parishes of Caerwent and Caldicot. Beyond my school years, and my initial working days at home, my horizons were extended to successive places of work – Whitehall Farm at Highmoor Hill, Caerwent Quarry, Penhow Quarry, various parts of the M4 motorway locally (as it was when under construction in the mid-late 1960's, and which was renamed the M48 after the construction of the Second Severn Crossing in the mid-late 1990's), various parts of the County of Gwent visited as a lorry driver, many different woodlands during more than eleven years' employment with the Forestry Commission, based in Wentwood Forest, and finally, many parts of the area studied as a result of my most recent working years – 1982 to 1997 – as a self-employed naturalist.

The end result is an assessment of the natural history of the area as reflected by my casual observations over this period of over forty years. It should be emphasised that it is not the product of a methodical study made with the intention of producing a detailed account of the subject. Furthermore, it is my aim to concentrate my notes, where relevant, on species in which the greatest population changes have taken place. For example, on a day when I originally recorded ten or twenty notable bird species, I may only refer to one or two of them here in order to illustrate their abundance then, as compared to their scarcity now. This can equally work in reverse. I may mention a species such as the Collarded Dove, at a time when they were regarded as rare, in contrast to their abundance today. In fact, because of space limitations, limited available knowledge in certain subjects, or the very nature of the subjects themselves, each chapter will be treated in a very individual way. Some, such as those on the fungi and the invertebrates will amount to lists, or little more than lists, respectively, while the chapter on plants will be treated under sub-headings such as the distinct land-form divisions already described, or in relation to habitat type – woodlands, meadows, and so on.

At the end of the chapter on mammals I will list the species which I know to have been recorded here, but my more detailed accounts are restricted to those species of most interest to me, or which show the greatest population changes. The index is based largely on scientific names followed by the relevant common names where these are known to me. These common names will have been taken mostly from works given in the bibliography, or from works specifically mentioned, or, as in the case of the Shingle Spider, it will be a name given to the animal by myself. Many of the less well-known species, of fungi or invertebrate animals for example, have not as yet been given common names.

Prehistoric Gwent

~

An excellent account of the geology of this area has already been given by D. Emlyn Evans in the *Flora of Monmouthshire* (A. E. Wade, National Museum of Wales, 1970), and here I merely dip into this account for the relevant detail, and add further comment where I am able.

The oldest rocks to be found at the surface here are called the Wenlock Shales and, because they do not form the lowest strata of the Silurian System, must date from a time rather less than 440 million years ago (Silurian period c.440 to 405 million years before the present time).

Following on from the Silurian, and covering the largest part of Gwent, are rocks of the Devonian age. These comprise marls, sandstones, cornstones and conglomerates, and are associated with soils which may be calcareous (marls and cornstones), or which may have an acidic content to varying degrees. This range of rock-type in Gwent is representative of parts of the Lower Old Red Sandstone and the Upper Old Red Sandstone, rocks of Middle Old Red Sandstone times being absent here.

The Devonian spans the period from c.405 to 345 million years ago. The succeeding Carboniferous period (c.345 to 280 million years ago), in the Gwent area, is represented by limestones (Lower Carboniferous), conglomerates and shales (Millstone Grit) and a complexity of sediments mostly comprising sandstones, grits and coal (Upper Carboniferous or Coal Measures). The last two occur at the surface in the Gwent Coalfield area which they dominate, but Coal Measures material has also been excavated during the construction of the Severn Tunnel, and was used to build some of the houses in Sudbrook. This material has also been strewn over the beach below Sudbrook Camp and still lies there in substantial quantity.

The Carboniferous Limestone has become perforated by cave systems and fissures some of which have yielded the remains of mammals and amphibians. The most notable cave system known to date in Gwent is that named Otter Hole, which lies partly beneath Chepstow Racecourse, and which is recognised by some as the finest in Britain, in respect of its calcium formations.

The Permian period is represented in Gwent only by volcanic rocks which occur at the surface in the area lying approximately mid-way between Llanllowell and the northern edge of Wentwood Forest. These rocks have been found at the surface at just two sites, and are of two distinct types – Monchiquite (which is the solidified molten magma) and the Vent Agglomerate (the rock forming the Earth's crust at the point of the eruption and which later re-solidified along with the ash and other residue of the explosion).

With the Triassic period (225 to 190 million years ago) we return to rocks of sedimentary kind. These are initially sandstones and marls laid down largely in a desert and lagoonal situation, but later, they culminate in marine deposits as a shallow sea flooded in over the desert.

In places where the relatively soft 'desert' rocks are found adjacent to Carboniferous Limestone rocks, commonly in the south of Gwent, 'Potato Stones' occur, sometimes in abundance. These are nodular agates (frequently geodes – that is, hollow and crystal-lined) – basically quartz stained by haematite to produce reddish-brown colours, but also, clear quartz crystal. I have also found poor specimens of these in the Minnetts forestry area above Llanvihangel Rogiet (to the West of Minnetts Lane, see map 2) where they lie in Carboniferous Drybrook Sandstone alongside, or close to, the Carboniferous Drybrook Limestone.

The youngest solid rocks in Gwent lie directly above the Triassic material and occur on top of Goldcliff point, Ringland Top, and at a number of other prominent sites between the Bishton area and Maes-Glas, Newport. These muddy sea deposits are fossiliferous and can yield a wealth of invertebrate and vertebrate animal remains. They are known as Liassic rocks and form the base of the Jurassic System (c.190 to 135 million years old).

Whatever rocks may have been laid down on top of the Lias here, they must, subsequently, have been removed by erosion, for the next 'rocks' we find here are mere thousands, and not millions, of years old. They are of Upper Pleistocene (late Ice-age) and Holocene (the last 10,000 years) date, and, in some cases (i.e. in caves and foreshore peat/clay deposits), yield the bones and teeth of a variety of animals. The foreshore deposits also contain much sub-fossil plant material as well as evidence of contemporary invertebrates such as beetles.

SELECTED LIST OF LIFE FORMS FOUND AS FOSSILS IN GWENT

SILURIAN

(MARINE)

Species of grapolites, corals (Favosites and the exquisite Halycites or Chain Coral), crinoids (also known as sea-lilies), brachiopods (also known as lamp-shells), bivalve, gastropod and cephalopod molluscs as well as primitive fish types.

DEVONIAN

(DELTAIC)

Relatively few fossils, mostly fragments of primitive fish-types called agnathans (jawless fish).

CARBONIFEROUS

(1) LIMESTONE SERIES (MARINE)

Quite large algal masses can be found, sometimes lying on the surface of the ground, in the Wye Valley (e.g. in Pierce Wood), brachiopods are very abundant and also corals such as Lithostrotion.

(2) MILLSTONE GRIT SERIES (DELTAIC)

Most commonly a range of molluscs – bivalves, gastropods and cephalopods (see 'Notes' for 9.9.72).

(3) COAL MEASURES (SWAMP FOREST)

'Tree' fossils such as Lepidodendron are very abundant, as are horsetails (Calamites) and other plant types. Also various brachiopods, molluscs and fish.

TRIASSIC

(DESERT WITH LAGOONS – MARINE)

Fossils come almost exclusively from the marine sediments at the top of the sequence but these are rather limited in Gwent. Bivalve molluscs and species of fish.

JURASSIC

(MARINE)

Animal fossils are abundant in the Liassic rocks here with bivalve molluscs (such as Plagiostoma and Gryphaea), ammonites and also reptiles, examples of both ichthyosaur and plesiosaur being found by Mr. Des Tucker at Llanwern. Although, apparently, scarce in such muddy conditions, fossil fragments of sea urchins have been found (e.g. in Pant-yr-eos Wood, south of Llanmartin).

PLEISTOCENE

LAST (DEVENSIAN) GLACIATION (VERY COLD, TERRESTRIAL)

Animal remains of this age, found in Gwent, should be termed sub-fossils since most of these found to date have not been converted to stone. Their preservation has been the result of their burial in the earth forming cave floors or the infil of fissures. The following list represents finds made by the author while working in Caerwent Quarry during 1969 and the early 1970's. The notes in brackets following the name of the species indicate the number of individuals represented by the remains found.

Mammoth (one adult and one juvenile)
Woolly Rhinoceros (one adult)
Lion (one adult)
Hyena (at least three adults and one juvenile)
Brown Bear (one adult)
Reindeer (one adult)
Wolf (one adult)
Badger (one adult)
Wild Pig (one adult)
Red Deer (one adult)
Bison (one adult)
Bank Vole (one)
Vole – *microtus sp.* (one)
Long-tailed Field-mouse (one)
Hare – species presumed to be the Mountain Hare (*Lepus Timidus*).

The last named species was discovered in an earlier find in Caerwent Quarry (c.1961) in a soil filled-fissure. Along with the bones of the hare were those of Hyena and Horse. Bones of Horse were also found in Caerwent Quarry Cave revealed in 1969, but they were found at a higher level than the rest and were not considered to be contemporary. The identification of this material was arranged by staff at Newport Museum and Art Gallery.

POST-SCRIPT SUMMARY OF PREHISTORY–1997

No further discoveries have come to my attention during the course of this year but it would be useful to add here those species which have previously been identified from sites in areas close to Gwent. Such species would, almost certainly, have existed here too.

Welch and Trotter (*Geology of the Country around Monmouth and Chepstow*, HMSO, 1961) informs us that material of Pleistocene Age from two caves in the Wye Valley just to the north of Gwent (King Arthur's Cave and Merlin's Cave) has been revealed by members of the University of Bristol Spelaeological Society in the past. In addition to species already listed for the Caerwent Quarry Cave these sites produced the remains of the following animals –

Cave Bear
Giant Irish Deer
Pika (*Ochotona spelaea*)
Sandford's Arctic Lemming (*Dicrostonyx gulielmi*)
Hensel's Arctic Lemming (*Dicrostonyx henseli*)
Lemming (*Microtus anglicus*)
Ptarmigan.

Arthur Bulleid (*The Lake Villages of Somerset*, Glastonbury Antiquarian Society/ Western Gazette Co. Ltd., Yeovil, Fourth Edition 1949) provides lists of birds, fish and mammals represented by material excavated at the Glastonbury and Meare Lake Villages. The period represented by the finds was judged to be of the 'Prehistoric Iron Age'.

The first list (birds) is based on material identified by Dr. C. W. Andrews

F.R.S. From this I have selected only those species considered unusual in the area today.

Pelican (*Pelicanus crispus*)
Common Bittern (*Botaurus stellaris*)
Scaup (*Nyroca marila*)
White-tailed Sea-eagle (*Haliaetus albicilla*)
Common Crane (*Grus grus*).

Of the fish remains discovered in the area Mr. C. Tate Regan identified –

Roach (*Leuciscus rutilus*)
Trout (*Salmo trutta*)
Shad (*Clupea finta*)
Perch (*Perca fluviatilis*)
Pike (*Esox lucius*).

Mammal remains uncovered at the Glastonbury Lake Village site (identified by Dr. J. Wilfred Jackson F.G.S.) include representatives of the following types –

Red Deer
Roe Deer
Wild Boar
Fox
Wild Cat
Otter
Beaver
Marten
Polecat.

These discoveries must shed further light on the probable fauna of Gwent during recent prehistoric times.

ADDITIONAL RECORDS/INFORMATION

Fungi

~

As in the case of most other life-forms to be found here, Gwent's fungi reflect the diversity of the area's geology and habitat. Because of the difficulties involved in a serious study of mycology, few people have attempted to record the range of species present, and this is true for myself too. Here is an ideal study-subject for naturalists wishing to 'make their mark' in the area.

Although it may be difficult, expensive and extremely time-consuming to identify even the majority of all species found, it is a relatively simple task to name the more distinctive types, and this is very much the level of my own studies. Therefore, as a complete amateur in this field, I propose to produce a list of fungi found in Gwent which may serve as a base-line upon which a more meaningful contribution can be built. The identification of species listed here has been made without the aid of either microscope or chemicals. The professional may well, therefore, regard some of those entered here as 'suspect'.

The order is based largely on Courtecuisse and Duhem (see bibliography) while the common names, where given, are taken from a range of sources, again, listed in the bibliography. Only where species are scarce or highly localised have I added the sites where they were found.

Reticularia lycoperdon (bark puffball).
Vibrissia truncorum – on submerged rotten branches in Wentwood Forest brooklets.
Claviceps purpurea (Ergot).
Hymenoscyphus fructigenus (Nut Cup Fungus).
Cordyceps militaris (Caterpillar Fungus) all specimens found were in acid soils.
Nectria cinnabarina (Coral Spot).
Hypoxilon fragiforme.
Daldinia concentrica (Cramp Ball).
Xylaria polymorpha (Dead Man's Fingers).
Xylaria hypoxilon (Candle snuff).
Neobulgaria pura.
Rutstroemia firma.
Chlorocibaria aeruginascens (Green Cup Fungus).

Coryne sarcoides.
Bulgaria inquinans (Black Bulgar).
Geoglossum fallax (Earth Tongue).
Morchella esculenta (Common Morel).
Rhizina undulata. (Pine Fire Fungus)
Helvella crispa (Common Helvel).
Helvella sulcata (Elfin's Saddle).
Peziza badia (Pig's Ears).
Peziza vesiculosa (Early Cup Fungus).
Sarcoscypha coccinea (Scarlet Elf Cup).
Aleuria aurantia (Orange Peel Fungus).
Scutellinia scutellata (Eye-lash Fungus).
Geopyxis carbonaria – Cadira Beeches area of Wentwood Forest.
Auricularia auricula-judae (Jew's Ear).
Auricularia mesenterica (Tripe Fungus).
Tremella mesenterica (Yellow Brain Fungus).
Tremella foliacea (Jelly Leaf).
Exidia glandulosa (Witch's Butter).
Exidia albida.
Dacrymyces deliquescens.
Pseudohydnum gelatinosum (Jelly Tongue).
Calocera cornea.
Calocera viscosa (Jelly Antler Fungus).
Stereum hirsutum (Yellow Stereum).
Stereum sanguinolentum.
Corticium quercinum.
Thelephora terrestris (Earth Fan) – Highlight area of Wentwood Forest.
Auriscalpium vulgare (Ear-pick Fungus) – Cadira Beeches area of Wentwood Forest.
Hericium flagellum (Coral Fungus).
Hydnum repandum (Wood Hedgehog).
Coltrichia perennis – Hardwick Plantation of the Minnetts forestry area.
Piptoporus betulinus (Birch Bracket).
Rigidiporus ulmarius.
Phellinus pomaceus.
Inonotus hispidus (Shaggy Polypore).
Inonotus dryadaeus.
Phaeolus sweinitzii (Sweinitz's Polypore).
Pycnoporus cinnabarinus.
Laetiporus sulphureus (Sulphur Polypore).
Ganoderma lucidum (Shining Ganoderma).
Ganoderma applanatum (Artist's Fungus).
Ganoderma adspersum.
Fistulina hepatica (Beefsteak Fungus).
Meripilus giganteus (Giant Grifola).
Daedaleopsis confragosa (Blushing Bracket).
Daedalea quercina (Maze Fungus).
Trametes versicolor (Zoned Bracket).
Grifola frondosa.
Dendropolyporus umbellatus – Reddings Enclosure, Park Wood near Usk.
Polyporus squamosus (Dryad's Saddle).
Polyporus leptocephalus.
Polyporus brumalis (Winter Ploypore).
Craterellus cornucopoides (Horn of Plenty).
Cantharellus cibarius (Chanterelle).

Clavulina cinerea.
Clavaria vermicularis (White Spindles) – Brockwells Farm fields.
Clavaria muscoides.
Clavaria inaequalis.
Clavariadelphus pistillaris (Dryads Club).
Ramaria invallii.
Ramaria stricta (Straight-branched Coral).
Sparassis crispa (Cauliflower Fungus).
Panellus stipticus.
Pleurotus cornucopiae (Branched Oyster Mushroom).
Pleurotus ostreatus (Oyster Mushroom).
Cuphophyllus pratensis (Meadow Waxcap).
Cuphophyllus virgineus (Snowy Waxcap).
Hygrocybe glutinipes.
Hygrocybe conica (Conical Waxcap).
Hygrocybe calyptriformis (Pink Waxcap) – fields near Cribbau Mill in the Cwm.
Hygrocybe punicea (Large Crimson Waxcap).
Hygrocybe coccinea (Scarlet Waxcap).
Hygrocybe psittacina (Parrot Waxcap).
Hygrophorus hypothejus (Herald of Winter).
Clitocybe geotropa.
Clitocybe nebularis (Clouded Clitocybe).
Clitocybe langei.
Clitocybe vibecina.
Clitocybe rivulosa.
Armillaria mellea (Honey Fungus).
Pseudoclitocybe cyathiformis (The Goblet).
Laccaria amethystina (Amethyst deceiver).
Laccaria laccata (The Deceiver).
Tricholoma album.
Tricholoma sulphureum (Sulphur Tricholoma).
Tricholoma columbetta (dove-colour Tricholoma).
Tricholoma ustaloides – Maryland Woods.
Tricholomopsis rutilans (Plums and Custard).
Lepista nuda (Wood Blewit).
Lepista personata (Field Blewit).
Melanoleuca melaleuca (Changeable melanoleuca).
Leucopaxillus giganteus (Giant Clitocybe).
Lyophyllum connatum.
Lyophyllum decastes.
Calocybe gambosa (St. George's Mushroom).
Nyctalis parasitica (Pick-a-back Toadstool).
Marasmius androsaceus (Horse-hair Toadstool).
Marasmius rotula (Little Wheel Toadstool).
Marasmius oreades (Fairy-ring Champignon).
Marasmius ramealis (Twig Marasmius).
Marasmius calopus.
Micromphale foetidum.
Collybia butyracea (Butter Cap).
Collybia fusipes (Spindle Shank).
Collybia maculata (Spotted Tough-shank).

Collybia dryophila (Russet Tough-shank).
Collybia kuehnerioma – Reddings Enclosure, Hadnock.
Collybia confluens (Clustered Tough-shank).
Collybia peronata (Wood Wolly-foot).
Baeospora myosura.
Mycena epipterygia (Yellow-stemmed Mycena).
Mycena polygramma (Steely-stemmed Mycena).
Mycena vitilis – Park Wood near Usk.
Mycena galericulata (Bonnet Mycena).
Mycena galopus (Milk-drop Mycena).
Mycena haematopus (Bleeding Mycena).
Mycena sanguinolenta (Small Bleeding Mycena).
Mycena pura (Lilac Mycena).
Megacollybia platyphylla.
Oudemansiella radicata (Rooting Shank).
Oudemansiella mucida (Porcelain Fungus).
Flammulina velutipes (Velvet Shank).
Strobilurus esculentus.
Cystoderma amianthinum (Saffron Parasol).
Cystoserma granulosum.
Lepiota cristata (Stinking Parasol).
Leucoagaricus leucothites.
Macrolepiota rhacodes (Shaggy Parasol).
Macrolepiota procera (Parasol Mushroom).
Macrolepiota gracilenta (Slender Parasol).
Agaricus campestris (Field Mushroom).
Agaricus silvaticus (Wood Mushroom).
Agaricus macrosporus.
Agaricus arvensis (Horse Mushroom).
Agaricus langei.
Agaricus silvicola (Wood Mushroom).
Agaricus essettei – Reddings Enclosure, Hadnock.
Agaricus xanthoderma (Yellow Stainer).
Agaricus praeclaresquamosus.
Coprinus plicatilis (Little Japanese Umbrella).
Coprinus disseminatus (Trooping Crumble-cap).
Coprinus domesticus.
Coprinus radians.
Coprinus micaceus (Glistening Ink-cap).
Coprinus niveus.
Coprinus comatus (Shaggy Ink-cap).
Coprinus atramentarius (Common Ink-cap).
Coprinus lagopus.
Coprinus cinereus (Dung-heap Ink-cap).
Coprinus picaceus (Magpie Ink-cap).
Psathyrella lacrymabunda (Weeping Widow).
Psathyrella conopilus.
Psathyrella candolleana (Fringed Crumble-cap).
Psathyrella hydrophilum (Watery Psathyrella).
Amanita ceciliae – Darren area of Wentwood Forest.

Amanita vaginata (Grissette).
Amanita fulva (Tawny Grissette).
Amanita muscaria (Fly Agaric).
Amanita pantherina (Panther Cap).
Amanita spissa.
Amanita rubescens (The Blusher).
Amanita phalloides (Death Cap).
Amanita citrina (False Death Cap).
Amanita porphyria – Five Paths area of Wentwood Forest (see map 1).
Pluteus cervinus (Deer Toadstool).
Pluteus salicinus.
Volvariella gloiocephala (Rose-gilled Grisette).
Entoloma clypeatum (Roman Shield Entoloma) – Llanmartin area.
Entoloma sericeum – field to the south of the Wyncliff.
Entoloma porphyrophaeum – in grass near Forester's Oaks, Wentwood Forest.
Entoloma incanum – Brockwells Farm fields.
Clitopilus prunulus (The Miller).
Macrocystidia cucumis.
Hebeloma crustuliniforme (Poison Pie).
Inocybe geophylla var. lilacina – Llanmartin area.
Cortinarius sanguineus.
Gymnopilus junonius (Orange Pholiota).
Gymnopilus penetrans.
Kuehneromyces mutabilis (Brown-stew Fungus).
Crepidotus mollis (Soft Slipper Toadstool).
Crepidotus variabilis.
Pholiota squarrosa (Shaggy Pholiota).
Pholiota aurivellus – Reddings Enclosure, Hadnock.
Stropharia aeruginosa (Verdigris Agaric).
Stropharia semiglobata.
Psilocybe semilanceata (Liberty Caps).
Hypholoma sublateritium (Brick Cap).
Hypholoma fasiculare (Sulphur Tuft).
Agrocybe aegerita.
Agrocybe praecox.
Bolbitius vitellinus (Yellow Dung-cap).
Conocybe tenera (Brown Cone-cap).
Panaeolus rickenii.
Panaeolus sphinctrinus.
Panaeolina foenisecii.
Anellaria semiovata.
Russula nigricans (Blackening Russula).
Russula emetica var. silvestris – Reddings Enclosure, Hadnock.
Russula krombholzii.
Russula drimeia.
Russula cyanoxantha (Charcoal Burner).
Russula virescens (Sea-green Russula).
Russula ochroleuca (Common Yellow Russula).
Lactarius torminosus (Woolly Milk-cap).
Lactarius acerrimus.
Lactarius pyrogalus.
Lactarius necator.
Lactarius blennius.
Lactarius deliciosus (Saffron Milk-cap).
Lactarius deterrimus.
Lactarius uvidus.
Lactarius rufus.
Lactarius glyciosmus (Coconut-scented Milk-cap).

Lactarius quietus (Oak Milk-cap).
Lactarius subdulcis (Sweet Milk-cap).
Lactarius mitissimus.
Hygrophoropsis aurantiaca (False Chanterelle).
Paxillus involutus (Brown Roll-rim).
Chalciporus piperatus (Peppery Bolete).
Suillus grevillei (Larch Bolete).
Suillus luteus (Slippery Jack).
Xerocomus subtomentosus (Yellow-cracked Bolete).
Xerocomus chrysenteron (Red-cracked Bolete).
Xerocomus badius (Bay Bolete).
Tylopilus felleus (Bitter Bolete) – Wentwood Forest.
Boletus edulis (Penny Bun).
Boletus luridus – Minnetts forestry area.
Leccinum versipelle (Orange Birch Bolete).
Leccinum scabrum (Birch Bolete).
Geastrum triplex (Earth Star).
Geastrum sessile – valley of the Mounton Brook below Shirenewton.
Sphaerobalus stellatus.
Scleroderma citrinum (Earth Ball).
Langermannia gigantea (Giant Puffball).
Calvatia excipuliformis.
Calvatia utriformis.
Lycoperdon pyriforme (Stump Puffball).
Lycoperdon perlatum (Common Puffball).
Lycoperdon echinatum (Spiny Puffball).
Lycoperdon foetidum.
Crucibulum laeve (Bird's-nest Fungus).
Cyathus olla (Bird's-nest Fungus).
Cyathus striatus (Bird's-nest Fungus).
Phallus impudicus (Common Stinkhorn).
Mutinus caninus (Dog Stinkhorn).

POST-SCRIPT SUMMARY OF FUNGI–1997

Potentially, material for this subject could fill several volumes and so, at the present time, the possibilities for additional species seem endless. Without undertaking any specific searches for new species the following came my way during the course of general rambles in Gwent this year.

10th May. St. Georges Mushrooms were noted in some abundance in the general area of the Goose and Cuckoo Inn (Llanover).
18th May. Panaeolus (Anellaria) semiovatus growing on horse droppings at Mathern.
24th July. Amanita crocea in woodlands near Ty-fry (Llangwm).
13th September. Amanita ceciliae growing below a hedgerow near Kilgwrrwg Church (31/463 984).

28th September.	Pink Waxcap (Hygrocybe calyptriformis) in fields at upper Cwm (31/458 936).
12th October.	A bracket fungus – Tyromyces albellus – found in the Minnetts forestry area above Rogiet.
18th October.	Waxcaps of at least six species found in the churchyard of St. David's, Trostrey. These included numbers of the Pink Waxcap (Hygrocybe calyptriformis).

ADDITIONAL RECORDS/INFORMATION

Plants

~

For a variety of reasons it is my intention to limit the contents of this chapter to my own personal records and notes. There is already a Flora of Monmouthshire (see bibliography) and the present B.S.B.I. recorder for Vice County 35 (T. G. Evans) is now in the process of producing an up-to-date account of the area's flora. Indeed, much of the information written here was collected while in the company of Trevor Evans.

There is obviously no point in referring to the common and mundane in this account, unless they have some definite relevance to soil-type or environment. Therefore, the following notes relate to the most characteristic or unusual species in their respective categories.

THE COALFIELD

This is principally an acid soil environment of valley and ridge, though the outer periphery is formed partly by the calcareous Carboniferous Limestone. The more central Coal Measures have such plants as Heather, Bell Heather, Cross-leaved Heath, Crowberry and Bilberry; Hard-fern occurs in woodland on the lower levels and on the higher moors while Lesser Skullcap, Marsh St. John's-wort, Bog Pimpernel and Ivy-leaved Bellflower grow in the wetter places. Sheep's-bit, Wood Sage and Harebell are likely to be found on the flanks of the valley sides, often in the afforested areas.

On the grassy slopes in the western part of the Gwent coal-field occur Great Burnet, Petty Whin and Wood Bitter-vetch, while the similarly named Bitter-vetch is found, in the greatest profusion I have ever seen, in the churchyard of St. Sannan's, Bedwellty.

Dense patches of Dwarf Elder are of frequent occurrence in this part of Gwent with records from the South Celynen Colliery spoil-heap, Blaina and Rhymney etc. Alternate-leaved Golden-saxifrage grows at the side of the lane in Cwm Lasgarn and I have seen a single plant of Woolly Thistle at the roadside leading to the Cwmcarn Scenic Drive. Of more regular and typical occurrence, in woodland and hedgerow, is the small tree known as Bird Cherry which, in Gwent, is almost restricted naturally to the Coal Field and the Northern Hills area.

THE NORTHERN HILLS

These comprise all uplands in the northern part of the area beyond the Coal Field – basically the Black Mountains, Sugar Loaf, Skirrid Fawr and Great Graig. In the Gwent portion of the Black Mountains the Bird Cherry grows abundantly in woodland and in hedgerows. In parts of the Honddu Valley it is often the major constituent species in long stretches of hedge. Also in the valley bottoms (valleys of the Grwynne and Honddu) grow patches of Sweet Cicely. As in the Coal Field, the hill-tops and ridges have a characteristic mix of Heather, Cross-leaved Heath, Crowberry and Bilberry, but in the area of Chwarel-y-Fan, at least, Cowberry occurs too.

In the grass-dominated areas typical species include Mat-grass, Heath Rush and Deergrass while in wetter places Hare's-tail Cottongrass and Purple Moor-grass often become dominant. The very wettest of places may have Common Butterwort and Round-leaved Sundew and where these wet places occur at lower levels we may find Water Avens and, on rock faces, Green Spleenwort.

THE TRELLECH PLATEAU

This relatively high-level area lies between the western edge of the Wye Valley below Monmouth, extending down to Tintern, running through to Devauden and then westwards to include the Wentwood Ridge, almost to Cats Ash. From here it then turns back north-easterly to run along the Wentwood escarpment, and then on via Golden Hill, Newchurch, Devauden, Llanishen and on to the area of Penallt south of Monmouth once more.

Virtually all of this plateau is dominated by the Devonian sandstones and conglomerates, but there is also a small 'oasis' of Carboniferous Limestone (Lower Limestone Shale) between Penallt Common and Tregagle. This range of rock types produces a mix of both calcareous and acid soils, the latter being particularly so over the Quartz Conglomerate and Tintern Sandstone.

These acid soils support Heather, Bilberry, the two common heaths, Climbing Corydalis and Trailing St. John's-wort, with a further range of calcifuge species in such wet areas as Cleddon Bog.

Sheep's-bit occurs in only a few places here and Heath Cudweed similarly (all of my records for the latter species coming from the Wentwood Ridge). Giant Bellflower can be found in the area of Penallt, Sneezewort near Pen-y-clawdd and Daffodil is a major feature of some localities within the area. Another common but very eye-catching plant, in the wooded areas especially, is the Slender St. John's-wort.

THE USK VALLEY

The major features of the valley of the River Usk are firstly, that it is generally broad and shallow, secondly, pebble banks and bars occur along much of the river (from near Llanllowell to the point at which the river enters Gwent), and thirdly, the soils of the valley are of a sandy nature, often both sandy and pebbly. These factors seem to suit such field plants as Bugloss and Field Woundwort, as well as the invasive Giant Hogweed which grows in great profusion along the river-banks. Pink Purslane would appear to be a coloniser which has spread from the Llanover area, and which now occurs downstream at least as far as Usk Town, while another alien, possibly originating from the Radyr, is Giant Butterbur, which now occurs along the Berthin Brook, just above its confluence with the River Usk.

Other, more common, aliens along the river-bank include Monkeyflower, Dame's-violet and Soapwort, while among the native species of note may be mentioned Meadow Saxifrage, Giant Bellflower, Spreading Bellflower, Small Teasel, Common Meadow-rue and unbranched Bur-reed. These all tend to be highly localised. The notable tree species of the Usk Valley is Black Poplar.

THE WYE VALLEY

The valley of the Wye seems deeper, and is certainly more narrow, than that of the Usk, and lacks the profusion of pebble banks. As in the valley of the Usk, we find along the Wye Giant Bellflower, Common Meadow-rue and, probably more abundantly, Small Teasel. In the Wye Valley however, we also have Wood Fescue, Fingered Sedge, Mountain Melick, Deadly Nightshade and Hornbeam, which is here considered to occur naturally at the western extreme for the species in Britain.

At least two other specialities occur in the lower part of the Wye Valley in Gwent. One of these is Salsify which occurs quite commonly on the riverside grasslands up-river from Chepstow, and flowers from late spring to early summer. The other is found in the general vicinity of Chepstow where it typically parasitises the native Ivy, but which, at Elmdale, on the Gloucestershire side of the river, has also been found to take its nourishment from the alien Fatsia japonica. This parasitic species is the Ivy Broomrape.

THE GWENT LEVELS

To the west and east of the Usk's outfall into the Severn Estuary we find, respectively, the Wentlooge Level and the Caldicot Level. This distinctive landscape is man-made and was initiated, it is currently believed, by the Romans. The Levels are presently under threat from a wide range of industrial, recreational and other developments, indeed a large part of the typical Levels landscape has already been lost to these new uses. As a result the floral and faunal communities here are under great pressure and have already been damaged.

The drainage ditches which carry freshwater into the Severn Estuary across these flat lands are called reens, and these have very characteristic populations of plants; Frogbit, Arrowhead, Whorl-grass, Cyperus Sedge, Flowering-rush, Curled Pondweed, Fools Water-cress, Common Reed, Water Dock, Branched Bur-reed, Yellow Iris, Water Fern and a variety of duckweeds typify the plant-life of these reens, although some may be rather local and of a sporadic occurrence. This, in part, is due to the fact that the reens are not only man-made but man-maintained too, and cleaning operations have a temporary effect on some species which require just the right conditions to enable them to develop.

The alluvial nature of the area produces a generally heavy and moist soil, largely of a clayey nature, and, in the dryer areas, this seems to be conducive to the growth of such plants as Greater Burdock, Hoary Ragwort, Wild Parsnip and Bristly Oxtongue.

The reens may have hedges growing alongside them, sometimes on one side, and sometimes on both sides, in which case the reen itself may become virtually hidden from view. Sunlight becomes restricted and so too does the plant and animal life dependent on it.

The basic constituent species of these hedges are Hawthorn, Blackthorn and willows of various species, with Almond Willow being something of a scarcity. These hedges may be kept at a low level by regular cutting, but when allowed to grow to full height they become a major habitat for resting, nesting and feeding birds, the Hawthorn in particular producing fruits for thrushes and others in the winter months.

Apart from some already mentioned, the more scarce and localised plants on the Levels include Brown Sedge, Grey Club-rush, Meadow Thistle and Brookweed while some species are thought to have disappeared completely. One of these is Floating Club-rush which I discovered in a reen lying between Wilcrick and Bishton in July 1974. This has not, to my knowledge, been recorded since.

THE SEVERN ESTUARY

The habitats to the estuary side of the back-ditch are reviewed here – the 'back-track', the sea-wall (sometimes referred to as the 'walking bank'), swarth-turf, salt-marsh, mud/gravel flats and Denny Island.

The seaward side of the sea-wall can be a complex of habitats, one merging into another, the whole situation complicated further in some places by the presence of a secondary, low-level, sea-wall. As a result of this, species named in relation to the swarth-turf may also be found commonly on parts of the salt-marsh too. However, there are species which are decidedly characteristic of one or the other, and these will be described separately.

The 'back-track' runs between, and parallel with, the 'back-ditch' and the main sea-wall. Many plant species occur here but of greatest interest are the Bird's-foot Clover (when it can be found) and both Common and Stiff Salt-marsh-grasses, which only occur in those places where the track is sufficiently wet and muddy.

The main or primary sea-wall ('Walking Bank'), constructed from a variable mixture of soil, clay, boulder and concrete, has a surprisingly distinct flora, even though many of the species occurring here grow in other habitats too. Of the sea-wall 'specialities' then, mention may be made of Sea Clover, Sea Beet, Sea Radish, Narrow-leaved Bird's-foot-trefoil, Knotted Hedge-parsley, Stone Parsley, Sea Wormwood and Slender Thistle. These species by no means occur generally along the sea-wall but are only of localised distribution, the Narrow-leaved Bird's-foot-trefoil, for example, being found in the vicinity of Uskmouth, and spreading east towards Goldcliff Pill.

The swarth-turf has pools, depressions and drainage gullies. These are often filled with water of a degree of salinity and may have Brackish Water-crowfoot growing in them if the right conditions prevail at the right time of the year. In the damper areas Saltmarsh Rush is often abundant while on the drier areas of turf occur Slender Hare's-ear, Strawberry Clover, Meadow Barley, Sea Barley and Sea-milkwort. Marsh-mallow is scattered here and there on both sides of the sea-wall and right down to the upper edge of the salt-marsh. Another rare species in the last named situation is Dittander. Sea Arrowgrass, Sea Plantain, Greater Sea-spurrey, Lesser Sea-spurrey and Thrift all occur on the swarth-turf but are also present on the salt-marsh. Between Black Rock and St. Pierre Pill is found a small area of intermediate habitat between these two distinct zones and this has an interesting combination of Sea Rush and Wild Celery not seen elsewhere in Gwent.

The salt-marsh of today is usually dominated by Common Cord-grass but this is not a native here and, although present in some places from an earlier date, was widely planted during the 1950's (Derek Upton, pers çomm). Characteristic co-habitants here include a number of glassworts (*Salicornia sp.*) and salt-marsh grasses (*Puccinella*), English Scurvy-grass, Sea Aster, Common Sea-lavender and Annual Sea-blite. Patches of Sea Couch grow at the top edge of the salt-marsh in some places.

The salt-marshes developed at the top of the mud-flats, and from here to the middle of the estuary, a typical sequence of estuarine zonation on the Gwent shore is mud-flat, gravel-bed, sand-bank. Of these it is the gravel-bed, with its occasional rocks and boulders surrounded by shallow pools, and general mix of gravel, sand, silt and mud which provides the opportunity for plant growth. The floral community here is dominated by 'sea-weeds' such as Bladder Wrack, Knotted Wrack and Saw Wrack, among others, but also by a type of flowering plant-eelgrass (*Zostera sp.*). The eelgrasses are particularly important here as low-tide-period food for various wildfowl, particularly Wigeon, but also, more occasionally, for both Brent Geese and Bewick's Swans.

Denny Island, a limestone outcrop in mid-estuary, has a variety of plants, the most famous and imposing of these being the Tree-mallow which forms a 'mini forest' on the island's cap.

Although these distinctive areas (Coalfield, Northern Hills etc.) cover most habitats there are still many in-betweens which I now hope to include by way of a habitat-type summary. These plants are the ones to be found in woodlands, meadows, waste places and in arable and farm-yard situations.

WOODLANDS

Some plants are so typical of this habitat that they are named after it – Wood Vetch, Wood Spurge, Wood Speedwell and Wood Millet. All of these occur in Gwent as does Wood Barley, but the latter tends to be rather scarce (with records from Upper Rodge Wood, Cwm Woods and the Minnetts forestry area). Other, more unusual, species include Marsh Violet (Wentwood), Saw-wort (Minnetts and woods above the British, Abersychan), Pale St. John's-wort (Minnetts), Stinking Hellebore (Cwm woods) and Green Hellebore (Salisbury Wood), while of slightly more widespread occurrence are Greater Butterfly-orchid, Lesser Butterfly-orchid, Bird's-nest Orchid, Lily-of-the-valley, Tutsan and Herb Paris. This last-named species is of interest because of its relative abundance at former rural industrial sites. I have noted it near an old lime-kiln in Upper Rodge Wood (Caerwent) where I once counted twenty flowering plants in just a small area, and also in the vicinity of the old iron furnace of the 1600's in Woolpitch Wood near Trellech.

The single most important woodland plant of the area, however, must be the Upright Spurge, formerly called Tintern Spurge since it is here that its greatest natural abundance occurs in the whole of the British Isles. As its old name implies, it is mainly a plant of the Wye Valley woodlands, but I have recorded it from the Minnetts and it is also present in Coed Wen (Penhow). Its presence is rarely apparent until tree-felling or some other disruption opens up the woodland floor to sunlight, when the species may suddenly appear in great profusion.

MEADOWS

As in many other parts of the country, the habitat of 'old grassland' is much diminished in Gwent and many sites have been lost altogether. Those still remaining have such plants as Green-winged Orchid, Early-purple Orchid, Autumn Lady's-tresses, Pyramidal Orchid, Lady's Bedstraw, Dwarf Thistle, Yellow-rattle and Cowslip. Rare species like Meadow Clary also occur.

Bee Orchids can be found in meadows, for example, in the northern part of RAF Caerwent and the Quarry Meadow (off Sandy Lane between Caerwent and Caldicot). However, I find this species far more commonly in places altered by man – road/railway cuttings, old quarries and land from which the top-soil has been removed. These 'impoverished' sites seem to be the most acceptable to the growth of the Bee Orchid.

In respect of lost sites it may be pertinent here to mention an area which was destroyed by the excavation of Caerwent Quarry. Here a formerly excellent site has been replaced by one whose potential is almost as good, but which will never, in reality, be retained for purposes of conservation. Rather ironically, the loss of wonderful calcareous pasture, 'parkland', woodland and limestone grassland/scrub when the quarry was excavated, gave rise to the discovery of Pleistocene mammal remains – the best found in Gwent to date (see pages 15 and 16).

The lost area consisted of a farm called The Woodlands, its fields, Rock House Wood, and a strip of grassy scrub on a steep slope along the northern edge of the wood.

The fields of highest elevation had very shallow soils overlying the limestone bed-rock, those in lower areas had deep soils over Triassic sands and sandstone. Over the years this area has been home to Barn Owls, Nightingales, Rosy Footman moths and Adders, among many others, but its plant communities have been even more impressive, especially in the context of the County of Monmouthshire as it was then (in the period leading up to the mid-1960's when new machinery and techniques accelerated the expansion of the excavated area). The plants found here at the time included Saw-wort, Wild Madder, Common Cow-wheat, Pyramidal orchid, Common Rock-rose and Wild Mignonette and this was in addition to the more usual flower-meadow plants found in nearby grasslands such as those at Brockwells Farm. The Wild Mignonette seems to be especially interesting on these Woodlands fields since other records of it in Gwent tend to come from disturbed soil sites.

WASTE PLACES

Often unsightly, downright ugly even, the 'wastes' associated with industry and various other forms of man's developments are often exciting areas of exploration for the botanist. In Gwent there are rubbish-dumps, docklands, railway sidings/embankments, old quarries and many other such places. Land filling with alien materials – ash, clinker, spoil and ballast. The chemistry and composition of this is often suitable for the germination and development of the more unusual species which may have arrived in such places as a result of man's activities.

The list of such species is never-ending, for the plants which do not occur here today, may well do so tomorrow, as a result of some new direction in importation or industry. Therefore, because of space limitations, I will enter only a short list of the more obvious species – Viper's-bugloss (Severn Tunnel Junction, Rogiet), Large-flowered Evening-primrose, Hare's-foot Clover, Annual Mercury, Sea Stork's-bill (R.A.F. Caerwent), Pale Toadflax, New Zealand Willowherb, Thorn-apple, Oxford Ragwort, Sticky Groundsel and Canadian Fleabane.

ARABLE LAND AND FARMYARDS

This final category comprises yet another man-made environment, that of the farm with its regular disruption of the soil and what grows in it. By introducing new crops we may also bring in new weeds too. A field of Maize near Rogiet in the 1980's also held a large amount of Amaranth (*Amaranthus sp.*), a plant only occasionally seen here before in waste places.

Many arable-land weeds have become rare in recent times because of improvements in seed cleansing or the wider use of selective herbicides, but some of them still persist. The following list consists of those recorded in the area and, as with the plants of waste-places, the more unusual species will be followed by the sites in which they were found. Corn Marigold, Small Nettle, Corn Spurrey, Field Woundwort, Sharp-leaved Fluellen, Round-leaved Fluellen (fields below Shirenewton near Kilpale), Bugloss (fields close to the River Usk at Llanllowell), Dwarf Spurge (Brockwells Farm, Dewstow Farm, Kilpale area and Common-y-coed, Undy), and Weasel's-snout (freshly exposed banks of the A40 trunk-road near Penpergwm.

Although farm-yards undoubtedly have a wide range of different plant species growing on them, Pineapple-weed being typical, there does seem to be only a few which are both scarce and characteristic. However, Good-King-Henry (Brockwells Farm and a roadside verge in Undy village) could be considered one of them, but Dwarf Mallow is a species which, to date, I have only seen in farm-yards (Great House Farm, Caerwent, and Church Farm, Wilcrick).

POST-SCRIPT SUMMARY OF PLANTS–1997

The status of some plants in Gwent does seem to be changing, some increasing while others are decreasing. Walks with Trevor Evans in August revealed a relative abundance of Cowberry (*Vaccinium vitis idaea*) on parts of the Blorenge/Blaenavon Moor but an apparent paucity of Bell Heather (*Erica cinerea*) where previously I seem to remember it as being of frequent occurrence. A concentrated search for this species must be put high on the agenda for the near future.

10th March.	The large Black Poplar tree down river from Usk Town has recently been snapped in half by strong winds (probably those of c. two weeks ago). From a remaining limb hangs a clump of Mistletoe.
21st May.	Dwarf Mallow growing (several plants) at the roadside in the middle of Caldicot.
3rd June.	Wood Bitter-vetch (*Vicia orobus*) noted at Bedwellty, Mynyddislwyn and above Llanhilleth, at the side of the lane leading up to St. Illtyd's Church.
7th June.	Among bushes of Broom c. fifteen flowering spikes of Greater Broomrape (*Orobanche rapum genistae*) were found around a playing-field at Gilwern.
13th June.	Along the Severn sea-wall in the area of the Rogiet (M.O.D.) Rifle-range we noted a profusion of both Narrow-leaved Bird's-foot-trefoil (*Lotus glaber*) and Sea Clover (*Trifolium squamosum*). The former species is obviously spreading further east along the sea-wall now.
17th June.	Quantities of Dwarf Elder (*Sambucus ebulus*) in hedgerow along the Abergavenny – Ross road between Penyffos-goch and Llanvetherine.
19th June.	Viper's Bugloss (c. five plants) on introduced material behind the sea-wall near Goldcliff Pill.
20th July.	A field to the south-east of Abergavenny, and west of Penpergwm, is found to be yellow with the massed flowers of Corn Marigold (*Chrysanthemum segetum*).
21st September.	Corn Marigold and Bugloss (*Anchusa arvensis*) in kale field near Llancayo Farm, Usk.
29th November.	During the autumn of 1995 Mrs. Margaret Braime discovered a patch of Water Hyacinth (*Eichhornia crassipes*) growing in the canal at Rogerstone. Today Mrs. Kate Harris telephoned to report more plants of this species in the same canal but a little further on to the north-west.

ADDITIONAL RECORDS/INFORMATION

Invertebrates

~

Because of the potential length of this topic I think it wise to list only representative species of my experience – adding further records of importance made by other workers, and then to bring the chapter to a close with a range of notes regarding certain species of particular interest.

In compiling the following selected list (from which many common species, and even major groups, have been omitted), I have taken the overall order of classification from Nichols, Cooke and Whiteley, and the works of M. Chinery, B. Skinner and D. Jones have provided the order for the insects and the arachnids (see bibliography).

PHYLUM COELENTERATA

Hydra sp. –	'Grass Pond' (Clytha – Bettws Newydd), 1990.
Tubularia indivisa –	Severn Estuary (Black Rock and Goldcliff).
Sertularia cupressina –	Severn Estuary (Goldcliff).
Common Jellyfish –	Severn Estuary; sometimes abundant in Newport Docks (see 'Notes' for 26.8.67).
Dahlia anemone –	Severn Estuary (Black Rock, Welsh Grounds off Caldicot, Goldcliff).

PHYLUM MOLLUSCA

Lepidochitona cinerea –	Severn Estuary (Welsh Grounds off Caldicot etc).
Common Limpet –	Severn Estuary (Goldcliff).
Flat Winkle –	Severn Estuary (Black Rock).
Common Periwinkle –	Severn Estuary (Uskmouth).

Rough Winkle –	Severn Estuary (Black Rock).
Round-mouthed Snail –	limestone areas of the Wye Valley where it is relatively common.
Hydrobia ulvae –	very abundant on Severn Estuary mud-flats and salt-marshes.
Whelk –	not known in Gwent as a living animal but great accumulations of 'fossil' shells occur as sub-surface layers on parts of the Severn Estuary foreshore – e.g. below Redwick (shown to me by Derek Upton).
Physa fontinalis –	found in reens, probably throughout the Gwent Levels, but recorded from the Wentlooge Level south of Celtic Lakes during October 1992.
Limnaea peregra –	very abundant in many freshwater habitats.
Limnaea stagnalis –	many sites – Neddern Valley, Gwent Levels, Monmouthshire Canal at Newport.
Limnaea auricularia –	one shell of this species collected along the edge of Llandegvedd Reservoir during the early 1990's.
Bithynia tentaculata –	found in reens, probably throughout the Gwent Levels, but recorded from the Wentlooge Level south of Celtic Lakes during October 1992.
River Snail –	empty shells of this species have been washed up on the Severn Estuary strandline but their place of origin is unknown.
Planorbis planorbis –	one of many species of ramshorn snail found in freshwater habitats in Gwent.
Planorbis corneus –	abundant in the Monmouthshire Canal in the Newport area.
Ancylus fluviatilis –	common in brooks and rivers in many parts of Gwent.
Succinea sp.–	one or more species of this genus noted from a variety of 'moist' places – Gwent Levels, Neddern Valley, Routs Wood (Underwood), near small brook close to Allt-y-bela (Gwernesney).
Clausilia bidentata –	often common where there are trees.

Marpessa laminata – often common where there are trees but notably abundant in parts of woodlands north of Rogiet.

Lapidary Snail – Wye Valley woods; ruins and walls of Llanthony Priory.

Goniodiscus rotundatus – Cilwrgi Farm area, Coed-y-paen.

Vitrina pelucida – probably widespread but recorded on the 7th June 1976 on Denny Island (identified by Adrian Amsden).

Pupilla sp.– found in soil with potted plants at Brockwells Farm but origin unknown.

Trichia sp. – Brockwells Farm.

Common Mussel – Severn Estuary where single specimens are scattered widely over the gravel flats (e.g. the Welsh Grounds). Great accumulations encrust the sides of the Newport Docks.

Swan Mussel – large specimens occur abundantly in St. Pierre Lake. Smaller animals found in the Gwent Levels reens. (2.8.75) – 'Hundreds of Swan Mussels are presently lying dead on the exposed lake-bed at St. Pierre, Chepstow'.

Duck Mussel – occurs in the River Wye, and possibly in the River Usk too (two shells were picked up on the side of the River Usk at Llanvair Kilgeddin in 1990.

Sphaerium corneum – probably found throughout the Gwent Levels but recorded from the Wentlooge Level south of Celtic Lakes during October 1992.

Common Cockle – 'fossil' cockle-bed off Uskmouth to the east side of the outfall.

Baltic Tellin – very abundant in mud of the Severn Estuary mud-flats.

Scrobicularia plana – localised but still common in parts of the Severn Estuary mud-flats.

Cuttlefish – (26.5.73) 'Cuttlefish washed up dead on the foreshore near Collister Pill, Undy'. Otherwise 'cuttle-bones' commonly cast up on Gwent foreshore.

PHYLUM ANNELIDA

Estuarine Rag-worm – abundant in the Severn Estuary, particularly on the mud-flats.

Neanthes virens – a single specimen was washed up on the tide-line along the Caldicot foreshore during the cold winter of 1962/1963.

Lug-worm – locally abundant in mud/sand/gravel mix of the Severn Estuary inter-tidal flats but much plundered for fishing bait.

Neoamphitrite figulus – Severn Estuary foreshore at Black Rock, Goldcliff, Uskmouth etc.

Lumbricus terrestris – this is the large common earth-worm and a very important part of some avian and mammalian diets. Very common.

Brandling Worm – very abundant in well-rotted farmyard dung-heaps but also found in more natural sites.

Allolobophora sp. – very common earth-worms which are responsible for obvious soil-casts in fields and on lawns etc.

Medicinal Leech – individuals of this species reportedly found in the area of Caerleon in recent times (1980's–1990's). Otherwise, Leechpool (near Portskewett) is said to be named after a specific leech-pool in the area.

Horse Leech – common in freshwater (and perhaps in slightly brackish water too). Recorded from Crick Brook, Neddern Brook, the 'back-ditch' near St. Brides Wentlooge etc. (1.5.59) 'Eight Horse Leeches in a deep pool of Caerwent (Neddern) Brook below Rodge Farm'.

PHYLUM ARTHROPODA

Daphnia sp. – the number of species present is unknown but by volume the water-fleas comprise a large part of the aquatic micro-fauna upon which many other species feed.

Balanus balanoides –	one of several acorn-barnacles recorded from the Gwent coast.
Idotea sp. –	one of this genus found among sea-weeds at Black Rock.
Sea Slater –	often abundant among sea-wall boulders along the Severn Estuary.
Water Louse –	common in freshwater habitats in Gwent.
Fairy Shrimp –	on the 16th April 1978 J. McGill, C. Carter and P. Whiting found specimens of the Fairy Shrimp in shallow pools near Pen-y-clawdd.
Oniscus asellus –	a common woodlouse in many habitats.
Philoscia muscorum –	a common woodlouse in many habitats.
Porcellio scaber –	a common woodlouse in many habitats.
Armadillidium vulgare –	a common woodlouse often found in and around buildings. Very common at Brockwells Farm.
Proasellus cavaticus –	one of many invertebrates of interest to be found in Otter Hole Cave, Chepstow (see bibliography).
Common Crayfish –	found in the River Wye and the River Monnow (Mrs. Pat Johns). (21.7.86) 'Today Mrs. Jean Roberts showed us numbers of Common Crayfish in the River Monnow near Tregate Bridge'.
Palaemonetes varians –	this common brackish-water prawn is found all along the Gwent coast and also in the brackish-water pond at Elmdale, on the Gloucestershire side of the River Wye at Chepstow.
Common Shrimp –	I can remember these being fished for using especially small mesh in a lave-net in the Severn Estuary off Caldicot (in the 1960's) where I assume they are still found.
Shore Crab –	still abundant along the Severn Estuary foreshore but in far smaller numbers than formerly (e.g. in the 1960's).
Hermit Crab –	found in the Severn Estuary up-stream as far as Goldcliff. (25.9.80) 'several Hermit Crabs on the inter-tidal flats off Nash – Uskmouth'.
Petrobius brevistylis –	found along the sea-wall of the Severn Estuary.

Silverfish –	probably widespread in some buildings throughout the area. Frequent in Brockwells Farmhouse.
Podura aquatica –	often forms dense 'rafts' on the surface of freshwater pools such as at Brockwells Farm and many other sites.
Ephemera danica –	one of many may-flies found in Gwent.
Potamanthus luteus –	apparently a British rarity. A nymphal specimen, given to me by Ms. Gillian Davies, originated from the River Wye above Monmouth.
Platycnemis pennipes –	one of many species of damsel-fly occurring in Gwent, most of them common and widespread.
Emperor Dragonfly –	a typical species of large dragonfly found widely in the area from low elevations (Gwent Levels) to higher elevations (valley ridge above Abercarn).
Sympetrum scoticum –	often abundant over pools in the Blaenavon – Blorenge area.
Sympetrum pedemontanum –	a single specimen recorded at Trefil during the summer of 1995 (Mr Ian Smith), apparently the first British record of this species.
Common Ground-hopper –	(12.4.74) 'one in Minnetts forestry area'. (21.7.75) 'one in the Bicca area of Wentwood Forest'. (see map 1).
Slender Ground-hopper –	(3.6.74) 'one on the edge of a reen south of Magor'. (23.6.74) 'one close to the brook in the Neddern Valley'.
Speckled Bush-cricket –	probably widespread in Gwent in the right sort of habitat.
Oak Bush-cricket –	probably widespread in Gwent in the right habitat.
Conocephalus dorsalis –	found in marshes and some salt-marshes – e.g. Wentlooge Level and Llanmartin Marsh.
Great Green Bush-cricket –	becoming rare (30.7.59) 'a single specimen at Brockwells Farm. (4.9.71) 'a single specimen found in Caerwent Quarry by Mr. Percy Evans'. (22.8.73) 'one found at Brockwells Farm'. (27.8.78) 'a single specimen found at Brockwells Farm'. (21.8.91) 'possibly two or

	three specimens, one of which was brought to me for identification from bramble bushes at Ifton Quarry, Rogiet (Mr. Cecil Morgan).
Dark Bush-cricket –	probably the commonest bush-cricket in Gwent and often remaining active into early November when suitable weather conditions prevail.
House Cricket –	formerly common-place in the days of the old-style fire places, e.g. at Brockwells Farm in the early 1950's. For a long time after that the House Cricket occupied burning rubbish-dumps but today changes have been made here also. Now these warmth-seeking insects are to be found in certain constantly heated buildings.
Common Cockroach –	formerly Crick Rubbish-dump – e.g. (8.6.73) 'large numbers of Common Cockroach present in Crick Rubbish-dump'. Otherwise, still present in some large kitchens.
Palomena prasena –	the commonest of several species of shield-bug in the area.
Reduvius personatus –	one of several species of assassin-bugs in Gwent. (6.6.95) 'a single specimen at Brockwells Farm'.
Deraecoris ruber –	(15.7.95) 'abundant on nettles along the River Wye between Redbrook and Wyesham'.
Water-cricket –	widespread in the right habitat which includes those reens on the Gwent Levels shaded by a double hedgerow, e.g. (September 1987) 'between Redwick and Goldcliff'.
Water Scorpion –	common in brooks, streams, pools etc., even at higher elevations such as Trefil Quarry Pool as witnessed on the 12th June 1982.
Long-bodied Water Scorpion –	recorded in the 1960's from Caerwent Quarry Pool, and (11.7.96) 'from pools at Golden Hill Farm'.
Saucer Bug –	probably widespread on the Gwent Levels at least, but actually recorded from the Wentlooge Level south of Celtic Lakes during October 1992.

Cercopis vulnerata –	a large and strikingly coloured frog-hopper found in many parts of Gwent.
Cicadella viridis –	a common leaf-hopper on the Gwent Levels and at Llanmartin Marsh.
Cinara piceae –	(13.11.75) 'noted regularly on Norway Spruce in Wentwood Forest this Autumn'.
Scorpion-fly –	a distinctive, common and widespread member of the order *Mecoptera*.
Camberwell Beauty –	(8.8.95) 'a single specimen of this rare vagrant butterfly was seen at Llandegvedd Reservoir by Mr. Chris Hatch'.
White Admiral –	an expanding species with records from the Wye Valley, Angiddy Valley, and the Minnetts forestry area.
Dark Green Fritillary –	rare in Gwent. (23.7.83) 'one in Great Barnets Woods near Chepstow'.
Small Pearl-bordered Fritillary –	found in many wooded/afforested areas in Gwent, but probably declining in numbers.
Grayling Butterfly –	strongholds for this species occur in stony places in the Coalfield, Trefil, and R.A.F. Caerwent. I also have one record – (20.8.80) 'Grayling Butterflies in Newport Docks'.
Brown Argus –	of rather sporadic occurrence – (31.7.76) 'on fields at Brockwells Farm'. (17.8.96) 'in flower-meadow area of Trevethin Churchyard'. (17.8.96) 'a mating pair at Brockwells Farm'.
Purple Hairstreak –	common where there are oak trees – Wentwood Forest, Upper Rodge Wood (Caerwent) and woods flanking the Neddern Valley near Caldicot. Also (25.8.96) 'a single specimen around oak foliage in Oldcastle Churchyard'.
White-letter Hairstreak –	a declining species noted at Brockwells Farm, Great Barnets Woods etc.
Green Hairstreak –	local in Gwent. (29.5.84) 'several seen on Grey Hill'. (17.6.93) 'several seen along the upper edge of the forest at Cwmcarn, to the west side of Twm Barllwm'.

Dingy Skipper – rather local in its occurrence in Gwent – Wentwood Forest rides, R.A.F. Caerwent (where it still flourishes in the 1990's), and formerly over land belonging to the Woodlands – e.g. (7.6.64) 'seen in the Lanneck in good numbers'.

Grizzled Skipper – this species may now (1997) be confined in Gwent to R.A.F. Caerwent, but formerly more widespread – e.g. (7.5.71) 'a single specimen in the Minnetts forestry area'.

Nemophora degeerella – a long-horn moth, frequent in woodlands.

Adela reaumurella – another long-horn moth commonly seen in dancing 'clouds' in woodlands in the Spring.

Coleophora caespitiella – very common in the Coalfield area particularly.

Coleophora laricella – often abundant wherever larch trees are grown.

Oak-leaf Roller-moth – sometimes extremely abundant in oak woodland – e.g. (6.7.80) 'huge numbers of imago in Wentwood Forest'.

Brown House Moth – Brockwells Farm-house and buildings. Otherwise, probably very widespread in Gwent.

White-shouldered House Moth – Brockwells Farm-house and buildings. Otherwise, probably very widespread in Gwent.

Nymphula nymphaeata – one of several china-mark moths in Gwent.

Cataclysta lemnata – probably throughout the reens on the Gwent Levels where duckweeds occur.

Hypsopygia costalis – often common on farms where hay or straw is stored – e.g. Brockwells Farm.

Pyralis farinalis – found around farms where cereal products are stored – e.g. Brockwells Farm.

Alucita hexadactyla – one of many plume-moths in Gwent. (25.3.93) 'one found in the western area of Newport by Mrs. Connie Harris'.

Wood Leopard Moth – Parc Seymour (Eric and Florence Loveys). Probably widespread.

Common Forester – scarce in Gwent – R.A.F. Caerwent and Croes Llwyd near Raglan (Mr. David Lewis).

Oak Eggar – both forms of this moth occur widely in Gwent in their respective habitats.

Small Eggar –	in July 1983 Derek Upton drew my attention to a larval-web of this species in a hedgerow close to Magor Pill.
Noctua fimbriata –	(28.7.80) 'a single specimen found near Five Paths, Wentwood Forest (see map 1).
Broom Moth –	widespread throughout much of Gwent and sometimes abundant – e.g. (24.9.74) 'larvae very abundant amongst Bracken on Gray Hill'.
Silurian –	very much a Gwent speciality for this moth was discovered by Dr. Neil Horton in the Coalfield area in 1972 and it still remains undiscovered elsewhere in Britain.
Alder Moth –	(4.8.93) 'one larva found at Wentwood Lodge in Wentwood Forest'.
Copper Underwing –	Brockwells area (many records of moths coming to 'sugar' in the 1960's). Imago often inhabit nest-boxes in some woodlands in the July to August flight period.
Green Silver-lines –	recorded from the Brockwells/Woodlands area in the 1960's and later (1970's) from the Minnetts forestry area.
Herald –	moths of this species are most often encountered during their hibernation in caves, cellars etc. e.g. (12.1.74) 'fifteen Herald Moths hibernating in cellars beneath a ruined house near Chepstow'.
Burnet Companion –	formerly common around the area of the Brockwells, more recently (1980's and 1990's) noted in abundance in R.A.F. Caerwent.
Drepana binaria –	one of several hook-tip moths in Gwent.
Thyratira batis –	although apparently widespread I have only come across one specimen of the Peach Blossom Moth, and that at the Woodlands in the 1960's.
Orange Under-wing –	(7.4.81) 'several on the wing during the day in the Highlight area of Wentwood Forest'. (see map 1).
Tissue Moth –	often found hibernating in lower Wye Valley caves.

Chimney Sweeper –	most common in the Coalfield and Northern Hills areas – e.g. (13.6.88) 'several flying over valley side moorland near Ebbw Vale'.
Geometra papilionaria –	one of several emerald moth species in Gwent.
Clouded Magpie –	several records, the most recent being (15.6.93) 'one in Great Barnets Woods near Chepstow'.
Swallow-tail Moth –	many records from the area of Brockwells Farm but also (9.7.79) 'one at Dingestow'.
Large Red Caddis-fly –	this is the largest of many caddis-fly species occurring in Gwent. Like this species, some of them produce exquisitely fashioned larval cases and some make them out of water-snail shells (species of *Limnephilus*).
Molanna angustata –	this caddis produces a very distinctive larval case as witnessed (28.4.83) 'Bettws Ponds near Newport'.
Down-looker Fly –	probably widespread in Gwent and certainly in Wentwood Forest.
Tabanus sudeticus –	several records from the Wentwood Forest. This is one of several horse-fly species in Gwent.
Bombylius major –	One of, probably, several bee-fly species in Gwent.
Hornet Robber-fly –	this is the largest and most spectacular of its family (*Asilidae*) in Gwent. It is also a National Rarity and, to date, recorded from just four sites in the area – Brockwells Farm, R.A.F. Caerwent, Rogiet Poor Land and a meadow adjacent to the River Usk at Llanvihangel Gobion. First recorded at Brockwells Farm on the 30th July 1959, and it still flourishes at this site in the late 1990's.
Poecilobothrus nobilitatus –	generally common where there are stagnant pools – e.g. (23.7.77) 'common on water-filled ruts in Wern Brake near Llanvaches'. (11.7.96) 'on pools at Golden Hill Farm'.
Volucella bombylans –	a distinctive but variable bee-mimic found commonly in many parts of Gwent.
Urophora cardui –	the common causer of swollen-stem galls on

Creeping Thistle and probably found wherever the plant is found.

Sepsis fulgens – concentrated swarms of these tiny flies occur during the summer in both Wentwood Forest and the Minnetts forestry area. At close range there is a pungent smell associated with them.

Lipara lucens – is the cauşer of the well-known 'cigar-galls' on Common Reed.

Phytomyza ilicis – is the causer of the common Holly leaf 'blotch-gall'.

Ornithomyia avicularia – probably the commonest of several louse-flies found in Gwent and associated with many species of birds.

Tachina fera – a largish fly commonly found on umbellifer flowers, especially Angelica, during the summer.

Mesembrina meridiana – one of the more 'handsome' of the house-fly group and most often associated with cow-pats and other livestock droppings.

Stomoxys calcitrans – is a particularly disliked 'house-fly' because it 'bites'.

Hypoderma bovis – the notorious Warble Fly, now much reduced in number because of an intensive eradication campaign.

Giant Wood-wasp – a common associate of coniferous woodland – e.g. Wentwood Forest where I saw many of the females but only one male of this species during my eleven years employment there (1970-1982).

Steel-blue Wood-wasp – a single specimen of an emerging imago was discovered in a piece of timber at the Gwent County Council Depot at Slough, Caerwent in the Autumn of 1978. It was found by Mr. Des Tucker and identified by Mr. Adrian Amsden (National Museum of Wales).

Hawthorn Saw-fly – one of several species of saw-fly occurring in Gwent.

Rhodogaster viridis – a very distinctive green coloured saw-fly recorded from the Minnetts forestry area and several other places.

Pontania proxima – the common causer of 'kidney bean' galls on willow leaves and one of very many gall-wasps in Gwent.

Apanteles glomeratus – one of many icneumon-wasps in Gwent.

Chrysis sp. – one of, possibly, several 'jewel-flies' (solitary-wasp parasites) in Gwent.

Yellow Meadow Ant – produces the distinctive ant-hills on old pasture.

Black Garden Ant – also produces ant-hills on occasions, but probably only in certain circumstances. Nest-mounds of this species occur on the valley side above Pengam in the western part of Gwent.

Jet-black Ant – only found occasionally, making 'carton nests' in tree hollows etc. Colonies persist in the same place for years if allowed to do so. (4.4.92) 'nest in hollow Ash trunk on southern edge of Minnetts forestry area' – and still present in 1996. Also noted at Brockwells Farm in 1995.

Wood Ant – typically, but not exclusively, associated with conifer woodlands in Gwent. Probably most abundant in the Trellech Plateau area.

Mellinus arvensis – one of the digger-wasps which burrows into sandy soils. This species associates with cow-pats on which it takes flies – the larval food.

Odynerus spinipes – one of the mason-wasps, formerly occurring in Caerwent Quarry, but common and regular along the River Usk, e.g. (28.5.90) 'several "lattice-tubes" of *Odynerus* projecting from the sandy river-banks in the Llanvihangel Gobion area'.

Common Wasp – nests in a wide variety of places – inside sheds and greenhouses or in the ground.

German Wasp – presumably a common species in Gwent.

Red Wasp – frequently found in Gwent.

Tree Wasp – not a common species but a number of records have been made over the years.

Norwegian Wasp – (23.6.95) 'nest in Pyracantha bush at Parc Seymour and brought to my attention by Mr. Jim Pitcher'.

Hornet – widespread in Gwent but more particularly in

the northern half of the area. However, – (25.9.83) 'Hornet's nest in hollow of fallen tree trunk at Llandevaud'. (Mr. Jim Pitcher).

Leaf-cutter Bee – probably several species occur in Gwent and have been recorded from many places – Brockwells Farm, Penhow etc. – (24.11.82) 'cells of Leaf-cutter Bee in soft wood (probably poplar) at Sudbrook Pulp-mill (Mr. S. Griffin).

Honey Bee – commonly occurring wild in Gwent and occupying hollow trees, buildings (very often churches) and occasionally produces a nest in the open – e.g. (22.6.95) 'comb amongst branches in canopy of small tree in the grounds of Usk Castle'.

Bombus terrestris – one of many bumble-bee species in Gwent.

Green Tiger Beetle – widespread in Gwent but probably not as common as formerly. Records from Minnetts forestry area, Wentwood Forest, Caerwent Quarry and, more recently – (8.4.95) 'very large numbers in R.A.F. Caerwent'.

Violet Ground Beetle – probably the best known of many ground-beetles in Gwent.

Necrophorus sp. – several species of burying-beetles are to be found in Gwent but none have been identified to specific level by me because of the necessity to kill in order to bring this about. In a scientific study situation this would be acceptable, but not for a casual recording scheme.

Devil's Coach-horse – a large, distinctive and common rove-beetle, noticeably abundant and widespread in the Autumn of 1996.

Aloconota subgrandis – a rove-beetle found in Otter Hole Cave near Chepstow, and apparently, in no other British cave (P. Chapman see bibliography).

Stag Beetle – there are only two of my own records for this area – (25.6.61) 'a male Stag Beetle flying at dusk over the road at Dewstow Hill between Caerwent and Rogiet'. (5.6.63) 'a single female Stag Beetle in the Minnetts forestry area'.

	In the early Summer of 1995 Mrs. Anne Jackson found a single male of this species at Little Wentwood Farm, Llantrisant.
Lesser Stag Beetle –	a common and widespread species where there is well-rotted wood.
Black Rhinoceros Beetle –	common where there is rotten wood.
Dor Beetle –	several species occur commonly on farmland in Gwent and provide food for Foxes and Badgers and a variety of other animals.
Minotaur Beetle –	sporadically common in the Wentwood area generally.
Aphodius fimetarius –	a common dung-beetle at Brockwells Farm and a frequent prey item for the Hornet Robber-fly.
Summer Chafer –	a still common member of the chafer group of beetles and an important food-source for, among others, Noctule Bats.
Bee Beetle –	this is the most distinctive species of what is generally a very distinctive group of beetles and recorded from many sites in Gwent, but none recently. (1.7.71 and 3.7.71) 'a single specimen seen in the Black Sow's Well area of Wentwood Forest. (1.9.71) 'one in the Minnetts forestry area'. (1.7.72) 'one at Uskmouth near the sea-wall'. (25.7.74) 'one in Wentwood Forest'. (5.8.74) 'one in Minnetts forestry area (Hardwick Plantation)'. (19.7.81) 'one near the Forestry Commission houses/offices in Wentwood Forest'.
Ctenicera pectinicornis –	(5.7.80) 'one in Wentwood Forest'. This is the only specimen seen by me to date.
Upland Click-beetle –	widespread over upland heath/commons/ moors – e.g. the Wentwood area and Grey Hill, the Black Mountains, and almost certainly the high ground of the Coalfield as well.
Glow-worm –	a very distinctive species for obvious reasons, and one in which there has been an obvious decline over the past half-century.

Pyrochroa coccinea – this is the largest and brightest of the two common cardinal beetles found in Gwent.

Mycetophagus quadripustulatus – (6.6.81) 'several adults of this species feeding on Oyster Mushroom in Llanwern Park'.

Endomychus coccineus – (14.3.78) 'two adults under bark of dead tree trunks at Brockwells Farm'. (6.1.80) 'a single specimen in Wentwood Forest'.

Eyed Ladybird – a typical, if relatively large, representative of the ladybird group of beetles and frequent in Wentwood Forest where it feeds on conifer-feeding aphids.

Attagenus pellio – this species represents the larder-beetles (*Dermestidae*), several of which occur in Gwent. The larvae are very distinctive and often called "woolly bears" – a name also applied to some hairy moth-caterpillars.

Death-watch Beetle – well-known and widespread pest in old timbers – e.g. at the fine old Gwent farm-house of Coed Cefn, Tregare (Steve and Valerie Jones).

Oil Beetle – occasionally noted – e.g. (4.5.79) 'a single specimen in Wentwood Forest'. (18.4.80) 'one in the Little Oak area of Wentwood Forest'.

Tanner Beetle – a large and rare longhorn-beetle in Gwent with one record of a dead specimen found in Park Wood near Usk by Mr. Graham Harris on 25th January 1995.

Wasp Beetle – a distinctive longhorn with many records in Gwent – (25.5.73) 'one in Slidy Hill Wood, Crick'. (2.6.78) 'one at Brockwells Farm'.

Strangalia maculata – a common and well marked longhorn often found on *umbelliferous* flowers.

Strangalia quadrifasiata – not as frequent as the last species but with several records – e.g. (24.7.74) 'a single specimen in Wentwood Forest'.

Strangalia punctata – (10.6.82) 'several on Common Rockrose in R.A.F. Caerwent'.

Rhagium bifasciatum – common around coniferous trees.

Clytra quadripunctata – a rare beetle associated with the nests of Wood

Ants – (9.7.80) 'one found in Wentwood Forest'. (1.7.95) 'one found in the Minnetts forestry area'.

Bloody-nosed Beetle – sporadically abundant in the Wentwood area generally – e.g. (15.6.80) 'nineteen in the Highlight area of Wentwood Forest'.

Chrysolina fastuosa – (11.8.86) 'a single specimen on Common Hemp-nettle near the Monmouthshire Canal at Malpas, Newport'.

Cassida rubiginosa – often found near thistles and not uncommon.

Apion miniatum – one of many species of weevil in Gwent.

Pine Weevil – a common pest in some conifer plantations.

Great Diving Beetle – a large and distinctive representative of the water-beetle genus *Dytiscus*. Widespread in Gwent.

Great Silver Beetle – a rare species found on the Gwent Levels – (6.8.94) 'one larva about to pupate in soil close to the 'back-ditch' at Newport Lighthouse'. Also noted (imagos) coming to mercury vapour light on Caldicot Level near Magor (Dr. Neil Horton).

Glomeris sp. – a pill-millipede frequently found in many parts of Gwent.

Polydesmus sp. – a type of millipede commonly found under the bark of rotting trees and in other damp places.

Geophilus sp. – a type of soil-dwelling centipede, some species of which have the ability to release a luminous fluid which helps us to locate them when they move about on the surface of the ground at night – e.g. (29.10.64) 'a *geophilid* centipede on the front drive at Brockwells Farm leaving a luminous trail this evening'.

Lamprochernes – one of the pseudo-scorpions – (15.4.76) 'one in beech-litter in the Little Oak area of Wentwood Forest'.

Cob-web Spider – inhabits the inner parts of buildings for most of the year, venturing outside during the very warmest weather. Very abundant at Brockwells Farm.

Spitting Spider – (17.6.84) 'a single specimen was discovered in a house in Woodlands Road, Newport, by Alun Price, but it is believed that it may have been accidentally transported from Weymouth, Dorset'.

Dysdera crocata – a common and distinctive spider often found in dark recesses around buildings.

Clubiona sp. – at least one species of grass-twist spider is found in Gwent with records from the Caldicot Levels, Llanmartin Marsh and the Wye River-side 'meadows' above Chepstow.

Zebra Wall Spider – the common jumping-spider of walls, wooden sheds and other vertical surfaces.

Misumena vatia – the common species of crab-spider in Gwent, typically inhabiting flower-heads in the Spring and Summer.

Micrommata virescens – several specimens, both male and female, recorded from Wentwood Forest in the period c.1972-1982.

Shingle Spider – the first record for the area came from the banks of the Sirhowy River on 26th August 1978 when one of this species was discovered near Pochin below Tredegar. Subsequently (1980 onwards) many records from the pebble banks along the River Usk from Llanllowell to well beyond Abergavenny.

Tegenaria sp. – the large house-spider, of at least one species, is common through most parts of Gwent, usually inside buildings.

Theridion pallens – best known for its diminutive but very distinctive 'sputnik' shaped egg-case. Widespread in Gwent – (30.9.77) 'egg-case found under leaf along lane between Crick and Broadwell'. (2.7.82) 'several in tall hedgerow near Tredegar House, Newport'.

Cave Spider – abundant in lower Wye Valley caves, cellars in derelict/ruinous houses and mine-shafts – e.g.

(19.10.59) 'Cave Spiders occupying small cave in Upper Rodge Wood near Caerwent'. Also found under sewage duct inspection-cover at Brockwells Farm.

Araneus diadematus – the most common orb-web spider and widespread in the Gwent area.

Araneus quadratus – a large and 'handsome' orb-web spider of more local occurrence than the last species and found in quite rank vegetation – e.g. the banks of trunk roads/motorways, in marshlands, etc. Records from Llanmartin, Rhiwderin, Kemeys Inferior etc.

Nuctenea cornuta – recorded in the 1980's from Llanmartin Marsh.

Araniella cucurbitina – widespread among bushes and trees where it constructs a very small orb-web amongst the foliage.

Linyphia sp. – many species of money-spider occur in Gwent and are notable for the gossamer they produce in the Autumn period.

NOTES

If space permitted, a very interesting aspect of invertebrate study in Gwent would be that of its ecology, and the communities which have developed in certain situations – the species found on Denny Island, those of the inter-tidal zone of the Severn Estuary, the species found in caves, particularly Otter Hole Cave (see bibliography), and those inhabiting marshland, reed-bed, heather moor – the list is endless. And what about man-made environments – quarries, coal-mines, conifer plantations and rubbish-dumps.

Apparently a distinct fauna has developed in and around sewage-farms, and of this fauna may be mentioned at least three species of money-spider. At periods of their dispersal, when they normally ride the air-currents on streamers of silken thread, they sometimes remain grounded through lack of air movement, the resulting gossamer being concentrated into surprisingly tough sheets which envelop the sewage-farm structure producing a tent-like effect.

Webs of other kinds can also be spectacular. Those of the small-ermine moth larvae for example, particularly the Bird-cherry Ermine, will defoliate bushes and trees of that species, and replace the leaves with a covering of silk. The Spindle Ermine will do likewise, but in by experience, not to such a dramatic extent.

Glow-worms produce a spectacular of a different kind, but these days few people ever get to see it. Childhood memories remind me of Glow-worms 'illuminating' local hedgerows to Brockwells Farm and the occasional one or two persisted, if only sporadically, until as recently as July 1990 when a single female was present for at least two consecutive nights at the roadside on Brockwells Hill.

Over the years I have recorded Glow-worms from many parts of Gwent, either as 'glowing' females at night, or as males, females and larvals during the daytime. My earliest record in any year was that of 18th May 1967 when one was noted at Ifton Quarry, Rogiet. The latest was a reported sighting (Mr. Ian Parret) for the 2nd October 1976 from Penhow Road, Wentwood Forest. I always associate the occurrence of 'glowing' females with dry, warm weather but this is not necessarily so.

It is more likely that when the females are ready to attract a mate they do so no matter what the weather. Witness my experience on the evening of 28th June 1980 when, on returning to Wentwood Forestry Commission houses from Cardiff at 10.45 my diary records – 'As we drove back it was raining steadily – the rain at Wentwood being moderately heavy. This did not, however, deter the luminous activity of ten female Glow-worms in the grassy areas around the houses'.

As I write (mid- late 1990's) Glow-worms are still being reported to me from Wentwood (Nial Harrhy) and from R.A.F. Caerwent (De-tec Security Services), but they can now be generally regarded as rare in Gwent.

Hornets are large and impressive insects of undeserved notoriety. Because of their 'folk-lore' status as fearsome stinging 'giants' people often find it difficult to believe that they are normally docile and non-aggressive. To me they have that almost friendly charm of the bumble-bee – capable of stinging, but reluctant to do so. Many naturalists are able to substantiate this view and have done so in a range of published anecdotes. The Hornet has now become one of my favourite insects. I have discovered them in many parts of inland Gwent.

On one occasion the nest was sited in a large and hollow tree trunk that had been cast up on the field adjacent the River Usk at Llanvihangel Gobion. With me at this time was a young German student who insisted on peering up into the hollow in order to see the nest. I thought at the time that this was pushing the Hornet's tolerance a bit too far but this was not the case at all for the workers flew in and out of the hollow alongside him without so much as a brief investigation – try that on with a wasp's nest!

On the 28th September 1996 Graham Harris showed me a Hornet's nest in a hollow oak tree between Usk and Glascoed. What was particularly interesting here was the fact that a Honey Bee's nest occupied a part of the same hollow. Each species had separate nest entrances – the Hornet's through the obvious large opening, while the Honey Bees used a smaller hole, c.2½' across, and about two feet further up the trunk. What was 'unusual' about this was the fact that these two insects are normally sworn enemies – the Hornets predating the Honey Bees. But as is so often the case in nature, predator and prey, when residing in close proximity to each other, seem to maintain a state of complete indifference.

Honey Bees themselves are intriguing insects which have fascinated man since his days as a hunter-gatherer, and in many parts of the world. This fascination didn't really hit me until very recently while carrying out a survey of wildlife in and around churches in Gwent. I found that a surprisingly high number of churches had Honey Bee's nests in their fabric, and in all sorts of different places. It wasn't as if a church had some unique architectural niche which the bees found especially suitable for their requirements. They were found to nest low down (c. 2½ ft. above the ground in Malpas Church) or high up (almost at the apex of the bell-turret on St. David's Church at Trostrey), under the roof or in the wall, on the north side, south side, east side or west – it doesn't seem to matter. What does seem significant is that churches are so often used by Honey Bees, and also that they are quite determined to use them too. For example, a nest was removed from beneath the roof of Mathern Church some years ago, but there is still a Honey Bees nest there, now sited in the tower. I am informed that bees have been smoked out of Caerwent Church tower on at least two occasions within recent memory, and removed from St. Michael's, Tintern Parva, perhaps even more times than that – but I understand that they are back there again now !

So what is it that attracts Honey Bees to churches in particular? – or is this really not the case? – it certainly seems to be so to me. Is it, perhaps, to do with nest location – the fact that the structure of a church is almost unique within its own locality, and therefore recognisable. Much more investigation is necessary before this conundrum can be satisfactorily explained.

The last species worthy of attention here is the Hornet Robber-fly, a British National Rarity. Surprisingly, for such a large and impressive insect, relatively little is known about its lifestyle and behaviour, authorities being at variance on many aspects relating to its larval stage especially.

It has, for example, been stated that this fly only inhabits dry heaths and unimproved pasture but on the 24th August 1989 I found two specimens on a field bordering the River Usk at Llanvihangel Gobion.

This field, I happen to know, had previously been treated with artificial fertiliser, and I wouldn't have described it as being particularly dry either.

I had for a long time believed that Hornet Robber-flies require, as well as a dry habitat, the presence of grazing animals, especially cattle, the important connection being the animal's droppings. Certainly they will also occupy places grazed by horses, as I discovered (19.8.82) at Rogiet Poor Land. However, I now believe that the presence of large herbivorous animals isn't totally necessary. Mike Sayce informs me that he has seen Asilus at Rogiet Poor Land when there were no animals grazing there at all, and had not been for some time. And secondly there is the question of the Asilus presence in R.A.F. Caerwent. To my knowledge, grazing animals had been excluded from this site for quite a number of years. Then, during the 1980's, sheep were brought back in to control the rampant Ragwort growth. Following this, cattle were also brought in and, on investigation (4.9.93) Asilus was found to be present. Only one individual was seen on this occasion but in 1995 more were present. The questions arising from this are – (1) was Asilus here all the time, simply taking advantage of the presence of the cattle when they arrived, or (2) does Asilus explore, actively seeking out new habitat? It may be that the Hornet Robber-fly is capable of existing in habitat devoid of grazing animals, but such sites do not encourage or permit a density of population. A profusion of cow-pats may well serve to concentrate food-sources (dung-flies, dung-beetles etc.) and this may be the reason for 'unnaturally' high concentrations of Asilus in such places too.

To date, I personally have never seen any predatory insect attacking Asilus, though apparently this does occur, at least with asilids in general (Colyer and Hammond, Warne, 1951). The Hornet Robber-fly itself takes a wide range of prey species but it is, nevertheless, selective to a degree. At Brockwells Farm I have recorded the following prey species for Asilus –

Meadow Grasshopper (*Chorthippus parallelus*)
flesh-fly (*Sarcophaga sp.*)
house-fly type (*Mesembrina meridiana*)
crane fly (*Tipula sp.*)
dung-beetle (*Aphodius fimetarius*)
social wasp (*Vespula sp.*)

POST-SCRIPT SUMMARY OF INVERTEBRATES–1997

On the 22nd March Mr. Gerry McQuade reported the sighting (just prior to that date) of a Red Admiral Butterfly flying in the Abergavenny area. This individual must have been a successful hibernator here. Interestingly, Mr. Derek Upton found one of this species at the bottom of a log-pile in his garden at Caldicot during the latter part of September, 1996.

In direct contrast to last summer when huge numbers of Painted Lady Butterflies migrated in from the south, summer 1997, to date, has not produced a single individual of this species that I have seen. Indeed, very few have been reported.

24th May.	In the Minnetts forestry area I noted 1 Grizzled Skipper Butterfly, 1 Eyed Ladybird, 1 beetle of the species Clytra quadripunctata, 2 Green Tiger-beetles.
25th May.	In R.A.F. Caerwent Grizzled Skipper and Dingy Skipper Butterflies were of frequent occurrence today. Two Green Tiger-beetles were also noted here.
23rd June.	A pyralid moth of the species Anania funebris was seen on the scrubby area between Pengam and Cefn Fforest.
23rd July.	Today the dipterids Tachina fera and the much scarcer Tachina grossa were noted feeding from flowers of Hogweed at Fairwater, Cwmbran.

During early July a swarm of Honey Bees invaded the Brockwells Farm buildings, setting up residence in an old meal-bin where, unfortunately, they could not be allowed to stay. As luck had it Mr. Barry Layton very generously came to the rescue and added the colony to his own stock.

Early in August Mr. & Mrs. H. J. Sadd came across a White Admiral Butterfly in the Draethen Woods which lies just beyond Gwent to the West. Other sightings of this species were made here by others too and this would suggest a total, if only patchy, covering of Gwent by this species now.

I saw my first Hornet Robber-fly of the year at Brockwells Farm on Friday the 8th August. On the following Monday I went into R.A.F. Caerwent with Mr. Peter Skidmore and here we found five of this species in areas where the cattle were grazing. We then came back to Brockwells Farm fields and found a female Asilus which had killed a male of her own species – a known feature of Hornet Robber-fly behaviour (Colyer & Hammond, Warne, 1951, page 118). This was the first time I had witnessed this.

On Wednesday 13th August I counted the Asilids on top of the south-facing bank of the Banky-field (Brockwells Farm) and found 41. On the following day (between 5.10 and 5.50 pm) I checked the whole of the Banky-field and found 47. On the 16th August I found that the number seemed to increase as the day progressed. At 1.15 pm I went out and counted 12 Hornet Robber-flies over the top of the south-facing bank. At 4.15 pm, over exactly the same area, I counted 32. On the following day I led a walk from Llanvihangel Gobion to Llanover along the line of the Usk Valley Walk. In the second field along the group found one (possibly two) Hornet Robber-flies and another close to Llangattock-Juxta-Usk, with a further four in the large field opposite Llanover. All of these fields were cattle-grazed and all of the flies were located on cow-pats. The sites at Llangattock and Llanover were new records for this species.

At the Brockwells the numbers of Asilus had continued to rise through the rest of August for on the 5th September 63 were counted on the Banky-field alone. This was to prove the best count of the year for the numbers gradually decreased through September but the mild conditions probably allowed some individuals to remain active until the 5th October when I found just two.

The remaining invertebrate records for the year are as follows –

15th August.	Two Grayling Butterflies on Gilwern Hill.
25th October.	While driving along the A48 between Chepstow and Crick the gossamer covering the fields became obvious as the lowering sun in the western sky illuminated the mat of threads as it would over the surface of water.
2nd November.	During the field-trip along the Monnow near Monmouth Graham Harris spotted a flying Hornet which seemed quite late in the year but wasps were still active on the 8th of the month.

ADDITIONAL RECORDS/INFORMATION

Fish

~

A variety of aquatic habitats such as ponds, reservoirs, canals, brooks, rivers, reens and estuaries ensure Gwent a rich and diverse range of fish species. Some prefer the faster flowing waters of the brooks and rivers, others are typical of slow-moving or still water, while yet others are adapted to life in the estuary. These fish are naturally divided into salt-water, freshwater and euryhaline species. That is, those which live in the sea, those which live in freshwater and the relatively few species which have the ability to move from one to the other.

Gwent's contact with the sea is the Severn Estuary where a great range of species may be found, but very rarely are. During the period of its operational life the Uskmouth Power Station was the source of a great deal of information regarding the fishes occurring in, or visiting, the Severn Estuary, for its 'pump-screen' acted virtually as a trap into which fell a surprising variety of species, many of them recorded by Brian Whittaker of Goldcliff (see appendix C).

What follows is a list of salt-water fish of my experience, taken in the order used by Muus and Dahlstrom (see bibliography).

Thornback Ray –	a species which probably enters Gwent waters on a regular basis. Derek Upton once showed me the tail from one of this species which he found cast up on the strand-line near Magor Pill.
Skate –	the egg-cases of this species are frequently cast up on the Severn Estuary foreshore strand-line.
Conger Eel –	commonly found under large rocks in shallow pools on the Welsh Grounds off Caldicot at low-tide.
Great Pipefish –	(23.6.81) 'a single specimen washed up dead in the River Wye at Chepstow' (Mr. Trevor Evans).

Cod –	frequent in the Severn Estuary during the winter months and often caught by anglers.
Bib –	a cod relative which is common during the winter period in the Severn Estuary.
Whiting –	comments as for the last two species.
Hake –	one very young specimen washed up dead on the strand-line at Goldcliff on the 1st June 1980.
Three-bearded Rockling –	(24.3.73) 'one washed up dead at Collister Pill, Undy'.
Bass –	a 'summer fish' in the Severn Estuary often caught by anglers and, formerly, by lave-net fisherman.
Grey Mullet –	and in particular, so I am informed, the Thin-lipped Grey Mullet, is common in the Severn Estuary in the warm months of the year. It is said to move into freshwater on occasions but I have no experience of this.
Swordfish –	the trunk of a single animal was washed up at Collister Pill, Undy on the 1st August 1971.
Common Goby –	found commonly in the Severn Estuary and apparently into the tidal parts of the River Wye for one of this species was found to be present in the entrance-passages of Otter Hole Cave when it was claimed as the first of its species to be recorded in a British cave (P. Chapman – see bibliography).
Red Gurnard –	(20.11.65) 'a single specimen washed up dead on the Severn Estuary foreshore at Undy'.
Sea Snail –	specimens of these unusual fish were shown to me by Brian Whittaker who took them from the 'pump-screens' in the Uskmouth Power Station.
Sole –	frequent in the Severn Estuary where they are sometimes caught by anglers.
Sunfish –	at least one of this species has passed through the waters of our area for a specimen was taken in the salmon-putcher baskets at Beachley in the mid 1990's.
Angler Fish –	apparently frequent in the Severn Estuary with specimens taken in the Salmon putcher-baskets at Goldcliff, and also by the stop-boat fishermen

who used to operate in the River Wye at Chepstow. Dead specimens are occasionally washed ashore as well as odd bones, some of which are very distinctive and therefore easily recognisable.

The euryhaline species which will be treated next, may be *anadromous* (moving from sea-water into fresh-water in order to breed), *catadromous* (moving from freshwater into sea-water in order to breed) or simply those which can exist in either environment, or which move from one to the other in order to feed.

Sea Lamprey –	*anadromous* species recorded from the River Wye, the River Usk, and also from Llandegvedd Reservoir into which they are presumed to have passed from the River Usk which is the reservoir's main source of water supply.
Sturgeon –	many records of this species over the years, mainly from the Severn, but at least one in the Wye. No personal experience of this species.
Twaite Shad –	anadromous species known locally (Monmouth area) as 'May-fish', that being the month during which they migrate up the Rivers Wye and Usk to spawn. Cleach-netting of this species takes place on the River Wye just beyond Gwent at Symond's Yat.
Salmon –	of regular occurrence in both Usk and Wye, and also up the River Monnow, at least as far as Osbaston Weir.
Trout –	the migratory form of the Trout, usually referred to as the 'sea-trout', apparently, present in Gwent waters. No personal experience of this species.
Common Eel –	*catadromous* species typically moving into Gwent waters as 'elvers' during April. This species commonly occurs in the Severn Estuary and also, probably all bodies of fresh-water.
Three-spined Stickleback –	found in the brackish waters of the Severn Estuary fore-shore, and also the reens of the Gwent Levels, the Neddern and Crick Brooks, the canal system in Gwent and the Pontypool Park ponds etc.

Ten-spined Stickleback –	found in reens on the Gwent Levels but formerly up the Neddern Brook as far as Caerwent Brook (1950's).
Flounder –	common in the Severn Estuary but also well up the River Wye, Usk, and presumably the Ebbw and Monnow as well. Also in the smaller tributary brooks such as the Sor Brook, Bettws Brook and the Olway Brook. I was informed by Mrs. Jean Roberts (28.3.85) that a Flounder was even found in the tiny brook which flows down through Buckholt above Monmouth.

The freshwater fish represent the largely artificial aspect of Gwent's pisci fauna, with so many introductions from other parts of Britain and, even the world. The species of my knowledge and acquaintance include the following (order taken from Muus and Dahlstrom – see bibliography).

Brook Lamprey –	probably found in most brooks and rivers in the area but recorded (15.2.59) from the Cas-Troggy Brook near Great Llanmelin, from the same brook at Earlswood and from the River Usk (Mr. Graham Harris) and probably many other similar waters.
Trout –	the non-migratory 'brown-trout' is found in rivers and brooks through most of Gwent, where pollution levels permit.
Rainbow Trout –	an introduced species commonly used to stock ponds, reservoirs etc.
Grayling –	apparently common in the River Monnow. No personal experience of this species.
Pike –	now introduced into most waterways in Gwent – the Monmouthshire Canal at Newport, St. Pierre Lake, Llandegvedd Reservoir etc. The latter site has produced the last two British rod-caught Pike records, the current one weighing 46lbs and 10 ozs.
Roach –	I have records from Monk's Ditch at Goldcliff, reens below Magor, St. Pierre Lake and the River Wye.
Dace –	abundant in the River Usk, Wye and monnow

Chub –	very abundant in the River Wye, present but less obvious in the Usk, and also present in the Monnow.
Minnow –	not known on the Gwent Levels though this fish is found in the Llanmartin Brook which ultimately flows through the Levels. Not present in the Cas-Troggy Brook but otherwise found in rivers and brooks all over Gwent, where pollution levels permit.
Rudd –	stocked into fishing ponds and ornamental pools.
Tench –	St. Pierre Lake (very abundant in the 1960's at least but the almost complete drying out of this lake in the mid-1970's may mean that many fish species which used to be present no longer are). Widely introduced as a prized anglers fish.
Gudgeon –	found, at least, in the Rivers Monnow, Wye and Usk.
Common Bream –	stocked fish at Bettws Ponds, Newport. Illegally introduced into Llandegvedd Reservoir.
Carp –	this Asiatic species has been widely introduced into many parts of the world, including Gwent. Two large specimens lived for many years in the moat at White Castle, where, during the period of his detention at Maindiff Court Hospital, they were occasionally fed by Rudolph Hess. Much later, I understand, they were stoned to death by visitors. Carp are now stocked into many pools, often the 'mirror' form of the species.
Stone Loach –	most rivers and brooks in Gwent contain this species but I have never recorded it from the Cas-Troggy/Neddern Brook.
Perch –	probably quite widespread but little personal experience. Illegally introduced into Llandegvedd Reservoir.
Bullhead –	probably found in most rivers and brooks in Gwent. Certainly very widespread. One interesting note was made on the 27th July 1974 when c.40-50 Bullheads were found dead in the Cas-Troggy Brook in the Cwm where men were using electric-shock treatment to take 'brown trout'.

POST-SCRIPT SUMMARY OF FISH–1997

Very few records relating to fish came my way this year but on the 16th February four Salmon (post-spawning spent fish) were found partially buried in the sand/silt on the banks of the River Usk near Llanbadoc Church.

In early June reports came to me of unusually large numbers of Mackerel in the Severn Estuary but beyond that the only note of interest came during mid-November when, with the late onset of autumn rains, the Salmon were seen jumping against Osbaston Weir on the River Monnow. River bailiffs reportedly stated that numbers of migrating Salmon were down this year.

ADDITIONAL RECORDS/INFORMATION

Amphibians and Reptiles

~

The species occurring in, and native to, Gwent are as follows (order taken from D. Frazer – Collins: *New Naturalist*, No. 69, 1983) –

Triturus cristatus	Great Crested Newt.
Triturus helveticus	Palmate Newt.
Triturus vulgaris	Smooth Newt.
Bufo bufo	Common Toad.
Rana temporia	Common Frog.
Anguis fragilis	Slow-Worm.
Lacerta vivipara	Common Lizard.
Natrix natrix	Grass Snake.
Vipera berus	Adder.

The three newt species can all be treated here together. Generally speaking newts, as we shall see, have fared rather better that the Common Frog, though exactly why this should be is difficult to say. Certainly, improved drainage and the in-filling of farm ponds has caused them problems, but it is also true that other water-bodies have been created – ornamental pools, fishing ponds and the large Llandegvedd Reservoir have all come into being over the past thirty years or so. Garden pools have played a significant role in aiding the newt population levels and this has certainly been the case at Brockwells Farm.

Our local 'speciality' is the Great Crested Newt, for, as far back as my memory (and diaries) take me, I can remember them in the area of Caerwent. In 1960 I recorded (12.6.60) 'There are currently large numbers of both Great Crested and Smooth Newts in Caerwent Quarry Pool'. Temporary set-backs came in the form of the stupid and thoughtless behaviour of certain quarry workers – (28.6.64) 'A few days ago a "pill" (gelignite) was thrown into the quarry pool and today numbers of newts are floating bloated on the surface'. This was, in fact, the second occasion on which this had happened in a short period of time. However, the pool was soon recolonised and I have further records for 19.4.70 and for the 28th June 1981 when 'large numbers' of both Smooth and Great Crested Newts were again present.

It may have been Caerwent Quarry Pool, or possibly the waters of the Neddern Valley, which kept both Great Crested and Smooth Newts in this area but whatever the case, they have always been here, at least in small numbers. Quite naturally, therefore, when we constructed a small pool at Brockwells Farm in 1987 it didn't take long to attract the local newt population and by 1995 the numbers were looking very healthy indeed. On the 6th April of that year I recorded 9 male Great Crested Newts in the pool as well as larger numbers of Smooth Newt.

Palmate Newts are known to be happy living at higher altitudes than the two foregoing species and so they are obvious occupiers of upland pools – Trefil, north of Tredegar, Prescoed near Coed-y-Paen, and Wentwood Forest for example. Perhaps because of this their populations may have a brighter future than those of the Smooth and Great Crested species since the lowland areas are more likely to be despoiled than the uplands.

Smooth Newts have been recorded from freshwater pools in the Newport Docks area and from the canal at Allt-yr-yn, as well as the Caerwent area generally. Great Crested Newts are common in the Raglan area (David Lewis), while I have recorded them from R.A.F. Caerwent and the Neddern Valley as well as from Caerwent Quarry and Brockwells Farm. Newts usually hibernate in dry-land sites, e.g. (17.2.60) 'one Smooth Newt found in middle of Yellow Meadow Ant nest-mound at Brockwells Farm'. However, in some circumstances, probably mild conditions, most, if not all of the winter may be passed in the water.

For me, living in the Caerwent area, the Common Toad was never a really abundant animal at all. We would get the occasional individual in the garden, and there were times when I noted their spawning presence in the Neddern floodwaters, but it wasn't until I became familiar with the Wentwood Reservoir mass spring migration that the species took on any great significance for me.

With the notable increase in road traffic during the 1970's the plight of the migrating toads moving down to the breeding pool at night, attracted our attention, and volunteers were enlisted (bucket patrols) to transport them safely across the road. This proved not simply to be a mercy mission, but also a means by which important data could be collected. For example, on the evening of the 9th April 1979 over 300 toads were moved off roads running down either side of the Wentwood Reservoir. On the evening of the 31st March 1980 the figure was 400.

Of the amphibians occurring in Gwent it is the Common Frog which has suffered the greatest losses over the forty-year span of my records. On the 12th March 1959 my diary recorded – '"thousands" of Common Frogs are to be seen in the Caerwent Brook area at present, many lie dead on the road, but also in the brook itself'. In the following summer a great exodus of tiny froglets from the Neddern Valley invaded all of the surrounding farmland. My diary at the time states – (28.7.59) 'For the past couple of months now the commonest animals in the fields have been the Common frogs. Whether it is dry or wet they are to be found in their hundreds in the shade of some tall growth (Spear Thistles etc.). These frogs are undoubtedly those which, only a few weeks ago, were to be seen in their "millions" down the Neddern. They have now made their way into the fields and woodlands where they have become the prey of a variety of mammals, birds and reptiles. It is interesting to note the different colour varieties that can be seen – yellow, light green, dark green, grey, light brown, dark brown, orange, dull black, wine-colour or emerald green'.

Later on, during the Autumn I noted – (30.10.59) 'Large numbers of small Common Frogs and one Smooth Newt were found "hibernating" (?) under rotting heaps of Ragwort which had been pulled in these fields during the summer'.

On the 13th March 1964 c.30 Common Frogs were seen spawning in an area of water amounting to about three square yards, in the Neddern Valley, but there-after the decline of these animals was so dramatic that by the late summer of 1971 I wrote – 'In the Hardwick Plantation of the Minnetts forestry area today I found a small Common Frog. These are becoming so scarce now in our area as to be noteworthy whenever they are seen'. In the spring of 1985 another comment illustrates the comparative scarcity of the species by that time – (13.4.85) '2 Common Frogs, 3 Smooth Newts and a single Great Crested Newt discovered during clearing operations in the "weed" congested acid-bath "pond" in R.A.F. Caerwent'. The ratio of frogs to newts on this occasion says it all! In about twenty-five years the Common Frog has plummeted from great abundance, almost to rarity.

Today the Common Frog population in Gwent is maintained largely by people with garden-pools. The frogs often 'infest' these small oases, on occasions to such a degree that the garden owners find it hard to believe that the species is anything but common. Yet they are the only ones who could possibly think so for in the countryside as a whole the decline of the Common Frog has been little short of catastrophic.

Of the reptiles found in Gwent, the Slow-worm is probably the most abundant and widespread. My records for this species come from most parts of the area – Highmoor Hill, Llanwern, Llanmelin, Wentwood, Garndiffaith, Llanelen, Tintern, Newport, Coed-y-paen, Llansantffraed, etc. In some places they can even be described as abundant – e.g. (2.4.77) 'On a walk in the Angiddy Valley at Tintern we found 7 Slow-worms, some of them very large specimens'.

The Common Lizard is of more local distribution but otherwise quite widespread. I once received a report that in September 1969 this species had been particularly abundant in the Tintern area that summer, but I have not personally seen them there. I have noted the Common Lizard from Mynydd Alltir-fach, Newport Docks, Wentwood Forest, Little Mill, Kemeys Inferior, Llandevaud, Blaenavon Moor, Cleddon, Llanvaches and Trefil – I have never seen them in the Caerwent area.

Of this entire group the Grass Snake is the species that is probably the most vulnerable, and which has shown the greatest decline in population. Early records show the species to be very abundant in the Caerwent–Caldicot area generally – (6.3.61) '"Quite a few" Grass Snakes out in the warm sunshine today in the shelter of a hedgrow at Brockwells Farm'. (31.3.61) 'Five Grass Snakes active at Slough Farm Marsh, Caerwent'. (16.4.63) 'Four Grass Snakes wound together in a tangle along the edge of the Upper Rodge Wood bordering Brockwells Farm land'.

In the winter of 1963, while moving stone-rubble from a long disused area covered with trees and bushes in Caerwent Quarry 3 Grass Snakes were found in their hibernation retreats, as well as 2 Slow-worms.

After this, and synchronous with the decline of the Common Frog, the numbers grew progressively fewer, but I still came across them on occasions in many parts of Gwent – (27.4.71) 'one in the Minnetts forestry area', (19.9.72) 'one in Llanwern Steelworks', (24.2.74) 'one at Long Ditch, Llanwern', (16.7.74) 'one near Noah's Ark on the Caldicot Level near Undy', (9.8.74) 'one at Wentwood Lodge in Wentwood Forest', (3.8.75) 'one at Bishton', (19.8.78) 'one near Wentwood Reservoir, and (12.6.90) 'one at Llanvihangel Gobion'. The last time I saw a Grass Snake at Brockwells Farm was on 29th June 1974 – I may never see one here again!

The Adder is also declining but not so obviously as the Grass Snake. At one time they were common in the area around Brockwells Farm. In the early 1950's I can remember my father killing one as it tried to enter our house. Adders occupied Rock House Wood (later erased by the excavation of Caerwent Quarry) and also the Shirefield Brake at the western end of Brockwells Farm. They were always common in the Minnetts forestry area, Wentwood Forest and many parts of the Trellech Plateau, the Coalfield and the Northern Hills. In fact, almost everywhere in Gwent where the right sort of 'rough' habitat exists – Heather-moor, woodland edge, scrub, heath, etc.

Adders hibernate below ground but the hibernation period can sometimes be quite short, or seemingly so anyway. This variation of hibernation period may depend on temperature, mild conditions encouraging continuing activity, cold conditions the opposite. As an illustration of this I have seen Adders out of hibernation by the last day of February on at least two occasions, and in 1978 saw one particular individual at Wentwood Lodge on several days leading into the Christmas period – the last day being the 26th December.

POST-SCRIPT SUMMARY OF AMPHIBIANS AND REPTILES–1997

The evening of the 5th March proved suitable for checking on the Common Toad migration down to the Wentwood Reservoir. The weather was mild and wet with drizzle falling during the afternoon and early evening. 187 Common Toads were counted on the roads running along either side of the reservoir and, also, 1 Common Frog. This figure compares reasonably well with those of previous years when figures quoted were the best over a period of several nights.

The rest of the year's records are as follows –

28th January.	Three Common Frogs found dead in the pool at Brockwells Farm, probably resulting from the ice-cover over the late Christmas/early New-year period.
7th February.	Frogspawn in small pond at Little Wentwood Farm (Anne and Walt Jackson).
26th February.	Two small clumps of Frogspawn in pond at Brockwells Farm.
13th March.	After checking on the Brockwells Farm Pool for the past seven days, I counted, this evening, 16 Great Crested Newts (9 males and 7 females), this being the highest number counted here this year.
16th March.	Today we found 1 Common Lizard on Mynydd Alltir-fach and another on Grey Hill while participating in one of our regular monthly field-trips.
13th May.	1 Common Lizard on Mynydd Varteg.
30th May.	1 Common Lizard on White Hill, Monmouth.

20th July. 2 Common Lizards on upland moor near Chwarel y Fan. Also one large Common Frog.

12th August. Today Mrs. Beryl Stopgate reported the presence of a Grass Snake in her garden at Rogiet. This individual is a resident in the area since it had been seen earlier in the year. On each occasion it was actively hunting Common Frogs in the garden ponds.

15th August. 2 Common Lizards seen on Blorenge/Blaenavon Moor.

8th September. 2 Common Lizards and one small Common Frog on upland moor near Chwarel y Fan.

ADDITIONAL RECORDS/INFORMATION

Birds

~

The bird life of this area has been most adequately dealt with by the Gwent Ornithological Society in a whole series of publications (see bibliography). However, since this book represents a largely personal account of Gwent's wildlife it may be useful to offer here my own notes on at least a small selection of species. For this excercise I have adopted the sequence used in *The Birds of Gwent*, 1977.

Cormorant

The Cormorant's success may have been rather too good, for, because of its particular diet, it has incited the wrath of fishermen, and during the 1990's, licences were granted to shoot at the birds. I use this rather strange phrase advisedly because I am informed that the wording on the licences is quite precise and does not mention the word 'cull'. Each licence permits c. six birds to be shot at but they must be single birds and not part of a flock.

My records tend to reflect this gradual increase in population. It is interesting that my earlier inclusion of records made along the Severn Estuary indicate a corresponding scarcity status at that time. Today they are so frequent along the estuary that they would not warrant a note in a 'casual' diary, however, the following notes may be of interest.

The main nocturnal roost for Cormorants in Gwent lies in the Wye Valley between Piercefield House and Lover's Leap. It is actually the same site as that used for nesting by the local Herons.

(28.1.68) 'c.25 flying into roost-trees in the Wye Valley', (12.4.71) 'Four Cormorants along the River Usk at Llanllowell', (4.6.72) 'a single bird along the Severn Estuary at Magor Pill', (29.9.73) 'one along the Severn Estuary between Magor and Undy', (19.2.74) 'c.70 Cormorants flying east high over the Usk Valley at Llantrisant, possibly passing from Llandegvedd Reservoir to the lower Wye Valley roost', (1.1.81) 'c.40-50 at the Wye Valley roost',

(3.2.83) '11 Cormorants flushed (7.00 am) from roost trees along the River Usk at Allt Farm, Llantrisant', (6.2.85) '23 on Bulmore pylon-roost near Caerleon', (13.8.93) 'a flock of 15 Cormorants flying down the Severn Estuary off Mathern', (18.4.96) '42 on Bulmore pylon-roost near Caerleon'. This last record was made at dusk, prompting the question – do the Cormorants use this roost nocturnally as well as diurnally? Perhaps it depends on prevailing weather conditions.

During the 1970's it seemed to me that most of the area's Cormorants roosted in the Wye Valley, but moved out to other feeding grounds and back again each day. A series of observations suggested that a regular route for these birds, roosting in the Wye Valley, but feeding in the Usk Valley, or Llandegvedd Reservoir, would be along a line passing over St. Arvans and Rogerstone Grange, along the southern edge of Chepstow Park Wood, the northern edge of Wentwood Forest, and thence into the Usk Valley near Llantrisant. It may now be (in the late 1990's) that more birds are roosting at sites in the Usk Valley.

To date (1996) the Cormorant has not been proved to breed in Gwent, though breeding has sometimes been suspected. Gwent Cormorants may originate from breeding colonies on Steepholm, Gower and on around the west Wales coast, or even further afield. In my diary for the 17th September, 1984, I noted – 'Today David Jones (of Malpas) phoned me to report on information recently received from the B.T.O. (British Museum of Natural History) re the ringed juvenile Cormorant that he found dead at the side of the River Usk at Usk Town during the summer. The bird was ringed as a nestling on Little Saltee (Island)off the coast of County Wexford, on May 28th, 1983'.

Garganey

This is a small duck which was, seemingly, never common in Gwent. Garganey did occur regularly (late 1950's and early 1960's at least) on flood-waters of the Neddern Valley, until improved drainage limited the time-span of flood water and rendered the area unsuitable. The Neddern wasn't the only site for the species in Gwent but Garganey are now considered a rarity and only occur sporadically on passage.

I first noted this species in the spring of 1959 when in April I recorded – '7 Garganey have been regular on the Neddern flood-water throughout the month, in the company of 27 Coot'. On the 20th April, 1959, a visit to the Peewit Field also produced an unspecified number of Garganey, but, if my memory serves, just a single bird. The birds remained in the Neddern Valley through May of the same year but on the 26th I noted that only 2 pairs were now present and, on the 29th, that it was mostly male Garganey to be seen. On the 5th August 1959 I even found a pair at the side of the River Wye, below the area of the Wyndcliff.

In 1960 my first Garganey record came on the 12th March when a single bird was present on the water. On the 24th April a pair was present but on the 12th and 17th of May only a single bird could be seen (sex not specified in my note at the time but presumably a male).

After this, the Neddern Brook in the Neddern Valley was cleaned out and deepened, which meant that although the flood water materialised during the winter, it drained away much more quickly and the Garganey only appeared briefly thereafter. If anything they seemed to switch their attention to the Magor Reserve where, in 1969 a duck with ducklings proved breeding for the second time in Gwent, and where I saw a pair on the 16th April of the following year.

In 1971 2 pairs returned to the Neddern but they were only present during March. Beyond this I have very few records of this species in the area, though Colin Elliot has provided the occasional record during the 1980's – e.g. (1.4.82) 'a pair seen on the Church Farm Pool'.

Shelduck

One of Gwent's most handsome birds, and one of great interest for a variety of reasons. Shelduck are most typically birds of the estuary, but they also occur, and breed, well inland, their main requirement being areas of open water, including a reasonably large river such as the Wye in its lower reaches. Rather strangely, I have always thought, Shelduck often nest some distance from that body of water, and, in consequence, frequently find it necessary to walk the precocial offspring a distance of two miles or more to reach the chosen stretch of open water. Think, for example, of a family of Shelducks walking down to the Severn Estuary from the Minnetts forestry area, or Wilcrick Hill, where they are known to have nested in the past. There are major roads and railway lines to cross, as well as a continually expanding strip of housing development to negotiate – a hazardous journey indeed!

Another fascinating aspect of Shelduck behaviour concerns the site of the nest itself, nearly always in a dark hollow (though there is the occasional exception) – small caves, hollows under trees, Rabbit burrows (hence the local name – Barrow Duck) etc., but do they also nest in Badger setts?, and if they do, are those setts occupied by Badgers at the time? I believe that this does happen – yet another instance of potential predator/prey species living together in harmony – like the Honey Bees and Hornets at the Radyr.

The social behaviour of Shelduck is also interesting. In the spring, presumably just prior to nesting, several pairs gather together on fields where they perform rather vocal displays – one of the most beautiful sights in the Gwent countryside. This behaviour is often associated with the proximity of Badger setts where, I believe, they sometimes nest.

After the nesting phase of the breeding programme has been completed, another aspect of social behaviour occurs when the Shelducklings are gathered together into groups (crèche) where they may be less vulnerable to predation.

My Shelduck records are as follows – (20.4.59) 'Shelducks on the flooded Peewit Field, (15.4.63) '3 pairs of Shelducks together on the flank of the River Bed Field, Dewstow Farm' (see map 3), (22.4.71) 'Shelducks frequently seen, and obviously breeding, in the Minnetts forestry area (several records that spring relating to two pairs), (26.6.71) '70 Shelducks (+32 Shelducklings) on the Severn Estuary between Magor and Undy, (18.4.72) '3 pairs in the Minnetts forestry area', (24.6.72) 'Today I found a female Shelduck incubating eggs in a small cave in the Upper Rodge Wood', (1.7.72) 'Shelduck pair with 7 young at Magor Pill', (31.5.77) 'Shelduck with young on Wentwood Reservoir', (31.5.78) 'Shelduck pair with 9 young on Wentwood Reservoir', (19.6.78) 'c.300 Shelduck (+ 24 Shelducklings) and 2 Ruddy Shelduck along the Severn Estuary near Collister Pill, Undy', (21.4.79) '2 pairs flying over Brockwells Farm fields', (19.4.80) '10 Shelduck on Wentwood Reservoir', (25.5.80) 'Shelducks (+ 9 Shelducklings) on Wentwood Reservoir', (28.6.80) 'Today I noted a pair of Shelduck on Caerwent Quarry Pool', (2.7.80) 'The Shelduck on Caerwent Quarry Pool now have two young with them' (incredibly, or so I thought, these two young were successfully raised to maturity), (13.5.81) 'Today we came upon a female Shelduck with 9 young walking down the lane leading from Llanvair Discoed towards the Wentwood Inn on the A48 – (the route to the Severn Estuary would presumably be down the St. Brides Brook but this is not necessarily so and I cannot remember seeing Shelducks, with or without young, on such a narrow water-way as a brook), (20.5.83) '14 Shelduck in R.A.F. Caerwent', (28.5.84) 'pair of Shelduck with 9 or 10 young close to Brockwells Farm buildings at 7.30pm', (7.6.84) 'Today a pair of Shelduck were present on Brockwells Farm Banky Field and one of them appeared to be cleaning our the old Fox hole on the south-facing bank', (14.6.92) 'Shelduck with 3 young on River Wye below Piercefield', (11.7.96) ' a pair with 6 young on the River Wye below Piercefield'.

Mute Swan

For a species that is widely recognised as the 'Queen's bird', and not regarded as truly 'wild', the Mute Swan's future seemed assured. So it came as a big surprise then, during the 1980's, to find this bird going into a population decline, the reason, apparently, artificially introduced lead into the water. My records for the Neddern Valley show a peak of numbers during the early 1960's, then came the big crash and subsequent, partial recovery.

(13.12.59) '21 Mute Swans on Neddern Valley floods', (10.1.60) '24 Mute Swans on Neddern Valley floods', (27.3.60) '40 Mute Swans on Neddern Valley floods', (18.2.61) '80 Mute Swans on Neddern Valley floods', (2.4.61) '62 Mute Swans on Neddern Valley floods'.

Whooper Swan and Bewick's Swan

My first sighting of these winter visitors came on the 9th January 1960 – 'On the Neddern Valley floods I counted 20 swans. Eight of the twenty were Mute Swans, the remaining twelve comprising a mixed group of Whooper Swans and Bewick's Swans. Six of these twelve were immature birds – a soft grey with pink and black bills. Of the remaining six adults 4 were Bewick's Swans and 2 were Whooper Swans.

After this date these 'wild' swans were recorded regularly with the Bewick's being the most abundant and regularly occurring. Records for Whooper Swans are as follows – (11.3.61) '5 on Neddern Valley floods', (10.2.62) '8 on Neddern Valley floods in the company of a single Bewick's Swan and a single Canada Goose', (6.3.65) '7 Whooper Swans on the River Wye at Whitebrook'.

Records for the Bewick's Swans are as follows – (21.12.68) '14 Bewick's Swans on the First Pool of the Neddern', (24.12.70) '7 on the Neddern Valley floods and 2 on the coast at Magor Pill', (27.12.70) '7 on Peewit Field floods near Llanvihangel Rogiet'.

From 1971 I became involved with the 'Birds of Estuaries' enquiry and largely forsook my Neddern Valley haunts. The Bewick's continued to visit the Neddern throughout, but my records now switch mostly to the Severn Estuary.

(2.1.71) '20 at Collister Pill, Undy', (9.1.71) '20 along the Severn Estuary between Magor and Undy', (10.12.72) '4 along the Severn Estuary between Magor and Undy', (1.12.73) '7 along the Severn Estuary between Magor and Undy', (19.3.81) '6 Bewick's Swans along the River Usk at Llanllowell', (11.2.90) '2 on riverside floods at Llanvair Kilgeddin'. During the latter part of this period they were also recorded regularly from Llandegvedd Reservoir and the Olway flood-meadows near Gwernesney. They continue to thrive.

Goshawk

Today (late 1990's) the Goshawk is almost a common breeding bird in Gwent, yet thirty years ago it was regarded as a rarity. Where did the population come from? Are they immigrants? Are they the result of a successful breeding boom in the largely post-shooting/pesticide era? Or are they, as many claim, the product of intentionally released birds by falconers, and if so, for what reason are they being released? My records chart the gradual build up of this species in the area, even though the notes were made on a purely casual basis. (19.6.71) 'Capt. Marshall of Llanarth reported to me today the sighting of a Goshawk over Llanarth Court land recently', (8.3.75) 'a Goshawk reported by Howard Slatter in Wentwood Forest in the Nant-y-pridd area', (28.4.75) 'Today a Goshawk flew into the trees at Wentwood Lodge in Wentwood Forest', (4.10.81) 'a single bird seen in the Reddings Enclosure area, Hadnock', (13.12.82) 'a single bird flying over the lower Wye Valley near the Wyndcliff', (24.8.91) 'Goshawk nest with young discovered by Jan and Tony Jenkins in Chepstow Park Wood', (27.3.94) '2 in R.A.F. Caerwent', (3.6.94) '2 displaying Goshawks over R.A.F. Caerwent', (16.4.95) 'a single bird over Cadira Beeches, Wentwood Forest', (18.8.95) '1 Raven and 1 Goshawk disputing air-space over the Cwm', (16.9.95) 'a single bird seen in R.A.F. Caerwent', (24.7.96) 'Today a Goshawk flew over Brockwells Farm and on towards Upper Rodge Wood'.

Partridge

Nationally the Partridge is in serious decline and this situation is also true for Gwent. Like many animal populations, that of the Partridge has fluctuated considerably over the years, and the very casual records entered into my diaries no doubt distort the picture considerably. However, with this species there is yet another factor which misleads the researcher and helps to paint a false picture, and that is artificial rearing. For, like other game species, this bird has been bred, raised in captivity and then released, and it would probably be an impossible task to find out exactly when, where and in what quantity these birds were added to the natural population. Nevertheless, it is all rather academic now for the species has become very scarce, the only area of Gwent which could reasonably be expected to produce any regular sightings of Partridge now being the Gwent Levels. It may well be significant that shooting syndicates operate here and possibly release birds for that purpose.

Within the span of my experience, the hey-day for the Partridge in the Caerwent-Caldicot area was in the 1950's and 1960's when they could be seen regularly and in good numbers. From the mid 1960's the populations became more localised but I sometimes recorded good numbers, on a local basis as late as 1971, but then came the obvious decline. The last regular, but small, numbers were recorded in the early 1980's.

A note in my diary for the 11th February 1968 demonstrates quite clearly that ten years after being seen so regularly and commonly there were none present, at least, not on that particular evening. Obviously, even by that time the status of the Partridge locally had diminished noticeably and the figures for 1971 may refer to released birds. All recent Partridge records that I have made are of birds on the Gwent Levels.

Water Rail

A mysterious bird of secluded places, typically rank marshland vegetation, where its activities are hidden from view for much of the time. Many records exist but at the present time one is left with the feeling that the species is undergoing serious decline.

I first saw this bird on Slough Farm Marsh, Caerwent on the 26th September 1959. It was seen regularly here for some time after that, and later still, further on down the Neddern Valley, throughout 1960 and well into 1961. The lack of records in the Neddern Valley after this probably reflect the improved drainage which I first noted as taking place on the 23rd January 1961, and which also reduced the occurrence of the Garganey here.

In 1970 and 1971 a friend living along the St. Brides Road, Penhow, (Derek Edwards) reported numerous sightings of a Water Rail along the brook which runs through the valley of that name, during the February – April period. In 1971 I began to watch the Magor Reserve and a Water Rail was seen regularly here from that time, at least until the period of the American Bittern visit ten years later – (27.12.81) 'This morning Colin Elliot and I went down to the Magor Reserve. As we drove along the northern edge of the marshland we came across the American Bittern only fifteen yards from the side of the road, and nearby were 3 Water Rails'.

Records also materialised from other parts of the Caldicot Level – (16.12.62) 'one in a reen near Magor', (30.12.77) 'one in the 'back-ditch' near Uskmouth ash-pans'. During the 1980's Colin Elliot, while photographing birds in the Tintern-Devauden woodlands, regularly saw a Water Rail along the tiny woodland streams during the 'winter period'. Indeed, it is noticeable that most of the records mentioned above relate to periods of the year other than the spring/summer. In fact, breeding has been confirmed in the area on very few occasions.

Oystercatcher

The fortunes of this bird appear to be on the up as far as my experience is concerned. Within the past forty years I didn't really 'operate' in the habitat of the Oystercatcher until I began my stint for the 'Birds of Estuaries' enquiry in 1970.

A pair of these birds had moved into the Collister Pill area during the early spring of 1971 and on the 23rd May Trevor Evans and I found the nest with two eggs. By the 8th June both eggs had hatched and the first breeding record for the area since the late 1800's was in place (*The Birds of Monmouthshire*, Ingram and Salmon, revised by P. N. Humphreys, Newport Museum Publication, 1963).

In the following year we found a nest with three eggs at the same site. This seemed to establish the Oystercatcher as a regular breeder along the Gwent coast for in subsequent years breeding birds moved onto the fields of the Levels just to the landward side of the 'back-ditch' and this situation persists to the present day. Oystercatchers now (late 1990's) breed here and there along the Gwent coastal strip as far east as Caldicot.

Lapwing

Here we have another example of serious decline. In the period of my childhood to teenage years the Lapwing was a regular and common breeder at two major sites in the immediate locality – the Neddern Valley and the Peewit Field near Llanvihangel Rogiet. As well as this there were many 'dry land' sites where breeding occurred throughout Gwent.

During the days of my Severn Estuary bird counts I recorded, on occasions, huge winter flocks, but even these now seem to be a thing of the past, and the nationwide picture is generally regarded as grim. Selected records for this species are as follows – (20.4.59) 'Lapwing nests with 4 and 3 eggs on the Peewit Field', (14.4.60) '"many" Lapwings nests in the Neddern Valley', (25.12.70) 'an estimated 10,000-15,000 Lapwings coming down to the Severn fore-shore below Magor/Undy at dusk', (12.4.71) 'Lapwings breeding on Usk River-side fields at Llanllowell', (13.4.71) '3 pairs of breeding Lapwings on the Neddern Valley. These numbers are well down on previous years', (11.5.71) 'Lapwings and Redshanks appear to be breeding in good numbers on the Peewit Field', (25.12.71) 'c.1,000 Lapwings on fields at Llanvihangel Rogiet', (24.1.81) 'Yesterday we saw a flock of at least 1,000 Lapwings circling over fields at Rogiet Pool. Today a similar number of Lapwings were circling over fields around Little Dewstow (between the Brockwells and Dewstow Farm)'.

Snipe

Because it is a wetland bird, the Snipe is, almost inevitably, a declining species in Gwent. Today, breeding records are few and far between, particularly in the area of the Gwent Levels which was formerly a stronghold of the species. A selection of records are as follows – (7.6.59) 'Snipe "drumming" in the Neddern Valley ("drumming" being the 'mechanical', as opposed to the vocal, form of territory declaration)', (26.9.59) 'large numbers of Snipe on Slough Farm Marsh', (31.3.60) 'Snipe "drumming" in the Neddern Valley' and again on the 22nd May. (16.4.70) 'large numbers of Snipe seen at Magor Reserve', (10.5.71) 'On fields at Church Farm, Wilcrick, we found a juvenile Snipe which was just beginning to fly', (12.6.71) 'Snipe obviously breeding on the Peewit Field', (17.4.72) 'Snipe "drumming" at Magor Reserve', (7.4.73) '18 Snipe on the Peewit Field', (18.3.74) '18 Snipe on rough, wet land at Newport docks', (17.5.81) '4 Snipe "drumming" at Trefil', (9.7.81) 'Snipe's nest with 3 eggs in the Magor Reserve'.

As well as these typical records I have also noted that Snipe sometimes take temporary shelter in what appears to be strange places. For example, I have flushed Snipe from long grass at Brockwells Farm on at least two occasions. On the 9th February 1978 I made the following observation – 'On Grey Hill I flushed a Snipe at 11.40 am from dry, Bracken-covered ground, and on my way back, at 1.20 pm, I flushed it again from a similarly dry area'. This observation equates with that of Woodcock, a close relative, on the 13th November, 1983 – 'On our way up to the top of the Sugar Loaf we flushed a Woodcock from Bracken c. 15ft. from the main path leading up to the top of the hill'.

Collared Dove

This is a species which has invaded Gwent within the past forty years. This 'natural' invasion began, for me, in this area on the 16th December 1967 when I noted one near Rogiet and another at Brockwells Farm. In the following January I saw 8 at Rogiet Rectory and by April of that year they were already becoming 'pests' on a local basis – (20.4.68) 'At the Innage

Farm, Mathern, today I saw a number of Collared Doves and was informed by the owner that the birds were now so numerous here that they were becoming a nuisance'. On the 30th April 1969 I noted 4 feeding with the chickens at Brockwells Farm, and this had become 12 by August of the same year. At sites of grain distribution, e.g. Triley Mill on the 4th October 1969, flocks of 30 or more were regularly seen. On the 8th April 1973 I counted 27 at this site and on the 30th July 1974 counted 13 together on wires at Dewstow Farm.

In fact, wherever grain is readily available, and this includes garden bird-tables, the Collared Dove becomes part and parcel of the scene. Gardens, especially if they include evergreen trees, provide the perfect habitat for this very successful colonising bird.

Turtle Dove

As the incoming Collared Dove flourished so that long-standing bird of the British countryside, the Turtle Dove, went into decline. My records corroborate its former abundance as a summer visitor, and then illustrate its decline into a state of virtual rarity today. On the 30th June 1959 my diary states- 'Turtle Doves "numerous" in the area of Brockwells Farm – Highmoor Hill'. Several more 1959 records followed, the last being on the 26th September.

In 1960 I saw my first bird on the 1st April at Brockwells Farm, with further records for the Minnetts forestry area and Neddern Valley. In 1961 I noted (27.5.61) 'Turtle Doves seen frequently in the Shirefield area', – followed by records from the Quarry Wood (to the south of Dewstow House) on the 23rd July.

Records seem to be lacking for 1962 but in 1963 I recorded Turtle Doves from the Shirefield Brake on the 16th May, Wentwood Forest on the 19th May, and then found a nest with 2 eggs in the Shirefield Brake on the 27th May. In 1964 I noted the presence of Turtle Doves at Highmoor Hill on 21st May and in various other places locally. In 1965 they were back in their territories by the 12th May and on the 25th July I noted – 'Many Turtle Doves along with Wood Pigeons on the wheat crop near Dewstow'.

It may be that my activities took me away from the haunts of Turtle Doves for the next couple of years but on the 4th June 1968 I noted – 'Numbers of Turtle Doves in Earlswood Bottoms', that being my only record for the year. Turtle Doves were again noted in the Earlswood Valley on the 15th June, 1969, in the Minnetts forestry area on the 12th May, 1970, and again on the 19th April, 30th April and 10th May, 1971, at the same site.

On the 13th June of that year I noted Turtle Doves in the Wentwood Forest and on the 20th June, saw a bird on the Severn Estuary saltings below Undy. It was, again, the 'Birds of Estuaries' enquiry which brought me into this environment for the next seven years and enabled me to record the Turtle Dove in this somewhat unexpected habitat on many occasions – (15.7.72) '10 Turtle Doves along the foreshore between Magor Pill and Collister Pill, Undy', (28.4.73) 'Two Turtle Doves seen on the fore-shore between Magor Pill and Collister Pill, Undy', (21.7.73) '2 at Collister Pill, Undy (4.5.74) 'a single bird along the foreshore below Rogiet', (13.7.74) 'one along the fore-shore between Magor Pill and Collister Pill, Undy', (5.7.75) '5 along the sea-wall between Magor Pill and Collister Pill, Undy', (21.5.78) 'a Turtle Dove on field near Collister Pill, Undy', and again on the 13th August and 20th August.

Turtle Doves were also commonly seen feeding at the side of narrow lanes in the area, possibly picking up grit. A typical record for this activity was noted on the 28th June 1971 – 'Several Turtle Doves noted in the lanes on a drive from Undy to Wentwood'.

The decline of the Turtle Dove in Gwent couldn't really be described as dramatic, it has been gradual, and in fact, still continues today. The last place in which I recorded this bird was in Chepstow Park Wood, within the present decade.

Cuckoo

As with many other long familiar forms of wildlife, there is a tendency to think of the Cuckoo as a declining species, and this is probably true. Personally, because of the bird's former abundance, I have no long-term records to check this belief against but, fortunately, I did record the occurrence, by both sight and sound, of the Cuckoo in Gwent during the years of 1976 and 1977. I am now able to compare the figures for these years, with those of the present year – 1997 (see Summary).

In 1976 I was away from the county for about eleven days during the period of the Cuckoo's presence. Neverthelesss between the 23rd April and the 2nd August I heard the Cuckoo's call on fourteen days and saw Cuckoo's on eleven days, these records representing at least 15 birds, those on the 28th June, 7th July and 2nd August being juveniles of the year.

In 1977, with no break in the period 30th April–15th June, the Cuckoo was heard on thirty-one days and seen on a further three days, these records representing at least 9 birds, but probably more. All of these records represent personal observations and do not include those received from other people.

Barn Owl

Under this heading I consider it desirable to include some records of the other owl species for, although the Barn Owl records are the more important, because of the dramatic changes in the bird's recent history, various aspects relating to the other owls are pertinent to the Barn Owl too, as will be seen from the following notes. (9.3.60) 'This evening a Barn Owl was flying around the area of Brockwells Farm at 5.40', (5.2.61) 'Barn Owl pellets found in old barn at Penhein', (5.4.61) 'one Barn Owl over Ballan Moor area of the Neddern Valley', (9.5.61) 'one Barn Owl in Minnetts forestry area', (10.5.61) 'a Barn Owl flew over the road at Pen-y-cae-mawr', (25.7.61) 'while Badger watching a Barn Owl passed over me on the edge of the Quarry Wood near Caldicot', (16.1.63) 'one Barn Owl over the Lanneck near Brockwells Hill', (8.4.63) 'one Barn Owl found dead at Caerwent Brook', (27.9.63) 'Today a Barn Owl was perched on the rock-face in Caerwent Quarry', (21.12.65) 'My third load (as a lorry driver for Penhow Quarries Ltd.) went to Temperance Hotel at Goldcliff, and then along the sea-wall towards Porton House. Down here on the Levels I have again seen numbers of Kestrels. Today, in only two visits, I saw 8-10 Kestrels and, on my second load, a Barn Owl. Stoats and Weasels are also obvious here, indicating, perhaps, a large population of Short-tailed Voles'. This situation continued into 1966 when Short-eared Owls were also seen regularly here – e.g. (14.1.66) '3 Short-eared Owls and a Barn Owl flying over the Porton Moors in daylight and obviously hunting'.

It was about this time that a temporary blip occurred in the Little Owl population. My diary for the 31st December 1967 states – 'Another bird which has declined sharply in numbers this past year or so is the Little Owl. Only a couple of years ago this was by far the most abundant species of owl in the Caerwent area'. However, during the latter half of 1968 a recovery was on its way and, although still not as abundant as previously, the Little Owl is frequently to be seen in many parts of Gwent now. A note in my diary for 21st July 1971 sets the scene at that time – 'A Little Owl was present here (Church Farm, Wilcrick) all evening and it now seems that this species has recovered from its decline of a few years ago and is now to be found almost everywhere. Not so the Barn Owl however, which I have failed to find in Gwent this year. Indeed, I haven't seen a Barn Owl anywhere since 1969'. On the 1st October 1972 I wrote – 'In the ruins of Piercefield House we found feathers and over 30 pellets of a Barn Owl – the first definite proof I've had of this species in Gwent since 1967'.

The most visible evidence of Barn Owl mortality comes in the form of road-accident fatalities and in the 1974-1976 period my work for the Forestry Commission took me down onto the relatively new stretches of trunk-road between the Coldra (Newport) and Monmouth (i.e. the A449 from Coldra – Raglan and the A40, that portion between Raglan and Monmouth). My records paint a disturbing picture for in 1974 I noted 4 dead Barn Owls on those roads, in 1975 a further 2 and in 1976 a further 4. There were, of course, other casualties on other roads during this same period. Although the Barn Owl is the species which is particularly vulnerable, it is not exclusively so as my record for the 7th April 1975 shows – 'one dead Barn Owl, a dead Little Owl and two dead Tawny Owls along the A449 between the Coldra and Usk'.

Fast moving vehicles are a problem for many British owls but it may be that they have something else in common too. The Little Owls which inhabited the line of hollow willows along the southern edge of the Peewit Field obviously preyed upon the roosting flocks of Dunlin on this particular area of wetland – (14.5.61) 'In hollows in some of these trees we found the headless bodies of several Dunlin and a Short-tailed Vole – all victims of a Little Owl'. Rather interesting then, my note of the 27th December 1962 – 'In an old shed on the Caldicot Level between Caldicot and Rogiet we found pellets of a Barn Owl plus several wings of wading birds – 6 Dunlin wings and the wing of a Knot. Whether the Barn Owl killed these birds is not known. Wings of Dunlin have also been found in hollow trees edging the Peewit Field, and these trees are the haunt of a Little Owl'.

Another interesting record of Barn Owls came by way of Noel and Linda Bellamy in the summer of 1991 when they located a nest with young in the limestone cliff-face below Chepstow Castle. This was a picturesque, almost romantic, setting in which to observe these beautiful birds.

From these records it will be seen that the Barn Owl is a species in serious decline, records from the 1980's and 1990's being few and far between. It should also be taken into account that during this recent period artificial Barn Owl breeding and release programmes have been put into operation so the few records coming from this period may well result from this particular activity. What is obviously the case is that the Barn Owl is unable operate successfully in a countryside through which pass fast roads. Even if other limiting factors are dealt with in order to aid its survival, it is unlikely that much can be done to solve the problem of fast-moving traffic.

Grasshopper Warbler

This is a bird of thick vegetation habitat typified by marshland, scrub, young plantation or similar vegetation types found on commons. In Gwent I have recorded this species in the breeding period from the Minnetts forestry area, Cleddon Bog, Magor Reserve, Grey Hill, Wentwood Forest, Slidy Hill Wood and R.A.F. Caerwent, but also, as they move towards these chosen breeding grounds on their inward migration, they will sing from hedgerows and other thick cover in all sorts of strange places.

Few people get to see Grasshopper Warblers on a regular basis, consequently they are usually identified by their very distinctive song, and that is generally the case with my records. During the 1950's this was a regular breeding bird in the Minnetts forestry area and my records show continuing occupation by this bird here up until 1971. At Magor Reserve up to three Grasshopper Warblers were singing during the spring of 1971 and at Slidy Hill Wood, then a young forestry plantation, we found a nest with eggs (4 eggs on the 8th June).

The earliest presence of this summer visitor, as noted by myself, was on the 7th March 1973 when one was singing from marshland vegetation at Newport Docks. A more unusual record concerns that of a Grasshopper Warbler singing from a cereal crop at Shirenewton on the 9th June 1984, this being the last occasion when I heard or observed this species in Gwent.

Firecrest

All of my observations of this species come from the Wentwood Forest during the period of my employment there by the Forestry Commission. There were comparatively few occasions on which I was able to use binoculars and so most of the records are based on hearing the bird's characteristic song.

I first heard the song of the Firecrest in 1974 but at that time was unsure of its identification. However, positive identification was ascertained in the following year with the aid of binoculars. On the 6th May 1975 there were 'several' Firecrests singing in the Forest and on the 8th there were three different birds singing near Cadira Beeches alone – how many could there have been in the Forest as a whole? In 1976 one bird was singing in the Port-a-slough area of the Forest and in 1977 a nest was located for the first time, just to the north of Cadira Beeches. On locating the position of the nest I was immediately intrigued, but also frustrated, by the fact that a female Chaffinch had also located it and was helping herself to the nest material, so systematically destroying the nest built by the Firecrests.

In 1978 I have only one record of a Firecrest singing at Wentwood Lodge but in 1979 I was again able to find a nest. This time the nest was being constructed amongst Ivy which grew well up into the upper part of a Scots Pine tree at the side of the road leading from Cadira Beeches to the northern edge of the Forest. Incredibly, as soon as we had located the nest so too did a female Chaffinch, and again began the process of removing the material, presumably to build her own nest. This incident took place on the 20th June of that year.

1980 produced records from four different areas of Wentwood Forest – Five Paths, Port-a-slough, the vicinity of the Forestry Commission houses/ offices and Nine Wells. In February 1982 I left my employment in Wentwood Forest so my regular records were curtailed at that time but I again saw the Firecrest there in the Bicca area in 1983 while on a casual visit.

Carrion Crow

With a bird as common as the Carrion Crow it should come as no surprise to learn that my casual records do not include it from early times, or from more recent times for that matter for, as a species, it continues to thrive. However, there are occasions when notable happenings take place, even in the most abundant of species, and it is these that I intend to include here.

The first concerns communal feeding areas. Although the Carrion Crow is a strongly territorial bird, at least in the breeding season, there are, nevertheless, some places of abundant food supply where large numbers of these crows may be seen together. One such a place was (and may still be, for all I know), Magor Pill, both on landward and seaward sides of the sea-wall. My records provide figures for the years 1972 and 1973 – (6.5.72) 'c.50 Carrion Crows on the fore-shore at Magor Pill, (20.5.72) '70 on the foreshore at Magor Pill, (4.6.72) '91 Carrion Crows counted on the foreshore at Magor Pill', (24.6.72) '97 on the foreshore at Magor Pill', (1.7.73) '85 Carrion Crows on the foreshore at Magor Pill', (7.7.73) '105 Carrion Crows counted on the foreshore at Magor Pill'.

The other aspect of Carrion Crow behaviour concerns the so-called 'trials'. These are, traditionally, a feature of the lives of Rooks as well as Carrion Crows, and perhaps of other corvids too. Anyway, I have only one such an experience and that took place at Brockwells Farm on the 16th May 1986 – 'A commotion in the Little Banky Field attracted our attention, a real cacophony of angry crow-calls. As we approached we could see that the disturbance revolved around three crows and as we drew nearer two of them flew away, the third could not for both of its eyes had been pecked out'. It can only be assumed that the local territory-holding pair, probably with young in the nest, has confronted the interloper who had not, for whatever reason, vacated the area. This obstinacy, or confusion, cost the unfortunate bird its life.

Nightingale

Like the Cuckoo, a bird of folklore status in Britain. The Nightingale has now gone from all of its former haunts in Gwent. It may occur briefly on passage, but to my knowledge no regular sites are now occupied by this renowned songster in Gwent. And all of this has taken place within the last forty years. The accompanying map (page 90) illustrates the saturation of summer Nightingale territory holdings in the early 1950's, but by the time my records began in 1958, the only regular sites were two at Highmoor Hill and that in the general area of Ifton Quarry near Rogiet – the rot had already set in. The following records commence in 1960, and show that the last regular singing bird was stationed at Highmoor Hill, the final entry, for Brockwells Hill, representing only the temporary occurrence of a bird passing through what was once a regular haunt on the fringes of the former Rock House Wood (see map 3).

(30.4.60) '4 Nightingales singing at Ifton Quarry'. (7.5.60) '4 at Ifton Quarry and another single bird at Highmoor Hill', (19.5.61) '3 at Ifton Quarry', (23.5.61) 'a Nightingale singing at Highmoor Hill', (26.4.63) 'one singing at Highmoor Hill', (22.4.64) '3 at Ifton Quarry', (1.5.64) 'one at Highmoor Hill', (3.5.64) 'a Nightingale singing in the Wye Valley at Hadnock', (18.5.64) '"several" at Ifton Quarry', (26.5.67) 'one singing at Highmoor Hill', (27.4.69) 'one at Highmoor Hill', (3.5.70) 'one at Highmoor Hill', (20.4.71) 'This evening a Nightingale was singing from thick growth at the side of the Brockwells Hill'.

Tree Sparrow

Going, going, almost gone, the Tree Sparrow still hangs on as a breeding bird on parts of the Caldicot Level, the precise location perhaps best left to the few who know. Their fall in numbers is nationwide and, on a local basis, documented in my records, particularly those from 1971 onwards. Prior to that, I knew the Tree Sparrow mostly as a breeder in small colonies on the Caldicot Level at places such as the Peewit Field, Undy and Redwick, but also as a component of winter flocks of seed-eaters, usually in the company

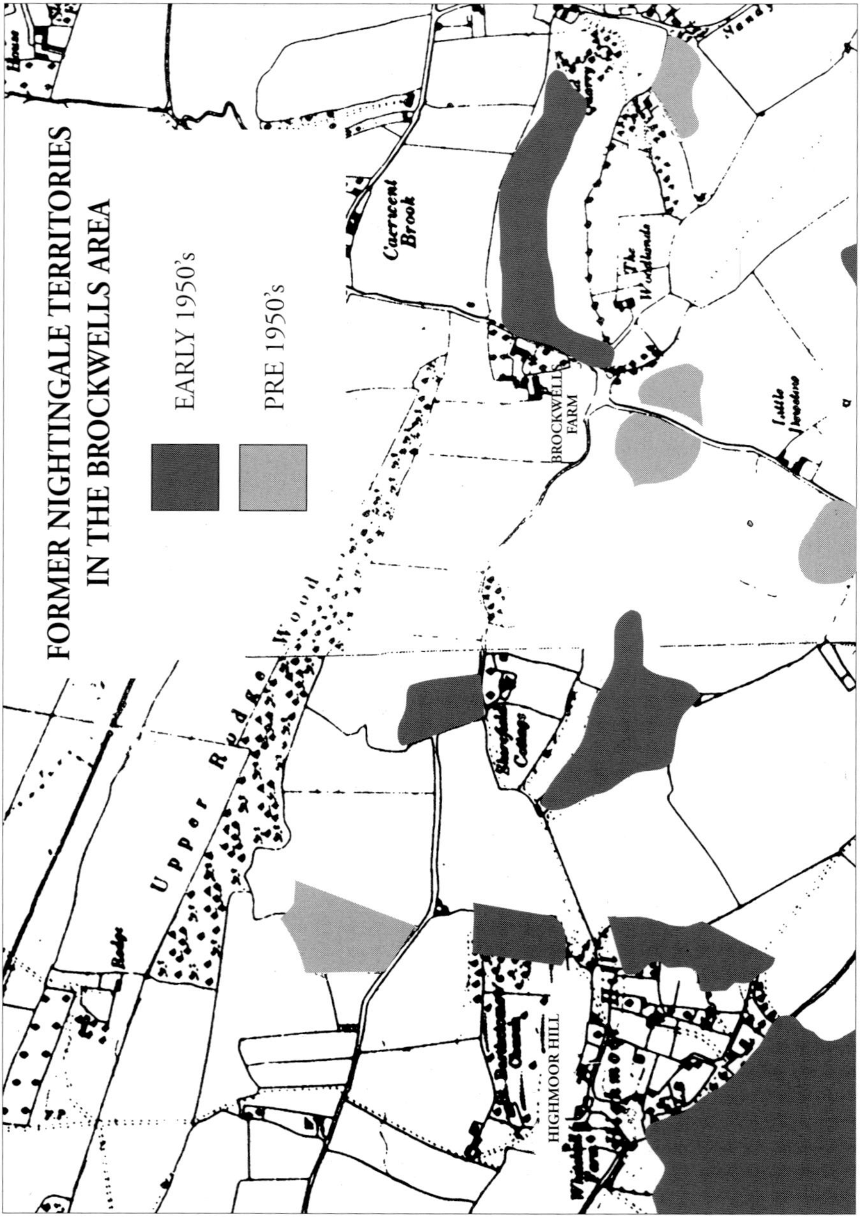
FORMER NIGHTINGALE TERRITORIES
IN THE BROCKWELLS AREA
EARLY 1950's
PRE 1950's
Caerwent Brook
BROCKWELLS FARM
HIGHMOOR HILL

of Chaffinches, Greenfinches, Linnets and Bramblings. Although characteristically a gregarious bird, the Tree Sparrow can also operate solitarily, as can be seen from the following records – (5.1.71) '2 in the Shirefield area of Dewstow Farm', (9.1.71) 'an estimated flock of 60-70 Tree Sparrows in the Slough Farm area of the upper Neddern Valley near Caerwent', (13.2.71) 'c.25 in a tall hedge bordering the Neddern Valley', (21.2.71) '20-30 Tree Sparrows near the St. Brides Brook, St. Brides Netherwent', (12.4.71) 'Tree Sparrows along the River Usk near Llanllowell', (25.4.71) '2 at Magor Pill', (7.6.71) 'Tree Sparrow feeding young in nest at Slidy Hill Wood, Crick', (12.6.71) 'Tree Sparrows nesting in the line of pollarded willows on the southern edge of the Peewit Field', (3.7.71) '"good numbers" of Tree Sparrows breeding in pollarded willows on Caldicot Level below Undy', (25.9.71) '"good-sized" flock of Tree Sparrows near Magor Pill', (11.12.71) 'mixed flock of Chaffinches, Tree Sparrows, with a single Brambling on a field in the Neddern Valley', (16.4.72) 'Tree Sparrows nesting in pollarded willows on Peewit Field', (23.9.72) 'small flocks of Tree Sparrows on Caldicot Level near Undy', (16.12.72) '"several" Tree Sparrows on Caldicot Level near Magor', (7.4.73) '3 Tree Sparrows near the Peewit Field and a further 12 near Collister Pill', (8.12.73) 'c.10 Tree Sparrows with flock of finches comprising c.150 Chaffinches and c.200 Bramblings on Fat Hen in kale crop near Allt Farm, Llantrisant', (24.2.74) 'a "few" Tree Sparrows at Bishton', (30.6.75) 'Tree Sparrows nesting in pollarded willows at Undy', (27.10.75) 'a single Tree Sparrow at Brockwells Farm', (5.1.76) 'Trevor Evans reports c.200 Tree Sparrows feeding with c.50 Goldfinches, c.20 Bramblings, c.20 Redpolls and 2 Siskins on the Maes-glas Rubbish-dump, Newport', (29.12.76) 'c.50 Tree Sparrows between Little Mill and Mamhilad', (20.8.78) '7 along Severn seawall between Chapel Farm and Collister Pill, Undy', (14.10.79) 'c.30 near St. Brides Wentlooge', (17.7.80) 'one along the River Usk at Llanllowell', (13.8.80) 'a "flock" of Tree Sparrows in the Kilpale area', (18.3.81) '2 along the Olway Brook at Llanllowell', (10.5.81) 'one along the River Usk at Llanllowell', (16.3.83) '2 along the River Usk between Llanvihangel Gobion and the Bryn', (22.4.81) '"several" along the Monmouthshire Canal between Malpas and Cwmbran', (24.1.93) 'Today there was a single Tree Sparrow in the garden at Brockwells Farm for the second time this winter. On this occasion it was feeding from the peanut dispenser on the upstairs window', (3.2.93) 'The single Tree Sparrow continues to feed from the peanut dispenser at Brockwells Farm', (20.6.96) '4 Tree Sparrows in tall hedges on the Caldicot Level west of Redwick'.

The reasons behind the varying fortunes of birds and other forms of wildlife are many indeed. Some of them are obvious to us, while others are far too subtle to be apparent until an in-depth investigation is mounted. Of the more obvious causes, habitat loss or change probably has the greatest effect and here in this area we have seen a great deal of that, particularly on the Gwent Levels.

As I mentioned the loss of the Woodland's fields to quarrying in the chapter on plants, so here can be included the loss of the Peewit Field, but in a very different way. The changes brought about here are not so obviously dramatic and terminal, yet they have still achieved the virtual destruction of a once vibrant habitat and animal community.

First the area of the Peewit Field was effectively drained, this most probably being accomplished by the pumps installed at Noah's Ark in 1961 (Stephen Rippon, 1996), though their impact could not have been immediate for, as will be seen in the following records, the Peewit Field remained a valuable 'wetland' site at least until the spring of 1972. Then, in 1995-1996, the link-road to the Second Severn Bridge was built alongside it, to those who witnessed its former splendour, a very great loss indeed. The following diary extracts should help to evaluate this wetland paradise that has now gone forever.

(20.4.59) 'On a visit to the Peewit Field today we found a Redshank's nest (4 eggs), Lapwings nests (4 and 3 eggs), Garganey, Snipe and Shelduck', (9.4.60) '2 Lapwing nests, 1 Redshank nest, 5 Yellow Wagtails, flocks of Dunlin and Redshank, a pair of Pintail and 11 Black-tailed Godwits on the Peewit Field', (19.3.61) '"thousands" of ducks – Wigeon, Shovelers, Teal, Mallard, Pintail, Tufted Duck and Shelduck on the Peewit Field', (31.5.61) 'This evening I went down to the Peewit Field. As I approached the wetland area large numbers of duck flew up, mostly Shelduck and Mallard. Here also were Lapwings, Redshanks and Snipe which evidently had young hidden in the vegetation. The Snipe kept flying around uttering a sort of "chack – chack" call and one of them was drumming', (27.12.70) 'A Little Owl was present in the line of pollarded willows along the southern edge of the Peewit Field. Also present – 7 Bewick's Swans, a covey of 5 Partridge and both male and female Stonechat', (11.5.71) 'Lapwings and Redshanks appear to be breeding in good numbers on the Peewit Field', (12.6.71) 'Tree Sparrows nesting in the line of pollarded willows along the southern edge of the Peewit Field. Other birds obviously breeding here include Meadow Pipits, Skylarks, Redshanks, Snipe, Lapwing and Yellow Wagtail', (4.3.72) 'I then drove around to the Peewit Field. As I approached, along the rough track, a flock of several thousand Dunlin passed over towards the Severn. When I walked across to the flooded area I found several thousand more Dunlin as well as 12 Bewick's Swans, 4 Pintail, 200 Redshanks, 50 Turnstone and 28 Shelduck. The combined Dunlin numbers would amount to about 8,000 – the number I have seen on the Severn Estuary recently', (2.4.72) 'The majority of the Redshank, Dunlin, Knot and Turnstone were spending the high-tide period on the freshwater of the Peewit Field. There was a pair of Shoveler here too and also Black-tailed Godwits in their ruddy breeding plumage', (16.4.72) 'c.2000 Dunlin, 200 Turnstone, 1 drake Shoveler, 15 Ringed Plover, 2 Black-tailed Godwits, 75 Knot, and several Tree Sparrows along the line of pollarded willows', (21.5.72) '3 Lesser Whitethroats singing from Hawthorn hedges around the Peewit Field. Tree Sparrows in the line of pollarded willows, Turtle Dove, Snipe and Yellow Wagtails', (16.3.75) '2 Little Owls in the line of pollarded willows at the southern edge of the Peewit Field'.

POST-SCRIPT SUMMARY OF BIRDS–1997

Bird populations are changing more obviously than those of any other group in the animal kingdom, but again, there appears to be both winners and losers. Riding on a current high are such birds as Common Buzzard, Little Egret and, apparently, the Hobby, while plunging ever lower in number are a great range of well-known favourites – a small selection might include Nightingale, Cuckoo, Lapwing, Tree Sparrow and Turtle Dove, but also less well-known species such as the Stock Dove.

In 1968 I noted 14 Stock Doves on the Caerwent Quarry cliff-face on the 29th December. In 1971, between the 27th February and the 11th April a regular four pairs were present, 6 birds were seen here on the 24th March 1972 and 5 on the 11th April 1977.

During the autumn/winter period good numbers of Stock Doves could often be seen feeding on the fields in various parts of Gwent – (14.2.67) 20-30 feeding on fields at Wyesham, Monmouth; (22.12.67) 7 feeding on ploughed land at Llanarth Court; (20.12.71) c.100 on Dewstow Farm's Shire-field, Caerwent; (10.3.72) 35 on fields at Highmoor Hill; (15.3.72) 10 on Brockwells Farm fields and 18 on Dewstow Farm fields; (29.1.74) c.40 feeding on field near the River Usk at Llanllowell.

Compare these figures with those recorded during the present year – (23.3.97) 1 Stock Dove cooing in the Cwm; (25.4.97) Stock Dove cooing in woods at Cleddon; (27.4.97) Stock Dove cooing at Penhein; (2.5.97) 8 Stock Doves on Neddern Valley fields and 1 near Caerwent; (25.5.97) c.4 in

R.A.F. Caerwent; (24.6.97) Stock Doves nest with one egg in Yew tree hollow, Llandevaud churchyard; (31.7.97) 3 Stock Doves seen during field-trip, Llanvihangel Gobion to the Bryn.

What must be remembered when comparing the foregoing records is that in 1997 I recorded *every* Stock Dove seen or heard. The previous records were restricted to those of particular note.

Despite regular visits to Caerwent Quarry during the first half of 1997 Stock Doves appeared to be totally absent.

It is likely that the Stock Dove is suffering from changes in agricultural practice, as are a large number of other species currently in decline, but there is also habitat loss. On pages 92 and 93 I commented on the one-time ecological significance of the Peewit Field near Llanvihangel Rogiet. Most of the sightings and records revolved around the former seasonally flooded area and the pollarded willows which formed a line running approximately east-west across the southern portion of the field. A visit during April of 1997 showed that the line of willow trees had been removed, the flood water effectively drained and the whole field planted with a crop of beans.

I heard the Cuckoo calling for the first time this year on the 8th May (some time later than many of my friends). This was during a walk at Earlswood. Subsequently calling birds were heard on ten occasions over a wide area of Gwent, but no birds were actually seen. These ten records may only represent eight birds, those heard at Brockwells Farm and Dinham (R.A.F. Caerwent) may well be one and the same and similarly, those heard at Nine Wells (Wentwood) and Earlswood. The other birds were all well separated as suggested by the following records – (13.5.97) 1 calling near Pontnewynydd; (20.5.97) 1 calling at Usk; (30.5.97) 1 calling at White Hill (Monmouth) and 1 calling near Fair Oak (Tintern), and (15.6.97) 1 calling on the Caldicot Level below Rogiet.

If we compare my Cuckoo records for 1997 with those made twenty years ago we could easily conclude that the species may be declining, but only very slowly (c.9 individuals estimated for 1977 as compared to c.8 for 1997). However, if we compare the number of days on which the Cuckoo was heard/seen we begin to see a much greater disparity and an indication that the species may be in serious decline. And if we include in this comparison, the figures for 1976, then the fall in numbers becomes even more obvious –

1976 – Cuckoos heard on 14 days and seen on 11 days.
1977 – Cuckoos heard on 31 days and seen on 3 days.
1997 – Cuckoos heard on 9 days and not seen at all.

Estimates for the number of individuals represented are –

1976 – at least 15 birds.
1977 – at least 9 birds.
1997 – at least 8 birds.

Changes in avian populations here are affected by a wide range of environmental factors – climate change, changes in land management and habitat loss being of prime concern. There is, however, another potential ingredient for change, not just for birds but for most other groups of animals too. That ingredient is artificial introduction, intended or otherwise.

On the 17th March a phone-call from Mr. Bobby Brown took me down to the golf-course at Llanwern where an Eagle Owl was found crouching under a hedgerow. I eventually caught the bird and returned it to its owner but the whole experience ultimately informed me of the number of such birds currently held in private hands and also the number which are escaping into the wild. There is obviously a distinct potential for the breeding of this species in the wild.

Other bird records for the year are as follows –

19th January.	At least 7 Goosander on the River Wye in the Tintern area.
29th May.	A pair of Tufted Ducks present on Park Wood Pond, Usk.
30th May.	1 Turtle Dove 'purring' near the Observatory, Trellech.
	4 Wood Warblers singing in Ravensnest Wood, Tintern.
9th June.	1 Wood Warbler singing at the Park, Abergavenny.
18th July.	While scanning the evening sky above the Upper Rodge Wood for Swifts and Noctule Bats a falcon came into my view through the binoculars. Its flight, form and actions identified it immediately as a Hobby. The time was now 9.43 pm. Over the next quarter of an hour a second Hobby appeared and the two were observed darting over the canopy of the wood and snatching what were almost certainly the July Chafer Beetles which occurred here in abundance at this time of year. A catch would be followed by the birds rising higher into the air and drifting slowly while eating the prey from the talon. Then would come another dive low over the canopy with tremendous acceleration, only to rise and drift again while savouring another meal. A Hobby was seen very briefly on the following evening, and then again on the evening of the 21st July, this being the last time I saw them here.

23rd July. Little Grebe with two young on the upper pool of Ynys-y-fro Reservoir.

28th July. This year's breeding success of Common Buzzards is obvious now in many parts of Gwent as deduced by the calling young.

31st July. 9 Goosander, 4 Green Sandpipers and 3 Common Sandpipers along the River Usk at Pant-y-goytre.

8th September. 4 Red Grouse flushed from the upland moor near Chwarel y Fan.

22nd September. Swallows have nested here at the Brockwells Farm this summer and what I presume to be the second brood left the farm building today.

29th October. c.6 Crossbills flying over Brockwells Farm today.

ADDITIONAL RECORDS/INFORMATION

Mammals

~

We have, in this area, about thirty-six regularly occurring mammal species, plus another handful of occasional 'visitors', mostly in the waters of the Severn Estuary, for example Grey Seal, Common Dolphin and Porpoise.

Many species have become extinct here since the end of the Ice Age, but some have done so in quite recent times. My age does not allow for an experience of the Red Squirrel in Gwent, though they may well have been around in small numbers at the time of my birth in 1944. However, the forty year record I have entered into my diaries does illustrate some significant changes in mammal populations, both good and bad.

At the end of this chapter I will list the species which I know to have been recorded here, but my more detailed accounts are limited to those species of most interest to me, or which show the greatest population changes.

Greater and Lesser Horseshoe Bats

I will treat these two species together for, in my experience, they often occur in similar situations. Certainly they are both regarded as rare mammals, and very special to Gwent.

Because of the sensitivity of the two species, and the general concern for their conservation, I will simply state that they are both to be found in underground caverns, both man-made and natural, in a number of places in Gwent. I will, however, make specific note of records from sites which no longer exist, or from which the bats have been excluded.

For example, my diary records that on the 7th October 1960, 9 Lesser Horseshoe Bats were found in the old 'gamekeeper's' hut in the Golden Valley below Shirenewton. Later the roof of this building collapsed, so destroying the site as far as the bats are concerned. On the 14th October 1961 I found a colony of Lesser Horseshoe Bats in an attic while visiting friends at Lower House Farm, Wolvesnewton, and very small numbers of this species in the Lower Cwm Mill during its derelict period (records made in 1974, 1975 and 1976).

The fact of the matter is that the Lesser Horseshoe Bat seems to be more widespread in the Gwent area than the Greater – I have only come across the latter in the Wye Valley area. Both species (and all other British bats) are protected by law and the Gwent Bat Group, founded by John and Molly Hines, is working constantly to protect them and their habitat. Since the time when bats became protected by law and a licence required to visit sites where they occur, I have ceased my recording operations in such places and left it to others. This is the reason for the lack of any personal recent records, not that the bats are no longer there.

Noctule Bat

These large bats are still very much a part of the fauna of Gwent, despite the fact that, as with many other species, they do not seem as abundant as was formerly the case. Certainly they are a very widespread species, my records coming from the Severn sea-wall (at Caldicot) and the mouth of the Wye below Chepstow, Ynys-y-fro Reservoir, Trellech Grange and Llandegvedd. I feel sure that they are to be seen hunting over all of the lower altitude areas at least.

They seem to be a species which travels widely in order to exploit temporary food bonanzas. At Brockwells Farm we only see them in good numbers when the July Chafers are abundantly on the wing. At Ynys-y-fro Reservoir, however, Noctules are plentiful as early as April and at such a bountiful site are likely to remain so for much of their active year.

The greatest number I have recorded in one place at one time is 23 over Brockwells Farm fields on the 2nd July 1976. The earliest record in the year was for a single Noctule over the Neddern Valley on the 18th March 1963, and the latest was of two over the Brockwells Farm fields on the 6th October 1972.

Brown Hare

My first full year of diary-keeping was 1959 when I recorded 26 sightings of Brown Hare. This period coincided with a reduced Rabbit population resulting from the disease known as myxomatosis which became evident around the middle of that decade. 1960 produced 52 recorded sightings but after that there was a fairly sharp decline until, in 1964 only 5 sightings were made.

The problem with these records is that they are only very casual, no attempt being made to seek out the species concerned, and lapses in record keeping are quite probable, with no actual objective in mind at that early time. However, it is noticeable that once Brown Hare numbers had fallen to an obvious low, that level was then maintained and the average sightings per year thereafter reflect that. Even in the current year of 1996 I have recorded the fairly average figure of 4 Brown Hare sightings.

What I am unable to explain is why some areas have more of these animals than others. Today, to my knowledge there are no Brown Hares in the vicinity of Brockwells Farm, yet in the spring of 1996 Colin Elliot counted eight in just two adjacent fields near Llangwm. One possible factor to play a role in this particular area however, could be a reasonably extensive area of set-aside. Other sites with known populations in recent times include the Penhein–Grey Hill area, and the Usk Valley near Llangibby.

It is probably true that the species maintains a generally low level of population through most of the region but, if the relatively new haemorrhagic viral disease of Rabbits lowers the numbers of that species significantly, then it will be very interesting to see if the Brown Hare population increases again as in the days of initial myxomatosis impact.

In the late 1950's I made a habit of walking out over the fields near Brockwells Farm to watch the dusk period activities of Brown Hares. They were plentiful at that time but by September 1962 my diaries recorded a change – Rabbits and Brown Hares were now equally abundant in the Caerwent area, this situation representing a step towards the decline of the Brown Hare. In the following year, on a walk around Dewstow Farm, I counted 15 Rabbits – they were obviously making a strong comeback. In 1968, ten years after my initial dusk-watching episode, my diaries recorded – (11.2.68) 'This evening I decided to go for a walk at dusk to assess the number of Brown Hares in the immediate vicinity of Brockwells Farm – but I failed to find one. Two years later I wrote – (23.4.70) 'From the Church Farm Pool field of the Neddern Valley we flushed a Brown Hare, the first I have seen for some time'. The Brown Hare had by that time reached the population level that it was to maintain until the present day. The Rabbit population continued to rise.

Water Vole

The recent history of the Water Vole in Gwent seems to be one of disaster, and it may be that, within this area at least, the species is doomed to extinction. It is said that various factors have conspired to bring about the demise of this native, but the final nail in the Water Vole's coffin is generally considered to be the Mink. This is an alien predator now more abundant here than almost any of its mustelid kin.

Over the past forty years I have noted the presence of the Water Vole in many parts of Gwent – (25.4.64) the River Wye at Bigswier, (12.5.64) reens near Caldicot Rifle-range, (30.6.64) Monk's Ditch, Goldcliff, (10.9.67) the River Monnow at Skenfrith, (29.4.71) Magor Reserve, (4.6.73) Newport Dockland area, (23.3.80) Magor Pill. On the 24th November 1967 I saw a Heron killing what I considered to be a fully grown Water Vole in a field at the Coldra (to the east of Newport) and, in July 1981, I was to make what may be, my last record of the species in Gwent, when Colin Elliot and I spent some time photographing these animals near Caldicot (8.7.81) '3 Water Voles along the Neddern Brook'.

What appears to be the disappearance of the Water Vole here coincides with the maximum expansion of the Mink in this same area. Whether we can draw the 'obvious' conclusion from this remains to be seen but it currently looks as if predation by this introduced predator may well end the existence of the Water Vole here, and in many other parts of Britain too.

Yellow-necked Mouse

Because of its similarity to the Wood Mouse, this animal is not generally known to the public of this area as a distinct species. It is larger and more brightly coloured than the Wood Mouse and, apparently, more likely to enter houses – a fact that is corroborated by our experience at Brockwells Farm over the years.

In recent times my encounters with this animal have become far more frequent because of an involvement with a Dormouse nest-box scheme, the Yellow-necked Mice occupying the boxes more frequently than any other small mammal in that particular woodland. On 24th September 1995 one of the nest-boxes contained, quite unusually, seven juvenile Yellow-necked Mice, and no nest-material whatsoever.

During my Forestry Commission years, and while working in the slades Wood (of the Minnetts forestry area), I made the following note in my diary – (26.4.71) 'When we packed up to go home at 4 o'clock I discovered a Yellow-necked Mouse in my lunch-bag. It had shredded my empty crisp-packet'.

The Yellow-necked Mouse is obviously an opportunist and this was illustrated by the activities of an individual at Brockwells Farm where I recorded – (17.12.92) 'Over the past few nights a Yellow-necked Mouse has been

Aerial view of Brockwells Farm, Caerwent.

Devil's Quoit, Llanvihangel Rogiet, with Store Fields and Minnetts forestry area in the background.

The Hall of Thirty in Otterhole Cave near Chepstow.

Columns and Straws in Otterhole Cave near Chepstow.

Botryoidal Stalagmite from Caerwent Quarry Cave.

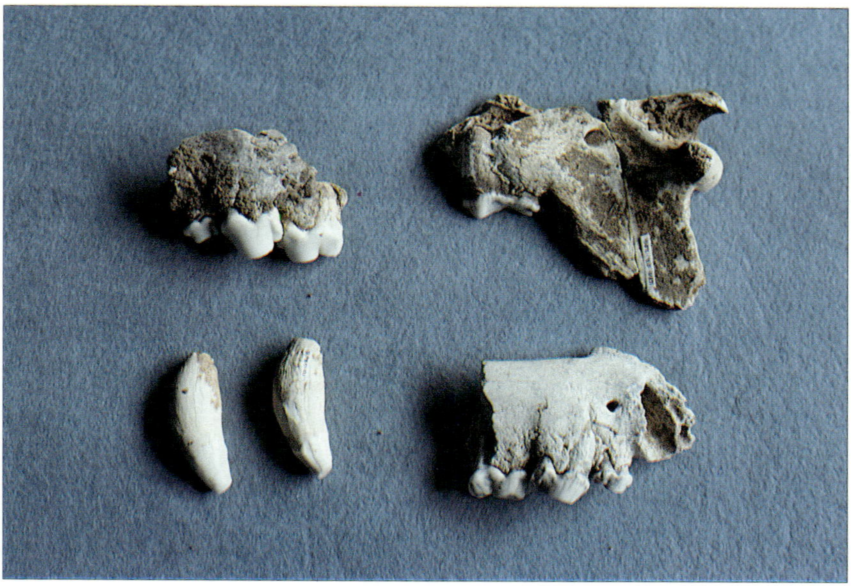

Hyena teeth and jaw fragments from Caerwent Quarry.

Freak growth of Wood Blewit from site near Parc Seymour.

Vibrissea Truncorum from shallow brooklets in Wentwood Forest.

Pick-a-Back Toadstools from Wentwood Forest.

Dahlia Anemone at Blackrock.

Greater Broomrape at Gilwern.

Ivy Broomrape at Chepstow.

Swan Mussel Shells from St. Pierre Lake, Chepstow.

Shore Crabs, Severn Estuary at Nash.

Hornet's Nest and Honey Bee Comb occupying the same hollow in oak tree near Glascoed.

Silurian Moth (Eriopygodes imbecilla).

Grizzled Skipper Butterfly in R.A.F. Caerwent.

Defoliation by Bird-Cherry Ermine in the Honddu Valley.

Mating Hornet Robber-Flies at Brockwells Farm, Caerwent.

Hornet Robber-Fly with prey at Brockwells Farm.

Shingle Spider (Arctosa cinerea) along the River Usk near Abergavenny.

Cave Spider (Meta menardi) in a lower Wye Valley cave.

Salmon jumping at Osbaston Wier, Monmouth.

Male Great Spotted Woodpecker with food for young at Fairoak, Tintern.

Victim of a Crow 'Trial' at Brockwells Farm, Caerwent, May 1986.

Water Shrew in the Minnetts Forestry area.

Torpid Dormouse disturbed by work operations in Wentwood Forest.

Lesser Rorqual or Minke Whale washed up on the foreshore at Nash in December 1977.

feeding from a bird peanut dispenser fixed to an upper-floor window'. On subsequent nights it also extracted nuts from a hanging feeder, lower down on the face of the house.

Dormouse

Another animal of folklore status, the Dormouse is in fact little known, and still far from being truly understood. It is, however, presently the subject of much study and it is likely that our current knowledge of this largely nocturnal mammal is to be greatly expanded and many early, erroneous beliefs dispelled. Already a number of formerly accepted 'facts' have been disproved. It was, for example, once claimed that Dormice did not occur in coniferous woodland, but this is now known to be incorrect.

While working for the Forestry Commission, based at Wentwood Forest, I came upon Dormice in conifer-dominated woodland on many occasions. On two such occasions the animals concerned occupied solid conifer blocks and were quite remote from any substantial number of broad-leaved trees or even area of scrub. For example (8.10.74) 'a single Dormouse in a nest c.18ft. high in Lawson Cypress plantation in the Port-a-slough area of the Wentwood Forest'. Or, (9.5.75) '2 Dormice in a nest 7 ft. above the ground in a Norway Spruce tree, one of a maturing plantation in the Wentwood Forest' (Cadira Beeches–Five Paths area).

The species of coniferous trees amongst which I have found Dormice are quite varied – Lawson's Cypress, Norway Spruce, Scot's Pine, Grand Fir and larch, and also in various stages of growth from young plantation to mature stand.

Again, some authorities believe that Dormice will not travel across the ground, even though they accept that hibernation is undertaken at that level. On the 26th June 1975 I found a flattened Dormouse in the middle of the main through-road in Wentwood Forest, close to Gilligan's Patch, a fact which appears to contradict this belief, and radio-tracking may ultimately prove this line of thought fallacious.

Another misunderstanding involves the collection of nest-material by Dormice. It has been stated that this is only collected above the level of the ground, in other words, directly from bushes and trees. Certainly, if Honey-suckle is present then the bark-strippings from the 'vines' of this plant are usually the preferred choice of material for the bulk of the nest. In the absence of Honey-suckle, Clematis bark-strippings may be used in areas where this is available. Green leaves straight off bushes and trees are commonly incorporated into the nest too but individual Dormice, in some circumstances, will use material from the woodland floor. On the 23rd June 1996 a nest-box I examined contained the nest of a Dormouse fashioned very largely from the dead and wilted leaves of Wild Garlic which had obviously been collected from the woodland floor at the base of the tree, where it formed the dominant field-layer plant. Inside the tightly-bound nest was a female Dormouse and three young. At this stage the yellow-brown leaves had lost their strong garlic smell which would otherwise have excluded them from the nest-material of any animal, or so I would have thought.

Dormice appear to be widespread in Gwent, in the right sort of habitat, records having been received from such areas as the oak-woodlands of the Coalfield (Abercarn – Miss Linda Joyce) and a locality near Skenfrith, as well as the better-known strongholds in the Wye Valley and Trellech Plateau, where they may, in some places, be regarded as common.

Stoat and Weasel

As with the Greater and Lesser Horseshoe Bats, it is convenient to treat these two closely related species together. Their numbers have remained fairly constant throughout the past forty years, though, according to my records, both appear to have increased in number temporarily in the mid-1970's, but then to have declined again to their former status and to have maintained that level until the present day. The population levels of Stoat and Weasel seem to be very similar, my total number of recorded sightings for the two species over the forty-year period being almost identical (48 and 50 respectively).

Reported 'hunting packs' of Stoats are in fact family groups with the virtually adult-sized young receiving basic training in hunting skills. I saw such a party at Trewen on the 29th June 1968. The Stoats were trying to cross the road, a fast stretch of the A48, and were strung out across it, moving about in short bursts of speed as if unsure of what to do when confronted with the vehicles bearing down on them. I expected to see a slaughter but, amazingly, all reached the other side of the road in safety.

I came across another such family group at the junction of the Crick and Neddern Brooks in the Neddern Valley. Using the cover of the rank waterside vegetation the inquisitive animals emerged, retreated and re-emerged, peering at me from close range while standing upright on their hind legs.

Many people have related to me their experience of the classic Rabbit kill by a Stoat – something I have never witnessed for myself. John Davies tells me that on leaving the Clytha car-park some years ago, he was mystified by the actions of a Rabbit which sat hunched in the road, screaming constantly. Almost immediately a Stoat emerged from the nearby hedgerow and killed the Rabbit. It seems that the Rabbit realises the inevitability of its death by the relentless pursuit of the Stoat, so much so that it simply gives up all hope and accepts its fate. This terror may well be exacerbated by the fact that the Rabbit is driven out of familiar surroundings into unknown territory, and simply does not know where to go.

The pursuit of the Weasel is equally determined. While walking along the Crick Brook on the edge of Crick Village I noticed a hunting Weasel nearby. In order to follow its prey it had to cross the brook but what was particularly impressive was the manner in which the action was executed. Being totally oblivious to my presence and totally fixed on its intent, the animal did not falter on reaching the water. There was no pause to consider whether to jump, swim or divert, the movement was a smooth and rapid continuation of its direct pursuit. Its eyes staring ahead it swam across the water – the running and swimming actions seeming as one.

At the Brockwells Farm on the 27th March 1982 I watched a weasel hunting in the roof of the shed, occasionally coming out into the guttering. Whether House Sparrows, whose commotion attracted my attention to the incident, were the intended prey I do not know, but at one stage one of the birds was seized and then released, or lost, again. (Also see 'Notes' for 25.5.81 relating to another aspect of Weasel behaviour).

Polecat

As this is a native British Mammal it is fortunate that we are presently witnessing a successful expansion of the population and range of the species. The main problem in charting the history of the Polecat is its similarity to the widely used, and often lost, domestic Polecat-ferret which may well have been derived from the species found in Britain and Western Europe (or its eastern European/Asiatic relative, the Steppe Polecat) in the distant past. Whatever the truth about its origins, the Ferret can be similarly marked and coloured to the wild Polecat and this may well lead to erroneous identification. However many reports are of road casualties and these can usually be checked out and the true identity determined.

My first report of a Polecat came from R.A.F. Caerwent (the Royal Navy Propellant Factory, as it was then) where one was said to have been trapped in one of the buildings. In 1971 (3.11.71) Stephen Locke (then Deputy Curator of Newport Museum and Art Gallery), reported the snaring of a Polecat at

Llanover. On the 8th September 1982 Tom Locke found, and brought to me, a Polecat which had been killed on the Usk–Chepstow road at Ty-fry (Llangwm). It seems that these animals have been widespread in Gwent for some time, but how plentiful they are is another matter. However, in the 1990's more reports materialised and it would appear that the lower Usk Valley has become something of a stronghold with sightings of family groups, for example those seen by Paul and Helen Sheppard in the Tredunnock–Newbridge area. There have also been a number of reported road casualties from this area including one along the 'Straight Mile' near Llantrisant which I saw myself.

Mink

The story of the Mink in Britain is one of great success, though from other view-points, including that of British conservation generally, this success must be regarded as something of a disaster.

Personally, my involvement with the Mink began on 29th April 1972 when I saw one on the Caldicot Level near Porton House, Whitson. Between then and September 1980 I had no further 'contact' with the species though reports came to me from the Olway Brook at Llanllowell on the 19th August 1974 and from the Caldicot Level generally when, on the 10th March, 1980, Derek Upton provided me with information relating to a series of Mink sightings. On the 7th September, 1980, however, I saw a Mink along the Windmill Reen near Redwick, and from that time on it became clear that the species was well established and widespread with reports from both Rivers Usk and Wye – e.g. (22.10.83) 'one along the riverbank near Chepstow Castle' (Mrs. Linda Bellamy), and from the Caldicot Level – (16.6.91) 'Today Mr. Wally Trigg reported the regular presence of Mink along the Chapel Reen, Goldcliff'. On the 3rd August 1994 Mr. Rhys Jenkins and I saw a Mink on the Wentlooge Level, close to the Peterstone Gout.

During the making of the television wildlife series, 'A Hundred Acres', along the River Usk, we located, and filmed at, a Mink den. On completion of our film we believe that local fishermen killed all the members of the Mink family, something we regretted at the time for the female had only been seen to bring Green Eels back to the den for the young.

The fact is that the Mink is a successful alien in the British countryside and, like all other alien species here, is detrimental to native wildlife conservation. However, its occurrence here is nothing to do with the Mink at all, and since we are responsible for its presence, the best we can do is to accept the situation and suffer whatever consequences result.

Fallow Deer

This early introduction into Britain is now well-established in some parts of Eastern Gwent. The original animals come from two major sources, the Forest of Dean herd and those from Hendre Estate, which now occur most commonly in the woodlands of the White Hill near Monmouth. These, probably collectively, have now extended their range down the Wye Valley and have notable populations at least as far as the Tintern area.

The other population, that of Wentwood Forest, is of more recent origins. A couple (or three?) of animals are said to have escaped from the zoo collection held at Whitson Court, and to have gradually made their way in a generally northerly direction until, in the Autumn of 1975, they were seen along the northern edge of Wentwood Forest near Pen-y-cae-mawr. A few more sightings were made after that but in the Autumn of 1976 a white Fallow buck was seen in the Nant-y-pridd area of the Forest. No one, that I have spoken to knows the origins of this animal but I suspect it to have been a deliberate introduction, possibly from Margam Park near Port Talbot. The initial colonisers from Whitson included at least one doe and so we now had the nucleus of a population. Consequently, on the 1st November 1997 it came as no big surprise when two bucks (one white and one brown) were seen with two does, and on the 27th July 1978, 'young' Fallow were reported from the Highlight area of the Forest.

Just when the white Fallow buck met his end I do not know but Nigel Phillips (of Tregarn) informed me on the 29th January, 1982, that such an animal had been knocked down and killed on the road (Cats Ash – Christchurch) near Mount St. Albans some time earlier. Despite this the seed, and therefore the gene, had been sown, and the herd continued to expand.

On the 25th April 1996 I saw five Fallow Deer crossing the main through-road in the Forest, between the Forestry Commission houses/offices and Cadira Beeches, just above Nine Wells. The group comprised a buck and four does, all of the standard brown colouration. However, in September 1996 Anne and Walt Jackson informed me of two white Fallow seen on the edge of the Forest in the Darren area – one a buck and the other a doe.

GWENT MAMMAL LIST

(Order as in the *Handbook of British Mammals*,
Corbet and Southern, 1977).

Hedgehog –	common and widespread to c.1250 ft. where there is human habitation – e.g. Brynmawr (Mr. Keith Jones).
Mole –	common and widespread.
Common Shrew –	common and widespread in most habitats.
Pygmy Shrew –	probably more widespread than the foregoing species, and more inclined to explore.
Water Shrew –	certainly not confined to an aquatic habitat but distribution largely unknown. Many records from the south of Gwent.
Greater Horseshoe Bat –	reasonable population in the Wye Valley at least.
Lesser Horseshoe Bat –	occupies buildings, caves and old mine-shafts in many parts of Gwent – Chepstow, Trellech, Wolvesnewton, Shirenewton and Portskewett.
Whiskered Bat –	owing to a close similarity to the Brandt's Bat the distribution of this species can only be assumed by me but casual records suggest many sites – Chepstow, Newchurch West etc.
Natterer's Bat –	present in Gwent but not known to me.
Daubenton's Bat –	present in Gwent and known particularly from the Wye Valley.
Serotine Bat –	a single record to date for Gwent–Cwmbran, 1985 (Mr. John Hines).
Noctule Bat –	widespread through much of Gwent.
Pipistrelle –	widespread through much of Gwent.
Barbastelle –	at least one record for Gwent – (Mr. John Hines).
Common Long-eared Bat –	known from many sites – Brockwells Farm, Wentwood Forest, R.A.F. Caerwent, Cwm etc.
Rabbit –	widespread in Gwent.
Brown Hare –	local in Gwent.
Grey Squirrel –	widespread in woodland and parkland areas.
Bank Vole –	widespread in suitable habitat.

Field Vole –	widespread in grassland habitats including marshland.
Water Vole –	once widespread in the right sort of habitat but now considered a rare species.
Wood Mouse –	widespread in suitable habitat.
Yellow-necked Mouse –	probably a local species but often abundant where it occurs.
Harvest Mouse –	present in rank grassland areas – forestry plantaions, reed-beds, marshland vegetation etc., but status notoriously difficult to assess.
House Mouse –	probably common in many places but no attempt made to assess populations or distribution to my knowledge.
Common Rat –	widespread in many types of habitat.
Common Dormouse –	relatively widespread in scrub and woodland, both broad-leaved and coniferous. Occupies those gardens with trees/shrubs which lie adjacent to suitable scrub/woodland and also tall hedgerows, presumably only where connected to suitable habitat.
Lesser Rorqual –	two strandings in the Severn Estuary in, or close to, Gwent – (1) Sedbury/Beachley (1973) and (2) Nash (1977).
Sei Whale –	one, reportedly of this species, washed ashore at Sudbrook in 1925.
Porpoise –	reports from the Severn Estuary and even well into the mouth of the River Wye at Chepstow.
Common Dolphin –	one of this species washed up on the foreshore at Mathern on the 3rd January, 1988, otherwise many 'dolphin' records from such places as Chepstow and Uskmouth etc.
Fox –	widespread in all parts of Gwent.
Stoat –	widespread wherever there is suitable prey.
Weasel –	widespread wherever there is suitable prey.
Polecat –	apparently numbers are increasing but still regarded, at least, as uncommon.
Ferret –	frequently lost by people hunting for Rabbits but no sign of the establishment of feral populations.
Mink –	widespread, typically near water.
Badger –	widespread in suitable habitat through much of

Gwent. Several known populations with erythristic individuals.

Otter – this species has declined dramatically over the past half century but is now (1990's) making a significant come-back. Old reports come from the River Wye near Whitebrook (Mr. Richard Vaughan) and the Neddern Valley in the late 1940's (Mr. Albert Davies). One Otter was shot in the Neddern Valley in 1958, which I later collected and of which I retain the skull. Otherwise there have been a profusion of recent records from many rivers and waterways in the area.

Common Seal – animals, apparently of this species are recorded occasionally in the Severn Estuary. Some reports (*The Cardiff Region, A Survey*, Cardiff University of Wales Press, 1960) suggest a breeding population in the Severn off Chepstow. Henry Arnold (1993) indicates a concentration of sightings in the upper Severn Estuary towards Gloucester but I have no knowledge of this. Noel and Linda Bellamy inform me of a seal seen at close quarters in mid-estuary above the 'old' Severn road Bridge.

Grey Seal – occasional records from the Severn Estuary.

Fallow Deer – captive animals, kept in several parts of Gwent. These occasionally escape so that the species has been seen roaming freely in many different areas, but mostly only temporarily. Main herds currently occur in the Wye Valley – Monmouth to Tintern, and in the Wentwood Forest.

Munjac – reports from the Monnow Valley (Osbaston), woods near Trellech, R.A.F. Caerwent and Wentwood Forest. This species is not known to me personally in Gwent as yet.

POST-SCRIPT SUMMARY OF MAMMALS–1997

In June Mr. Chris Jones (Gwent Bird Recorder) observed a Grey Seal in the lower Severn Estuary off Sluice Farm, Peterstone. This is rather an unusual mammal to be seen in Gwent but the estuary does spring such surprises from time to time.

Brown Hares would normally be of more usual occurrence but this year I have only seen one of this species in Gwent though Mrs. Doreen Mathews tells me that they continue to be seen regularly in the Llangwm area.

This year I made a particular effort to record the numbers of Noctule Bats flying over Brockwells Farm fields during the summer evenings. Memories are of dusk gatherings of these bats, along with Swifts, especially during the month of July when the greatest number of bats seemed to coincide with the emergence of hordes of Summer Chafers (Amphimallon solstitialis). Memories are, however, notoriously unreliable.

On the evening of the 15th June I was pleasantly surprised to find the two species flying together – 2 Noctule Bats and 2 Swifts. These figures, even though very small, can only be approximate since both bats and birds fly out of, and back into, vision with such regularity that it is impossible to determine whether a new arrival on the scene is literally new, or one already counted. For this reason the figures recorded are of individuals seen together at one time and therefore represent the absolute minimum number present. My records for Noctule Bats and Swifts during the rest of June, and much of July, are as follows –

16.6.97 –		c.60 Swifts.
22.6.97 –	5 Noctule Bats	3 Swifts.
23.6.97 –	9 Noctule Bats	10 Swifts.
24.6.97 –	4 Noctule Bats	12 Swifts.
25.6.97 –	13 Noctule Bats	4 Swifts.
28.6.97 –	15 Noctule Bats	15 Swifts.

For the next eleven days I was away from Gwent. On my return I found that the July Chafers had emerged and were flying at dusk. Figures for the rest of July are as follows –

11.7.97 –	2 Noctule Bats	2 Swifts.
13.7.97 –	3 Noctule Bats	2 Swifts.

16.7.97 – 2 Noctule Bats.	
17.7.97 – 8 Noctule Bats	2 Swifts.
18.7.97 – 4 Noctule Bats	1 Swift.
19.7.97 – 2 Noctule Bats.	
20.7.97 – 1 Noctule Bat.	
21.7.97 – 2 Noctule Bats	1 Swift.
22.7.97 – 2 Noctule Bats	1 Swift.
23.7.97 – 1 Noctule Bat.	
24.7.97 – 1 Noctule Bat	3 Swifts.
27.7.97 – 3 Noctule Bats	2 Swifts.
28.7.97 – 5 Noctule Bats	1 Swift.

The first point of interest is that in 1997 the Noctule Bats and Swifts typified the June evenings much more than those of July. Secondly, and more interestingly, Noctules occurred in greater numbers before the Summer Chafers were on the wing than they did when the beetles were active in July.

Whereas the best we can say for the Noctule Bats is that they are still with us in reasonable numbers, the Fallow Deer seems to be a species which is expanding. This year they were reported from Wentwood (Mr. Graham Harris) and from the lower Wye Valley (Des and Ruth John), but a visit to White Hill (Monmouth) on the 30th May revealed signs of great activity in that area.

The remainder of the mammal records are as follows –

19th January.	1 Brown Hare in woods between Tintern and Penterry.
16th February.	Otter spraints and scent-mounds along the River Usk in the Llancayo area. Plentiful footprints of Mink here also.
7th June.	Otter prints along the edge of the Berthin Brook near the Radyr, Usk–Glascoed.
30th July.	Mink reported dead on road between Usk and Llanllowell (Graham Harris).
17th August.	1 Mink seen along the River Usk near Llangattock-juxta-Usk.
29th August.	Mrs. Anne Booker reported the finding of a nest in the middle of a lane in a wooded area near Trellech Grange. Inside the nest was a Dormouse! Just a few days later (early in September) Mrs. Anne Booker reported the presence of a family of Harvest Mice in the vicinity of Cleddon Bog.
10th October.	2 dead Dormice were brought into the home of Mr. Eric and Mrs. Florence Loveys (Silver Birches, Parc Seymour) by

their cat. It is believed that the Dormice were caught in the well-wooded garden here.

19th October. 4 bats were found hanging in a cluster from the ceiling of a building at Brockwells Farm. In the absence of a close scrutiny I would suggest that they were probably Whiskered Bats.

ADDITIONAL RECORDS/INFORMATION

Diary for Winter 1962-63

~

Within the span of my diary-keeping years by far the most dramatic winter was that of 1962/63. Not only was it memorable for the amount of snow it produced, and the severity of its frost, but also for the number of wild geese which were drawn into the area, the like of which we will probably never see again.

The following notes are entered as a basis of comparison with any future winter of such extremes that we may have to endure.

25th December 1962

Today it is again frosty and cold with a fresh wind and sunshine lasting all day. This morning I went out at 10.15, walking down to the Neddern Valley, and across to Ballan Wood. The Neddern Brook was frozen over and Philip Hodges was breaking the ice for Harry Jones's cattle to drink. Fieldfares and Redwings were feeding in the hedges and down on the fields. In the Ballan Wood Long-tailed Tits were feeding in the trees along with Great Tits, Blue Tits and Coal Tits.

26th December 1962

Today it has been milder with sleet falling during the morning. This later turned to rain. Tonight it is freezing.

27th December 1962

This morning everything is covered in a blanket of snow. Stephen Farrar and I went walking, first up the woods in the Shirefield area, and later, down to the Caldicot Levels between Caldicot Halt and Rogiet (Fisherman's Lane).

30th December 1962

The snow has remained on the ground since Thursday (27th Dec.) and last night the wind freshened and between midnight and 8.00am snow fell. The wind, which became strong, blew the fresh snow into drifts and this morning we came downstairs to find piles of snow about 2½ feet high inside both front and back doors. The snow had blown in through every hole and crevice. The key in the front lock was covered in it's own mini-mound of snow three inches high.

When we went outside we found that Tom Williams (White Hall Farm) had to transport his milk churns on the tractor, but even then he only managed to get down the back-lane as far as Dewstow's Little Wood (Shirefield area) because the snow had drifted as high as the hedges. We had to take the milk churns off the tractor, lift them over the hedge and carry them down across our fields to the top of Brockwells Hill. As we were carrying them down the field we saw about 25 grey geese (probably White-fronted Geese) flying over Dewstow Farm land.

We then walked down to the Severn Estuary below Caldicot. As we were crossing the Rifle Range about 10 grey geese flew along the Severn. Everywhere down here there were flocks of larks as well as Chaffinches, Greenfinches, Tree Sparrows and Yellow Buntings.

31st December 1962

Today was our first day back at work after the Christmas break (at Caerwent Quarry). Weather conditions had not improved at all, in fact we had another shower of snow during the night. I reached the cabin about 7.35am. Bert Butler and Bert Harding were already there. When it became light we took shovels up Sharbee Hill in order to dig snow away from Tommy Ball's van. When the van was free Tommy went back home to Woolaston (Gloucestershire). At about 11.50am we all went home. The snow now lay in even greater quantities than I had at first thought. On the Caerwent–Caldicot road the drifts were eight feet deep in places, the road being almost impassable, even to pedestrians.

1st January 1963

Snow has again fallen during the night. I went to work at 7.30am and returned home at 1.00pm. At about 10 o'clock Ken Bass and I went down to Rogiet via Caerwent, Crick and Caldicot. On Jack Knight's kale (Bradbury Farm, Crick) were literally hundreds of Wood Pigeons. In Alf Smith's fields (Manor Farm, Ifton, Rogiet) two brown hares were searching for grass under about 12 inches of snow.

This afternoon Ray Harris and I walked up the Shirefield area having failed to walk through the depths of snow leading to the Neddern Valley. On the fields in the Brockwells–Shirefield area Tree Sparrows, Chaffinches and Skylarks were feeding.

3rd January 1963
Today snow has been falling almost continuously. Drifts have now doubled their size in lanes which were free yesterday and are now almost blocked again. Early this morning (c.7.45) I walked up Sharbee to ascertain the condition of the road and, just past Hall's house, found the snow to be level from one hedge top to the other. At about 10.00am Ken Bass, Ern Stanley and I had to go up to Mr. R. Newman's house (Quarry Director) at Woodcroft to clear a lane of snow-drifts and to dig his car out. On the way back we cleared the paths of an old-folks home next to the Live and Let Live Inn at Tutshill. I arrived home at about 1.20pm.

5th January 1963
This morning the snow is still here. I walked down to the quarry at c.7.55am and found that a Trackscavator had been working all night along the Caerwent–Caldicot road. We worked until 12 noon after which I walked down to the Neddern Valley. In many places the feathers of Skylarks and Redwings littered the snow – probably the victims of Sparrow Hawks. This morning, while we were working in the quarry, a skein of c.20 geese flew over in V formation towards the north. There are now some signs of the snow beginning to melt.

6th January 1963
Today the thaw continues. Snow is melting on roads (those used by cars), around houses and on field banks. In other places the snow is as before, but now it is riddled with foot-prints for we have had no fresh snow-fall in the last few days.

This morning we walked up to the woods in the Shirefield area. Hundreds of Wood Pigeons were feeding on Harris's kale (Dewstow Farm). Among these were the occasional Stockdove. A Tree Sparrow was also seen here and, lying in the snow, the feathers of Green Woodpecker and Skylark – probably Sparrow Hawk victims.

7th January 1963
Today the cold temperatures returned and the thaw has ceased. One of the recent features of this cold winter has been the fact that Skylarks have been

so abundant and confiding, feeding on our backyard here at Brockwells Farm, and also on the gardens close to the house.

Today I was informed of a skein of 50 geese flying over Highmoor Hill in the last few days.

10th January 1963
The cold easterly wind still persists but the sun is warm enough to melt the snow a little in some sheltered places.

13th January 1963
On last Friday morning at 8.40 c.60 wild geese (almost certainly White-fronted Geese) flew from the south-east directly over Caerwent Quarry. Later on 5 Mute Swans flew over the quarry towards the Neddern Valley. Skylarks still occur daily around the Brockwells Farm house on yards, gardens and the lawn.

Yesterday a party of 10 geese flew over the Shirefield area where the Wood Pigeons (and few Stockdoves) are still feeding on the kale. Today a single Common Snipe flew over the fields of the Brockwells Farm in the direction of the Neddern. Shortly after a very large flock of geese was to be seen in the same area. Here the bed of the brook is frozen solid and the geese seem to be everywhere. They are obviously desperate for food and are continually being flushed by people working or, walking in the area.

This evening the weather forecast was for more of the same, with the hardest frosts ever recorded. Tonight freezing fog is falling.

15th January 1963
This winter's unusually hard weather has produced many interesting reports; on Saturday Dick Vaughan informed me that the River Wye was frozen over near Whitebrook. On Monday this had cleared but it was still frozen at Bigsweir. Also on Monday the River Exe was frozen at Exeter, and many miles of the River Severn were frozen over too. Both today and yesterday we had a slight thaw but everything became frozen again at night. The forecast is now for more hard frosts.

Today at c.7.50am a Barn Owl flew down the Lanneck (a field running adjacent to, and parallel with, Caerwent Quarry). At about 11.15 this morning we noticed a Great Spotted Woodpecker feeding around some old tree stumps at the top end of the Quarry. Bert Butler and I went up to have a closer look and the bird moved around the back of one of the stumps. We walked closer and closer until we came within two yards of the stump. On coming into our view the woodpecker flew off but only as far as the next stump, about fifteen yards away.

This evening at about 7.20 my father called me outside to listen to a flock of wild geese which were passing overhead. The calls were very clear. The night was fairly cold with no wind and a clear sky, the stars showing perfectly.

18th January 1963

On Wednesday 16th January a Barn Owl was again noted in the general area of Caerwent Quarry. We walked up to the quarry face at about 9.45am and on the tree stumps was a female Great Spotted Woodpecker. After dinner it began to snow quite heavily and on the following day a bitterly cold wind was blowing from the east.

Today it is again bitterly cold. A flock of c.60 grey geese flew over in the direction of the Neddern Valley. Later my mother and father told me that they had seen a flock of c.100 geese flying north towards Wentwood at about 10.30am.

19th January 1963

Today it is again bitterly cold with an even stonger east wind. The snow has not been greatly reduced for the past three weeks. Today another skein of c.50 wild geese were seen flying into the wind towards the Neddern Valley, but it seems that the wind was too strong for them and they swung back around and along the Upper Rodge Wood on a completely opposite course. Later we picked up a dead goose on the Church Farm (Caldicot) fields, close to the Neddern. This bird was a White-fronted Goose – probably a bird in its first winter. The white on its forehead was just starting to develop but there were no black bars on its underside. I took the bird home to weigh it and it proved to be a mere 3½lbs.

Tonight at 6.30 it is snowing heavily and this is being blown by quite a fresh wind.

20th January 1963

This morning the wind has fallen away but the snow had been blown into little drifts scattered over the fields. Over the Caerwent Quarry area a flock of 60 wild geese flew overhead in the general direction of Highmoor Hill.

This afternoon we went up to the area of Itton Court where we found a field of kale stripped of its leaves by Wood Pigeons.

23rd January 1963

The rain of last Sunday night made the stones in the Quarry very slippery but the roads didn't seem to be that bad. Yesterday it was again very cold and on the previous night 30 degrees of frost were recorded in the south of England.

Today it is again very cold with 30 degrees of frost last night in many places. Our water tap was frozen for the first time this morning and remained frozen all day.

This morning, while working at Caerwent Quarry, we had to carry water from Mrs. Herbert's well (Rock House – just across the Llaneck from the Quarry) to supply the air compressor which drives Bob Arnold's drill.

26th January 1963

Freezing fog has been a feature of recent days. The early morning news forecast a thaw spreading down from the north which has mild weather already. This morning it was cold, although the sun appeared several times, but the afternoon was sunny and warm. The white cloak vanished from the trees as if by a miracle and hedges and woods were full of the sound of sliding, melting snow.

27th January 1963

Today the thaw continues. The difference in the snow is quite remarkable. After being crisp and crunchy yesterday morning it was now soft and slushy – although seemingly maintaining its original depth.

3rd February 1963

On Monday 28th January it was mild again. 8 geese were seen flying over the Neddern Valley in the direction of the Severn Estuary. The next day the cold temperatures returned and 10 geese were seen flying north over the Neddern. The next day was also cold, as was Thursday when 33 geese flew over the Brockwells towards the north.

On Friday it was very cold early on but became milder later with snow falling. At about 2.30pm a large flock of c.70 – 100 geese flew over the Neddern Valley. I have been told that floating ice has been causing blockages on the River Wye in the Redbrook, Whitebrook and Bigsweir areas.

Today it has been comparatively mild and sunny. We walked down to the Neddern Valley and noted that the Crick Brook was again frozen. Last Tuesday the water had been running over the old ice.

7th February 1963

On Monday last it was cold with snow falling all afternoon up until c.6.00pm. On Tuesday there was a cold east wind and during the night it must have snowed again because on Wednesday morning I walked out to find two inches of fresh snow which had been blown into small drifts.

Today a thaw has set in. At about 11.15am I went down to Redwick in the lorry with Les Jones. Down here on the Caldicot Levels the snow is melting more quickly than it is around the Brockwells and large pools of water lie on many fields.

10th February 1963

At c.1.10pm 84 wild geese flew over the Brockwells in a northerly direction. At 5.20pm Ray Harris and I saw another large flock of geese flying over the Neddern Valley towards the east.

On Saturday morning the wind was back in the north-east. At 7.30am I saw 21 wild geese flying over Caerwent Quarry towards the north.

Today the north-east wind is bitterly cold. Ice still lay in the Neddern Brook but fresh water was flowing over it to a depth of about nine inches. Before long it began to snow quite heavily.

16th February 1963

On Monday it was fairly mild and in the morning I heard both Dunnocks and Chaffinches singing. 16 White-fronted Geese flew over Caerwent Quarry towards the north.

On Wednesday I heard Chaffinch, Song Thrush and Missel Thrush singing. It was wonderfully mild and in the fields there was far more grass showing than there was snow.

On Thursday there was a cold wind and on Friday it gradually became milder with snow and then rain falling. At about 3.00pm it began to snow again and this soon started to stick. When I walked out on Saturday 15th about four inches of snow lay on the ground. I went in to work (Caerwent Quarry) and we had to go up to Woodcroft to clear snow from Mr. Newman's drive again. This afternoon hundreds of Wood Pigeons were feeding on the kale in the Shirefield area.

24th February 1963.

Today, after more snow showers during the week, the thawing process seems to be winning. The weather remains very cold however, with hard frosts at night. If this is the last of the snow then it has been lying on the ground now for virtually two months. This afternoon we walked up to the Minnetts forestry area and I saw my first Fieldfares since the beginning of the snow.

3rd March 1963

This morning I walked down the Neddern. Snow is still lying in patches and the brook is still frozen over. Lapwings have been flying over the Caerwent Quarry area in batches of about twenty in a fairly continuous flow. This has been the case for most of the week. It is now evident that such small mammals as mice, voles and moles have been active beneath the blanket of snow. On the ground can be seen runs carved about half an inch into the earth and on the banks of the Neddern Brook are the runs of Water Voles which can be seen in the earth and in the snow.

*   *   *

These notes were to be my last concerning the hard winter of 1962/1963 and from here on my records show a gradual move into the spring.

Selected Notes from the Diaries

~

26th April 1959
In the Cwm, the valley of the Cas-Troggy Brook south of Earlswood, five small nests made of fibres and bramble leaves were found. One of them was sited in Hawthorn and four in low bushes c.2-5 ft. above the ground on sloping land in the general area of Cribau Mill. In the last of these nests was a sleeping Dormouse.

29th July 1959
Today, for the first time, I saw a High Brown Fritillary butterfly. It is interesting how each successive year produces its particular 'crop' of butterflies. In the summer of 1955 Clouded Yellows were very common while 1958 seemed to be the year of the Silver-washed Fritillary. This year the White-letter Hairstreaks are more plentiful than usual and we have now seen our first High Brown Fritillaries as well.

21st November 1963
An injured male Crossbill was brought into the Caerwent Quarry office today by Les Jones, one of the lorry-drivers. The bird had been found near the Llandegvedd Reservoir site which is now under construction.

25th May 1964
This evening we worked on again until 9 o'clock (in Caerwent Quarry). When I got home I went straight out for a walk, through the Upper Rodge Wood and then into the Shirefield area of Dewstow Farm. Here I saw a Brown Hare, then a Rabbit, and then a further two Brown Hares. The wind was in a northerly direction so I decided to circle around to the far side of the Shirefield Wood and sat down for a while. Tawny Owls were feeding their young which called continuously. As it began to get dark I walked through the wood and came out at the edge of the narrow strip field known as the River-

bed Field. Under the opposite hedge I could see three or four Fox cubs. (*Note* – Today (1997) this area now forms part of the Dewstow Golf Club course).

25th June 1964

Last week I worked 93 hours and took home £13.16.3d. This week I worked 96 hours and took home £13.13.0d.

5th August 1964

In the woods behind Cleddon Hall we found a young Hedgehog which appeared to be blind, although it was wandering along the forest track quite happily on its own. There was no sign of any eyes at all – just shrivelled skin.

17th March 1965

While working on the construction of the M4 viaduct over the Neddern Valley I noted that the bed of the valley bottom is filled with peat, and rather smelly. In this peat can be found the branches of trees which can be squeezed to a pulp in the hand.

19th September 1965

I spent the rest of the day picking Hazel nuts which are very abundant this year. I picked over two large basketfuls in woods near White Hall Farm, Highmoor Hill.

7th May 1967

Today we were given a guided tour of Whitson Zoo by the new manager, my old friend Stephen Farrar. Here they are in the early stages of development with a collection which includes Sun Bears, Llamas, Red Deer, Golden Pheasant, Reeves Pheasant, Racoons, Peacocks, Terrapins, Macaws etc.

26th August 1967

At Newport Docks we first looked over some old steam engines that were lined up ready to go for scrap, and then we went down into the Docks proper. Here we saw two old barges completely constructed out of steel reinforced concrete. In the waters of the Docks the Common Jellyfish are to be seen in abundance, pulsating their way through the water. We then went on board the iron-ore carrying 'Iron Horse' which had come into the Dock that morning.

16th May 1968
Last night I visited Roy Williams (of Portskewett) who gave me a vertebra from the whale which was washed up on the beach at Sudbrook in 1925. He also showed me a photograph taken of the whale at the time and the measurements indicated a total length of over 48ft. This whale was a Rudolphi's Rorqual or Sei Whale (*Balaenoptera borealis*) which is one of the baleen whales.

28th September 1968
Today, just below the school at Llanfrechfa, I watched a Hedgehog for about two minutes or perhaps more. It was walking around in a circle on the farm-drive, covering the same area all of the time. There was no obvious reason for this behaviour and the Hedgehog continued even when our two lorries were driven past it at a distance of about two yards. The Hedgehog was still walking around and around when we eventually drove away.

30th December 1968
Today I started the delivery of hay to the N.C.B.'s Victoria Provender Plant at Ebbw Vale. The plant processes the hay and then distributes it to various coal-mines for pit-pony feed.

13th July 1969
This morning I walked into Caerwent Quarry where I found a small colony of Sand Martins excavating holes in the sand-bank below what was formerly the Lanneck, a long and slender field running the length of Caerwent Quarry and belonging to Mr. Harry Rhymer of the Woodlands. There were at least four pairs.

25th March 1970
On my way down through Caerwent Quarry I noticed that the most recent 'blast' has exposed the end of the cave where the Pleistocene mammal remains were found, and the machine has moved the rock and revealed the soil/rubble of the cave floor. I went over to investigate this and found that the rubble was liberally strewn with bones and bone-fragments. I probed amongst the loose rocks for a while and was lucky to chance upon some jawbone pieces and teeth of a large carnivore. This cave was originally exposed as a result of blasting the face of the Quarry on the 29th September 1969. The length of the cave is estimated at about 60 feet.

22nd March 1971

At Crick a huge flock of Starlings passed over us from the south-west. They must have numbered upwards of 20,000 birds.

8th May 1971

At the back of St. Peter's Cave, in cliffs above the River Wye, but below Bulwark (near Chepstow), we found a large concentration of amphibian bones (frogs or toads) in a heap of earth at the back of the cave.

17th May 1971

A young Raven which appeared to be an orphan (one parent found dead below the nest-tree in Wentwood Forest) was taken into our care on the 3rd May 1971. Here follows a note of my observations to date – 'I first took the young Raven out onto the lawn. At present its eyes are a slate-grey colour with brown just beginning to show around the pupils. On the ground the bird moves by both walking and hopping which is executed in a rather ungainly, vulturine fashion. Other corvids are attracted by the young Raven's calls. The bird has a gift for successfully catching insects which may fly near, especially bees or flies which have a droning flight. The insects captured are crushed at the bill-tip, and occasionally eaten. It is a very inquisitive bird and tests everything with its bill, ranging from metals and stone-work to vegetation, particularly flower-heads'.

24th May 1971

This evening Trevor Evans visited me and also Franklyn Perring and Margaret Barrow. They had just come from Sudbrook where they had found plants of Subterranean Clover (*Trifolium subterraneum*) growing on the embankments of the ancient fortress.

28th June 1971

This evening Trevor Evans and I drove to Common Coed where we photographed the Cut-leaved Selfheal (*Prunella laciniata*). We counted 16 plants of this species in one small patch covering about a square yard.

9th October 1971

While carrying out my regular count of birds along the Severn Estuary (Magor Pill to Collister Pill) I again saw the Dowitcher and made the following note – 'I was pleased to find that the Dowitcher is still flying with the Redshanks. Today I saw it on two occasions and was able to get very good flight views but have yet to see the bird on the ground. The Dowitcher readily engages in the Redshanks aerial manoeuvres when they suddenly dive from about 30 feet down to about 2 feet to skim over the surface of the water, twisting and turning as they do'.

7th August 1972

Later we went down to Collister Pill on the Severn Estuary below Undy. As dusk approached the influx of roosting Black-headed Gulls began. We knew that the numbers of this species at this time of year could be well into the thousands but our estimate for this evenings congregation could be as many as 8,000.

9th September 1972

Later Emlyn Evans (of the National Museum of Wales) took us to Rhymney Bridge where we were shown a very interesting section of rock exposure in the Millstone Grit Shale which was highly fossiliferous. The fossils here included fresh, or brackish-water mussels and other *bivalves*, plant remains and some *cephalopod* species including fine *goniatites*.

9th October 1972

This evening Trevor Evans and I went down to the lake at St. Pierre. Owing to the very dry conditions of the latter half of this summer the water level was unusually low and we found massive numbers of Swan Mussel shells left on the surface of the mud or in the shallows. Most of these shells were empty but I found two which still held body contents. The largest of the shells measured about 6½ inches.

15th October 1972

We then drove along to the Tramp's Cave (at the side of the Wye Valley road on the Tintern side of the track leading down to Livox Quarry). On entering the cave I was amazed at the structure of the rock which was unlike anything I had seen before. Instead of being solid it was a mass of naturally cemented limestone chips. In other words, a hardened limestone scree. Cave Spiders were very plentiful in here and their white, globular egg-sacs hung everywhere. Clinging to some of the empty sacs we found three Herald Moths.

8th June 1973

At dinner-time we took a walk up to the Crick Quarry Rubbish-tip which is fast being filled in. I was told that the quarry itself operated solely to supply base material for the Royal Naval Propellant Factory (now R.A.F. Caerwent) when it was being constructed in the late 1930's and early 1940's. Amongst the rubbish I again noted the abundance of the Common Cockroach.

19th June 1973
This evening I received a letter from the Bristol-based ornithologist Norman Lacy. In the letter he confirms the presence of a Spoonbill at Collister Pill (Undy) and also that of a Marsh Warbler at Magor Reserve.

19th September 1973
This evening I walked out over the fields (Brockwells Farm) and from the long grass on the north-facing Banky Field the dog flushed a Corncrake. It flew for almost 300 yards and landed clumsily in the top of a low hedge.

18th March 1974
At the shallow end of St. Pierre Lake, alongside the causeway, we found three dead plants of the Thorn Apple (*Datura stramonium*). In the water we noticed several Pike swirling about slowly, and quite close the surface. Checking on the text-book we found it highly likely that these fish were spawning.

9th May 1974
Today Neil Harrhy and I again put food out for the Brown Rats in the dried up bed of the Cas-Troggy Brook (opposite Trewen) and we were surprised to find that we had now attracted eight of them to our temporary 'feeding station'. We put some of the food on sticks so that the rats had first to locate it, and then climb up the sticks to get their reward. It seemed as though food location was being carried out almost exclusively with the nose. I also found that the rat's tail may be employed in a prehensile fashion as a fifth limb when climbing up a slender and vertical rod.

12th August 1974
This evening Trevor Evans and I drove up to the Narth area where we walked through Manor Wood and found a small patch of Oak Fern. We next visited Pen-y-fan Bog and, nearby, talked to two local ladies who informed us that, in their youth, the local people wouldn't walk past the Pen-y-fan Bog at night because of the 'hoppity lanterns'. These are more commonly known as 'Will o' the Wisp' or 'marsh gas' and are produced by the spontaneous ignition of methane which rises from the rotting vegetation of the bog.

7th September 1974

Today the weather has deteriorated again and the westerly winds have become gale-force, possibly the strongest I can remember. I went down to the Severn Estuary to carry out a bird count between Magor Pill and Collister Pill but the use of binoculars was virtually impossible. The two most unusual birds seen were a Grey Phalarope, which was down in the comparative shelter of the 'back-ditch', and a Gannet.

The Gannet was battling against the viciously strong winds but it could make no headway at all. After coming down to rest on the water for a while, and then being driven inland for a while, it was finally forced on upstream towards Chepstow.

8th September 1974

Today we met at Cobbler's Plain (Devauden–Llanishen) to search for Harvest Mice under the direction of Mr. Stephen Harris (Dept. of Zoology – Royal Holloway College). Mr. Harris showed us examples of nests that he had previously found here and as a result of his visit and talk we now know that we have Harvest Mice at Wentwood, Shirenewton, the Minnetts, Cobler's Plain, Magor Reserve and Llandevenny.

10th October 1975

Des Tucker (of Dunromin, Sandy Lane near Caerwent Quarry) has discovered two worked flints in the Pleistocene matrix of the Caerwent Quarry Cave, and these have been identified as being of Cresswellian age.

23rd August 1976

The incredible dry/hot spell continues and forest fires rage. Today Wern Brake (F.C. plantation to the south of Grey Hill common land) ignited once more and two fire-engines had to be called in. The diary of this fire is as follows – The fire starts at c.1.30pm on Monday 16th August. On the following day the 'hot-spots' were still bursting into flame and this continued until midday on the Wednesday. On the Thursday, Friday, Saturday and Sunday all was quiet but today the fire re-ignited.

In Wentwood (and in other forests) the Norway Spruce trees have been splitting because of the dry, hot conditions. At 7.20pm we were called out for fire-duty in Ebbw Forest (Abercarn). The actual fire was in a plantation of pine on Mynydd Maen.

6th September 1976

This evening we walked across the Brockwells Farm fields to study some unusual formations (parch-marks) that have appeared in the Laye – the low strip field which separates the south-facing and north-facing banks of the Banky Field. The shapes, basically rectangular, but one long and slender and at right angles to the other two, were outlined by the new green grass after the rains which began on the 28th August, the shapes themselves still being covered with dead, brown grass. (*Note* – These shapes appeared again after the drought summer of 1995).

26th February 1977

At 5.0pm we drove down to Wilcrick Hill where massive numbers of Starlings congregate to roost at this time. Uncountable thousands of birds are involved and these will probably be moving east into Europe before too long in time for their breeding season.

The Starlings have been providing a dusk spectacular here for the past week and after making a series of by-passes in several individual flocks which swirl and contort as the birds move in fantastic synchrony, they finally plunge into the trees on the side of the hill above the little church in a drone of wing and vocal sound.

5th May 1977

This evening Derek Upton told me about some of the unusual things that he had seen caught by the Caldicot lave-net fishermen in the Severn Estuary tidal gullies known as the 'Lake' and the 'Lubee'. These include Cuttlefish, a Seal and a Shelduckling.

11th September 1977

Today I noticed that virtually all of the Hornet Robber-flies were resting in the sunlight on dry cow-pats. In fact, on one cow-pat we also found another, smaller species of Robber-fly which had killed a small dipteron and was feeding from it there alongside a spider which had killed a Brown Argus butterfly.

16th June 1978

This year Wentwood Forest's larch trees have become heavily infested by the larvae of the Larch-leaf Miner-moth (*Coleophora laricella*). Some trees look as though they are turning to their autumn colour already.

24th June 1978

This morning a flock of about fifty Starlings were feeding on our Front Field (Brockwells Farm) and a group of Swallows were flying low over them, repeatedly skimming over the feeding flock and often flying in circles in order to keep themselves just above the Starlings. It certainly looked like a case of one species using the activities of another to their own advantage – the Swallows picking off the flying insects that the foraging Starlings had disturbed.

14th April 1981

Along a stretch of the A449 trunk-road embankment near Kemeys Inferior, and over a distance of about a hundred yards, I counted 81 Drinker Moth larvae.

4th May 1981

This afternoon I went down to the Goldcliff foreshore with Brian Whittaker. Here we found the hydroid *Tubularia indivisa*, complete with reproductive bodies. Another extremely abundant hydroid here was the Whiteweed (*Sertularia cupressina*). Brian also identified the following sea-anemones – *Tealia felina*, *Sagartia troglodytes* and *Anthopleura thallia*.

25th May 1981

We drove back around the narrow Penterry lanes to Devauden and came upon a Weasel that was carrying another Weasel virtually as big as it was – but which we assumed to be a young one though why it couldn't run itself is not known.

28th December 1981

I called in to see Brian Whittaker who now has three Sea Snails (*Liparis sp.*) in his aquarium. These were collected from the 'pump-screens' in the Uskmouth Power Station. Until today I had always been mystified by the name 'sea snail' but seeing one of these small fish affixed to the glass side of the aquarium by its 'sucker', and with its tail curled right back along its own side, its appearance was distinctly slug-like if not snail-like.

19th June 1981

During the past week it has been obvious that several pairs of Yellow Wagtails are now feeding young in Dewstow Farm's corn-fields. It is equally obvious that they cannot find sufficient food in that environment for they seem to do all of their food collecting in our unimproved Brockwells fields – often around the feeding cattle.

19th April 1983
In the grounds of Brynglas House (Newport) I climbed one of the Giant Redwood trees and found that the Tree Creeper/Wren/Coal Tit roosting hollows were distributed up the main trunk to a height of at least 30 or 40 feet.

4th October 1983
Over the last week or so the number and movement of Jays has been very noticeable and this morning, in a period of less than two hours, I noted 21 Jays moving over the Brockwells in an east to west direction. One group of nine birds alighted in the long grass on the north-facing Banky Field, and some on top of the roadside hedge. This strikes me as unusual behaviour and it seems very likely that these are Continental Jays.

21st December 1983
Today my uncle (Charlie Titcombe) collected a permit to cut wood in the Poor Wood near Llanmelin (Starkey Common – this is also known locally as 'Sharpee') and I helped him to cut and transport the wood to Caerwent. While here we disturbed a Dormouse from its nest at the bottom of a dead tree we were cutting. The nest was made almost entirely of Clematis bark shredding's.

18th January 1984
Today I found a pair of gull's wings on the south-facing bank of the Banky Field (Brockwells Farm) and was rather surprised to find them to be the wings of a Kittiwake. This was probably a wind-blown bird that had become the victim of a Fox.

15th April 1984
In the Wye Valley, between Brockweir and Llandogo, we met an Elver fisherman who told us that the first reasonable catch of the season had been made on the previous night. He had come down to the river to make sure of a place for fishing at 2.50pm – the Elvers were not due until 7 o'clock this evening. This indicates the level of competition these days.

10th August 1984
This evening we visited the Minnetts forestry area and then walked down into the fields above the Rogiet Windmill (ruin). On the lower edge of the wood all of the Wild Cherry trees bore an abundance of sweet, black cherries. We also found a tree of this kind at Wentwood on the 2nd August

last and I cannot remember seeing anything like it before. The fruits are jet black in colour, very sweet to taste, and yet there appears to be no evidence of birds or other animals eating them.

24th September 1984
Earlier this month Mr. Roy Thomas found the larva of a Convolvulus Hawk-moth in his garden at Trewen. This was passed on to me and eventually the caterpillar burrowed into the soil and pupated. On the 18th September I uncovered it and found that, although it had made a cell in the earth, it still had not pupated. Since that time I have inspected the now shrunken larva daily and it wasn't until today that it finally pupated. At the present the colour of the pupa is a pale lime-green and the 'jug-handle' (proboscis sheath) is much smaller than book illustrations have led me to believe. (*Note* – on the 25th September the pupa had achieved a glossy brown appearance and the 'jug-handle' is now as the book illustrations depict it). (*Note* – the moth emerged successfully on the 7th July 1985.)

27th November 1984
This evening Mr. Terry Ryan brought me the corpse of a petrel which, after examination, proved to be that of a Leach's Petrel. The bird was found on a ship that had come into Newport Docks.

14th January 1985
We are currently in the middle of a hard spell of weather with snow and frost persisting now for some time. The conditions have been much worse in the east and south-east of the country. Possibly because of this I was called down to Vinegar Hill, Undy, this afternoon to see a Bittern that was perched, uncharacteristically, on top of a laurel hedge in a back garden. When the bird became aware of my presence it pointed its bill skywards, so that its plumage would blend in with the reeds that were not there!

6th May 1987
This evening the calls of Whimbrel caused me to look up and, eventually, to locate a wavering V formation of c.40 – 50 birds, as high in the sky as would permit me seeing them with the naked eye – and then only because the sunlight was illuminating their undersides. (*Note* – 7.5.87 – 'Tonight, a bright moonlit night, Whimbrels could be heard passing over-head at 10 o'clock)'.

12th April 1988

We measured the girth of the two large Beech trees at the eastern end of Chepstow Racecourse (Piercefield Park) at 15' 7½" and 18' 7".

(*Note* – In the early part of 1996 one of these trees was literally snapped off, presumably by strong winds).

6th May 1990

Today I visited the stretch of the River Usk upstream from the Clytha car-park to check on the small fish which, during the current hot spell of weather, have been congregating in the shallows in dense masses so as to appear, at times, almost black. These small fish are largely a mixture of Minnows and Gudgeon. I also came across a young Trout of some 4½ inches in length which was suffering from a condition known as 'whirling disease', this being caused by the spores of *Myxosoma corebralis*.

6th October 1993

In England and Wales at least, this past September has been the wettest for ten years, corroborating the prediction that 'a month with two full moons in it is a wet one'.

27th April 1994

This morning we met Graham Harris at Usk. He showed us the scent-mounds of an Otter along the River Usk between the Island car-park and the Town Bridge.

8th January 1995

Today, near Usk, Graham Harris showed me what appears to be the only example of Mistletoe growing in an oak tree in the area (Gwent). The oak was the Pedunculate Oak (*Quercus robur*).

Wildlife in Gwent's Churches and Churchyards

~

When initially planning to make this study I consulted a book entitled *Ancient Gwent Churches* (Starling Press, 1979) in which the authors (John R. Guy and Ewart B. Smith) describe 146 churches, some of which are ruinous, or even, no longer in existence.

From these I selected 129 sites which I deemed to be suitable, and added to these one other, Llanelly, now in the 'new' county of Monmouthshire. Of the 130 churches chosen at least eight are not, currently (1996/1997) being used for their intended purpose. One is up for sale (Llanfaenor, October 1996) and another is ruinous (St. Mary's, Chapel Hill, Tintern), having been burnt out in a fire during 1977. However, with the exception of Llanfaenor (which never seems to have had a churchyard as such, just a narrow grassy strip between church and surrounding wall), all still retain their churchyards and these continue to be used and maintained.

This study can be divided into two major parts – the wildlife of the churchyard, and that of the church itself. The former is largely based on the flora but the latter has more to do with the availability of access into the church building or fabric for a range of different animals – bats, birds and insects for example.

Three major features of typical church structure present themselves for use by a variety of animals – (1) the TOWER, where present, usually has a variety of openings which permit access to the interior, traditionally perhaps to Barn Owls and bats, but otherwise to a whole range of animals; (2) the PORCH, if suitable, is frequently used by nesting Swallows or roosting bats, but otherwise, by a range of nesting and resting species. Many porches, however, are fitted with solid doors or wire-mesh doors, which exclude most animals. Swallows and bats will obviously make a certain amount of mess in the porch and this is sometimes judged to be intolerable so attempts are made to exclude them. During the course of the survey (1996/97) I found 45 Swallows nests in church porches in Gwent (or, as at Trellech, under the lych-gate roof).

(3) The 'UNDER CHURCH', whether a crypt or simply a ventilation space below the church floor, often has access from the outside to wildlife species of suitable size via the ventilation holes. These would normally be screened by some form of metal mesh but this is often removed, or rusts away, and permits entry to the like of mammals, amphibians, reptiles and invertebrates such as hibernating butterflies and moths, or spiders which would be more permanent residents.

Honeybees commonly build nests in the church structure but the actual situation varies widely from holes in the masonry to hollows beneath the roof, or beneath the roof of the porch as at Llangattock Lingoed. In 1996/97 I found 16 churches which held Honeybee nests but it would be very interesting to know how many there would be if they had not been evicted. Honeybees have previously been removed from the tower of Caerwent Church (on at least two occasions), from St. Brides Netherwent Church and from Mathern Church where they have now returned. Restoration work at the church of St. Brides Wentlooge in 1996 has almost certainly resulted in the removal of a Honeybees nest here also. It seems a little strange that Honeybees should use churches to nest in so regularly, and apparently so persistently, and it is interesting to speculate as to why this should be.

The churchyard's wildlife depends upon the type of maintenance employed, on the underlying geology, and on the nature of the surrounding terrain. The maintenance varies according to a mixture of option and choice on a local basis. If possible, a neatly trimmed and manicured churchyard would probably be the ideal for all people other than wildlife conservationists, but the work involved has to be paid for, or, the parish must be fortunate enough to have an enthusiastic volunteer with time and ability on his/her hands. Otherwise, if the powers that be inclined towards the conservation of wildlife, then a much more 'natural' churchyard is likely to be preferred with lots of wild flowers and their attendant wild animals.

Another factor which may play a part in this respect is local belief or tradition. The churchyard to the north of the church (churches are typically aligned East to West) is sometimes referred to as the 'Devil's side' and, given the choice, parishioners may not wish their deceased to be buried there. Consequently many churchyards do not have graves in this particular area and so, to minimise the work of maintenance, this area may be left unmown. This permits the plants to flower and seed, which in turn provides food and shelter for animal life.

Yew trees, either one or many, are typically associated with churchyards, but other trees are often planted here too. Churchyards in Gwent often have lime trees, either planted in rows – perhaps bordering one or more sides of the churchyard, or otherwise forming an avenue leading to the church porch, as at St. Mary's Goldcliff or St. Cadoc's, Penrhos.

Some churchyards in the area have unusual species of trees planted in them, outstanding among which must be St. Cadoc's at Trevethin, a possible result of the Hanbury connection. Here, among other scarce churchyard plantings, are Lucombe Oak trees (*Quercus X pseudosuber*).

Giant Redwoods provide nesting facilities for some birds, but roosting potential for others – notably Treecreepers, Wrens and Coal Tits, all of which may roost in hollows excavated in the soft, deep bark. Churchyards containing trees of this species currently are Marshfield, Itton, Caerleon, St. Brides Wentlooge, Penterry, Caldicot, Tredunnock and Llandewi Rhydderch. Pen-y-clawdd is unusual in having a Coast Redwood in its churchyard.

During the course of the survey at least 40 churchyards were found to have nests of the Yellow Meadow Ant. Particularly notable in this respect was the churchyard of St. Peter's, Blaenavon. Sometimes said to indicate 'ancient pasture' or undisturbed ground, these ant-hills must indicate a healthy invertebrate fauna for the ants have a wide range of species associated with them and occupying their nests.

Gravestones, in all their variety of shape, size and composition, often attract the growth of lichens. Some smooth and polished stones are usually devoid of these but stones of a textured surface, such as a sandstone, are often largely covered by them. Some gravestones at St. David's, Rhymney, have the Map Lichen growing on them, almost certainly because of the elevation here, and the chemistry of the stone itself – Map Lichen is said to be strongly calcifuge.

Gravel-topped graves also attract invasion by plants such as Navelwort. Again, the chemistry of the chippings is probably significant in determining the presence, or otherwise, of certain species.

Another feature recorded during the survey were those churchyards described as 'having a good mix of plants'. The basic criteria for inclusion in this category was a range of species in excess of fifty, not including trees and shrubs. One of the difficulties here is the fact that a churchyard may have 'a good mix of plants' but because of a rigorous mowing regime, the actual number of species is difficult to determine. It could be argued, however, that because the plants are not allowed to grow, flower and seed, they therefore play little part in the ecology of the locality, and should be disqualified on that basis alone.

The churchyards regarded as having 'a good mix of plants' are listed in appendix D. Of these there are a small number which are outstanding in terms of their floral diversity. These are listed in appendix E. In appendix F are listed those churchyards which contain scarce or unusual species. These are generally those listed in appendix E, but not invariably. Perhaps the most interesting plant found in a Gwent churchyard is that growing plentifully at St. Mary's, Chepstow, which is otherwise rather unexciting, botanically. The plant concerned is the Ivy Broomrape, and this is here only by virtue of the Ivy which it parasites, and which is allowed to flourish here by those responsible for churchyard maintenance. This is a nationally scarce species and, in Gwent today, occurs only in the Chepstow district.

This account of the wildlife, in Gwent's churchyards is based upon a two-year survey – there is obviously a great deal yet to be done in order to achieve a reasonably accurate understanding of the full wildlife potential here. Further avenues of study could include that of the stone-dwelling lichens, the terrestrial fungi, and the animals using parts of the inner church. Herald moths and Small Tortoiseshell butterflies have already been noted as hibernating in the dark recesses of church towers such as that of St. Jerome's, Llangwm Uchaf, and a Hornet's nest is reported to have occupied the roof-space of St. John's, Llangwm Isaf, some years ago. With the necessary permission this could prove to be a fascinating line of study.

POST-SCRIPT SUMMARY OF WILDLIFE IN GWENT'S CHURCHES AND CHURCHYARDS–1997

During the year I revisited many of the churches included in the survey of 1996 and came to the conclusion that a meaningful appreciation of what these sites really support can only be achieved after many years of surveying at varying periods through the seasons.

Yellow Meadow Ants were found to be present at many more sites bringing the present total up to almost half of the original 130 sites. In churchyards where nest-mounds occur, but not Yellow Meadow Ants, I can only conclude that the nests have been taken over by other species such as the Red Ant (*Myrmica rubra*).

One plant which has been reported to me, but which I have yet to see, is the Dropwort (*Filipendula vulgaris*) in the churchyard at Penallt 'OLD CHURCH'. Trevor Evans informs me that this is the only known site for this species in Gwent.

Additional records for this subject area are as follows –

7th May.	A specimen of Coast Redwood (*Sequoia sempervirens*) noted in the churchyard at Caldicot.
20th May.	Common Star-of-Bethlehem in flower in Llanover churchyard.
3rd June.	Wood Bitter-vetch growing commonly in the churchyard at Bedwellty.
6th June.	Burnet Companion Moths (*Euclidia glyphica*) in Bedwellty churchyard.
10th June.	Dusky Crane's-bill (*Geranium phaeum*) flowering in Penallt churchyard.
18th October.	At least six species of waxcap fungi are now to be seen in the churchyard at Trostrey – Meadow Waxcap (*Cuphophyllus pratensis*), Snowy Waxcap (*Cuphophyllus virgineus*), Pink Waxcap (*Hygrocybe calyptriformis*), Scarlet Waxcap (*Hygrocybe coccinea*), Conical Waxcap (*Hygrocybe conica*), and Parrot Waxcap (*Hygrocybe psittacina*).

ADDITIONAL RECORDS/INFORMATION

Appendix A

~

GLOSSARY OF TERMS

In the pages of this book, in the form of place names or land features, will be encountered a small number of words perhaps not immediately familiar. Some of these are of local origin. In this glossary I hope to interpret such words, either officially, or by way of their local meaning and usage. There are also some 'technical' terms and abbreviations which may also require explanation. Official definitions, in brackets, have been taken from sources listed in the bibliography.

BACK-DITCH This is specifically the large reen running behind, and parallel with, the Severn Estuary sea-wall. It often contains brackish (slightly salty) water.

BRAKE (Wasteland covered with brush-wood). Locally, tends to be extended also to a small wood, or a small wood which has been cleared, but then allowed to go back to nature.

B.S.B.I. Botanical Society of the British Isles.

ERYTHRISTIC A term applied to animals, usually their pelage or plumage, displaying erythrism (Red colouring, especially exceptional or abnormal).

IMAGO The final or adult stage of insect life.

PILL (A waterway, especially in Monmouthshire). Locally a pill is an outlet into an estuary, and therefore implies tidal association. Examples include Hunger Pill (estuary of the Wye), Collister Pill (estuary of the Severn),

Julian's Pill (estuary of the Usk), New Gout Pill (estuary of the Ebbw) etc. Gout, as in New Gout Pill, describes an enlarged pill or out-spill into the estuary, as in Peterstone Gout, Tabb's Gout etc. In Caldicot Pill we have a double location – (1) the outfall of the Neddern Brook into the Severn Estuary, and (2) that part of Caldicot lying close to the Severn sea-wall. There is also a line of houses known as Pill Row (Caldicot).

REEN (A major field drain which collects from smaller drains). Drainage ditches on the Gwent Levels are called reens and most, if not all, have specific names – e.g. Windmill Reen, Stutwall Reen etc.

RIDE Locally, refers to a broad track through woodland – more than a path – something of a size that a vehicle can be driven along.

SALTINGS Generally implies a salt-marsh or an area close to a tidal regime which becomes, even if only infrequently, inundated by the salty water – perhaps on the very highest tides.

SWARTH On a local basis, generally applies to areas of grassy turf close to the estuary of the River Severn – a part of the saltings, but not all of the salt-marsh. Relatively dry turf, only inundated by the highest tides, but having a range of salt-tolerant plants.

VICE-COUNTY (Part of a county divided for floristic purposes). The original system was devised by H. C. Watson. The vice-county largely pertinent to the area considered here is vice-county 35.

Appendix B

~

LIST OF SITES (GIVING GRID REF. LOCATIONS)

In the following list villages are identified by pin-pointing the position of the church. Larger areas, such as Wentwood Forest, are given a central grid reference point. Brooks are identified at the point of their confluence with the main river and, where an asterix follows the grid reference number, this indicates that the site as named, no longer exists. For example, Crick Rubbish Tip, now filled and landscaped. Place name spellings are taken from the relevant Ordnance Survey Map, that is, when they occur on it. If site identifications do not appear in the list check the map section.

Abercarn (centred at 31/ 215 950)
Angiddy Valley (confluence of Angiddy Brook and Wye at Tintern – 32/532 002)
Ballan Wood (centred at 31/493 895)
Beachley (centred at 31/550 910)
Bedwas (Church) 31/172 892
Bedwellty (Church) 32/166 004
Bettws Brook (confluence with the Usk at Crindau – 31/315 897)
Bettws Ponds (31/298 901)
Bettws Newydd (Church) 32/363 058
Bigsweir (32/539 051)
Bishton (Church) 31/386 873
Blackrock (32/215 125)
Black Rock (31/513 881)
Blaenavon (Church) 32/251 088
Blaina (32/200 080)
Broad Meend (32/505 043)
Brockwells Farm (31/471 896)
Brynglas House (31/311 902)
Brynmawr (32/190 120)
Buckholt (32/507 161)
Bulmore (centred at) 31/360 915
Caerleon (Church) 31/339 906
Caerwent Brook (31/475 898)
Caerwent Quarry (31/474 895)
Caldicot (Church) 31/483 886
Caldicot Rifle Range (31/475 871)*
Cats Ash (31/374 908)

Celtic Lakes (31/282 846)
Chapel Hill (Church) 31/530 000
Chepstow Park Wood (centred at) 31/490 980
Chepstow Racecourse (centred at) 31/525 955
Christchurch (Church) 31/347 894
Chwarel y Fan (32/258 294)
Cleddon Bog (32/510 040)
Clytha (car-park) 32/361 085
Cobblers Plain (32/481 008)
Coed Cefn (32/428 104)
Coed Cwnwr (31/410 992)
Coed-y-paen (Church) 31/334 985
Coldra (31/360 897)
Collister Pill (31/452 857)
Common-y-coed (31/433 891)
Cribau Mill (31/454 940)
Crick Rubbish Tip (31/486 908)*
Cwm (31/460 930)
Cwmcarn Scenic Drive (commences at – 31/240 936)
Cwm Lasgarn (32/285 046)
Cwmyoy (Church) 32/299 233
Denny Island (31/459 810)
Devauden (Church) 31/484 991
Dewstow (31/466 890)
Dinham Castle (31/481 923)
Earlswood (Common) 31/452 955
Ebbw Vale (Church) 32/168 092
Elmdale (31/533 944)
Garndiffaith (centred at) 32/265 045
Glascoed (32/333 017)
Goldcliff (Church) 31/365 832
Goldcliff Point (31/373 819)
Golden Hill (31/426 976)
Great Barnets Woods (31/515 940)
Great Graig (Graig Syfyrddin – 32/404 211)
Great Llanmellin (31/456 922)
Grey Hill (31/434 936)
Gwernesney (Church) 32/415 018
Hadnock Farm (32/530 147)
Henllys (Church) 31/268 910)
Highmoor Hill (31/460 895)
Ifton Quarry (31/464 886)
Itton (Church) 31/493 953
Kemeys Inferior (31/382 926
Kilpale (31/468 922)
Little Mill (32/323 030)
Livox Quarry (31/543 976)
Llanarth (Church) 32/375 109
Llandegvedd Reservoir (32/330 000)
Llandevaud (Church) 31/397 909
Llandevenny (31/410 870)
Llandewi Fach (Church) 31/333 959
Llandewi Rhydderch (Church) 32/350 129
Llandogo (Church) 32/527 041
Llanelly (Church) 32/232 148
Llanfaenor (Church) 32/431 169
Llanfoist (Church) 32/286 132
Llanfrechfa (Church) 31/321 936
Llangattock-juxta-Usk (Church) 32/330 096
Llangattock Lingoed (Church) 32/362 200
Llangattock-Vibon-Avel (Church) 32/457 157
Llangeview (Church) 32/397 007
Llangibby (Church) 31/374 967
Llangwm Isaf (Church) 32/429 006
Llangwm Uchaf (Church) 32/433 006
Llanllowell (Church) 31/393 986
Llanmartin (Church) 31/394 894
Llanmartin Marsh (31/385 895)

Llanover (Church) 32/318 094
Llansantffraedd (Church) 32/358 099
Llanthony Priory (32/289 279)
Llantilio Crossenny (Church) 32/399 149
Llantilio Pertholey (Church) 32/312 163
Llantrisant (Church) 31/392 969
Llanvaches (Church) 31/434 918
Llanvair Discoed (Church) 31/446 924
Llanvair Kilgeddin (Church) 32/356 087
Llanvetherine (Church) 32/364 172
Llanvihangel Crucorney (Church) 32/325 206
Llanvihangel Gobion (Church) 32/346 093
Llanvihangel Pontymoile (Church) 32/302 012
Llanvihangel Rogiet (Church) 31/452 878
Llanvihangel Tor-y-mynydd (Church) 32/464 018
Llanwenarth (Church) 32/276 148
Llanwern (Church) 31/371 879
Long Ditch (31/380 877)
Lydart (32/500 090)
Maes-glas (31/300 855)
Magor Pill (31/439 848)
Maindiff Court Hospital (32/316 154)
Malpas (Church) 31/303 903
Marshfield (Church) 31/262 826
Mathern (Church) 31/523 909
Minnetts forestry area (centred at – 31/450 890)
Mitchel Troy (Church) 32/493 104
Monkswood (Church) 32/346 027
Mount St. Albans (31/362 910)
Mynydd Alltir-fach (31/424 932)
Mynyddislwyn (Church) 31/193 939
Mynydd Maen (centred at 31/260 970)
Narth (32/525 065)
Nash (Church) 31/343 836
Neddern Valley (centred at – 31/486 894)
Newchurch (Church) 31/454 976
Noah's Ark Pump (31/445 868)
Oldcastle (Church) 32/325 246
Olway Brook (confluence at – 31/388 979)
Osbaston (32/500 140)
Panteg (Church) 31/311 991
Peewit Field (31/452 872)
Penallt (Church) 32/523 107
Penhein (31/450 933)
Penhow (Church) 31/424 908
Penhow Quarry (31/424 913)
Penpergwm (centred at – 32/325 100)
Penrhos (Church) 32/416 117
Penterry (Church) 31/520 987
Pen-y-cae-mawr (31/410 950)
Pen-y-clawdd (Church) 32/453 079
Pen-y-fan (centred at – 32/530 055)
Peterstone (Church) 31/268 801
Piercefield Park (centred at – 31/530 955)
Piercefield Wood (Pierce Wood centred at – 31/535 957)
Porton House (31/389 827)
Portskewett (Church) 31/498 882
Radyr (32/366 018)
R.A.F. Caerwent (centred at – 31/473 915)

Redwick (Church) 31/413 842
Rhiwderin (31/260 875)
Rhymney (Church) 32/112 080
Ringland Top (31/354 885)
Rogerstone Grange (31/506 966)
Rogiet Pool (31/456 878)
Salisbury Wood (centred at – 31/424 898)
Sedbury (31/547 935)
Sharbee (31/478 895)
Skirrid Fawr (32/332 183)
Slidy Hill Wood (31/488 905)
Slough Farm Marsh (31/476 902)*
Sor Brook (confluence at – 31/348 914)
South Celynen Colliery*
St. Arvans (Church) 31/517 965
St. Brides Netherwent (Church) 31/428 896
St. Brides Wentlooge (Church) 31/293 824
St. Maughans (Church) 32/462 172
St. Pierre Lake (31/513 905)
St. Pierre Pill (31/521 895)
St. Peters Cave (31/538 928)
Sudbrook Camp (31/505 874)
Sugar Loaf (32/273 188)
Symonds Yat (32/560 160)
Tintern Parva (Church) 32/532 007
Tredunnock (Church) 32/380 949
Trefil Quarry (32/120 135)
Tregagle (32/526 080)
Tregarn (31/382 904)
Tregate (Bridge) 32/477 173
Trellech (Church) 32/501 055
Trellech Grange (Church) 32/492 017
Trevethin (Church) 32/283 020
Trewen (31/457 909)
Trostrey (Church) 32/360 044
Tutshill (31/538 949)
Underwood (31/385 890)
Undy (Church) 31/440 869
Upper Rodge Wood (centred at – 31/465 900)
Usk (Church) 32/379 008
Uskmouth (centred at – 31/330 830)
Vinegar Hill (31/433 874)
Welfare Centre (Dinham) 31/480 904
Wentwood Forest (centred on Wentwood Lodge at 31/417 945)
Wentwood Inn (31/449 908)
Wentwood Reservoir (31/430 930)
Wern Brake (31/440 927)
Whitebrook (32/535 065)
White Castle (32/379 167)
White Hall Farm (31/460 897)
White Hill (32/480 123)
Whitson Court (31/371 848)
Wilcrick (Church) 31/410 880
Wolvesnewton (Church) 31/454 998
Woodcroft (31/544 957)
Woolpitch Wood (centred at – 32/485 047)
Wyesham (32/520 122)
Wyndcliff (31/527 974)
Ynys-y-fro Reservoir (31/283 890)

Appendix C

~

FISH FROM USKMOUTH POWER STATION (PUMP SCREENS) RECORDED BY BRIAN WHITTAKER

Salmon (*Salmo salar*)
lamprey sp.
Smelt (*Osmerus eperlanus*)
Common Eel (*Anguilla anguilla*)
Pipefish sp.
Bib (*Trisopterus luscus*)
Poor Cod (*Trisopterus minutus*)
Whiting (*Merlangius merlangus*)
Lumpsucker (*Cyclopterus lumpus*)
Three-bearded Rockling (*Gaidropsarus vulgaris*)
Bass (*Dicentrarchus labrax*)
Sand Eel (*Ammodytes tobianus*)
Sand Smelt (*Atherina presbyter*)
Thick-lipped Mullet (*Crenimugil labrosus*)
Crystal Goby (*Crystallogobius linearis*)
Pogge (*Agonus cataphractus*)
Sea Snail (*Liparus liparus*)
Three-spined Stickleback (*Gasterosteus aculeatus*)
flatfish (of several species)
Goldsinny (*Ctenolabrus rupestris*)
Sea Stickleback (*Spinachia spinachia*)

Appendix D

~

GWENT CHURCHYARDS HAVING A 'GOOD MIX OF PLANTS'

BEDWAS (St. Barrwg)
BEDWELLTY (St. Sannan)
BETTWS NEWYDD (dedication unknown)
BLAENAVON (St. Peter)
CHAPEL HILL (St. Mary)
CHRISTCHURCH (Holy Trinity)
CWMYOY (St. Martin)
GOLDCLIFF (St. Mary Magdalene)
GWERNESNEY (St. Michael)
HENLLYS (St. Peter)
LLANARTH (St. Teilo)
LLANDEWI FACH (St. David)
LLANDEWI RHYDDERCH (St. David)
LLANDEVAUD (St. Peter)
LLANELLY (St. Elli)
LLANFOIST (St. Ffwyst)
LLANGATTOCK-JUXTA-USK (St. Cadoc)
LLANGATTOCK LINGOED (St. Cadoc)
LLANGATTOCK VIBON AVEL (St. Cadoc)
LLANGEVIEW (St. David)
LLANOVER (St. Bartholomew)
LLANTILIO PERTHOLEY (St. Teilo)
LLANVACHES (St. Dyfrig)
LLANVETHERINE (St. James the Elder)
LLANVAIR KILGEDDIN (St. Mary)
LLANVIHANGEL CRUCORNEY (St. Michael)
LLANVIHANGEL GOBION (St. Michael)
LLANVIHANGEL PONTYMOILE (St. Michael)
LLANVIHANGEL TOR Y MYNYDD (St. Michael)
MITCHEL TROY (St. Michael)
MYNYDDISLWYN (St. Tudor)
NEWCHURCH (St. Peter)
OLDCASTLE (St. John the Baptist)
PANTEG (St. Mary)
PENALLT (St. Mary)
PENHOW (St. John the Baptist)
PENTERRY (St. Mary)
PEN Y CLAWDD (St. Martin)
RHYMNEY (St. David)
St. MAUGHANS (St. Meugan)
SKENFRITH (St. Bridget)
TINTERN PARVA (St. Michael and All Angels)
TREVETHIN (St. Cadoc)
TROSTREY (St. David)
WILCRICK (St. Mary)

Appendix E

~

GWENT CHURCHYARDS WITH EXCEPTIONAL FLORAL DIVERSITY

BEDWELLTY (St. Sannan)

LLANGATTOCK LINGOED (St. Cadoc)

LLANGEVIEW (St. David)

LLANVIHANGEL TOR Y MYNYDD (St. Michael)

PENALLT (St. Mary)

PENHOW (St. John the Baptist)

TREVETHIN (St. Cadoc)

Appendix F

~

GWENT CHURCHYARDS HAVING SCARCE/UNUSUAL PLANTS

BEDWELLTY (St. Sannan) – Great Burnet, Bitter Vetch, Sweet Cicely and Wood Bitter-vetch.

CHEPSTOW (St. Mary) – Ivy Broomrape.

LLANGUA (St. James) – Giant Bellflower.

LLANOVER (St. Bartholomew) – Field Woundwort.

LLANVIHANGEL TOR Y MYNYDD (St. Michael) – Early Purple Orchid, Goldilocks Buttercup.

LLANWERN (St. Mary) – Dwarf Elder.

TROSTREY (St. David) – Meadow Saffron.

Appendix G

~

CHURCHYARDS WITH YELLOW ANTS

The presence of Yellow Meadow Ant hills (nest-mounds) is regarded as an indication of little disturbed ground and their presence in churchyards can also be regarded as a sign of ecological importance. At least forty churchyards in Gwent have been found to contain ants of this species. Other churchyards, such as Bettws Newydd, were found to contain ants of other species, such as the Black Garden Ant, but these have far less ecological significance. The churchyards found to contain nests of the Yellow Meadow Ant are as follows:

Bassaleg
Bedwas
Bedwellty
Blaenavon
Chapel Hill
Cwmcarvan
Cwmyoy
Goytre
Grosmont
Llanarth
Llandewi Rhydderch
Llandogo
Llanvihangel Crucorney
Llanvihangel Llantarnam
Llanvihangel Pontymoile
Llanvihangel Ystern Llewern
Llangattock Juxta Usk
Llangattock Lingoed
Llangattock Vibon Avel
Llangovan
Llanhenog
Llanover
Llantilio Pertholey
Llantrisant
Llanvetherine
Llanwenarth
Llanwern
Malpas
Mitchel Troy
Monkswood
Panteg
Penallt
Penhow
Rockfield
St. Mellons
St. Pierre
Skenfrith
Tintern Parva
Trevethin
Trostry
Undy

THE WENTWOOD FOREST DIVIDED UP INTO DISTINCT AREAS

1. WENTWOOD FORESTRY COMMISION OFFICE/HOUSE AREA
2. GILLIGAN'S PATCH
3. FORESTERS OAKS
4. CADIRA BEECHES
5. BLACK SOW'S WELL
6. PORT–A–SLOUGH
7. CHAPEL CORNER
8. NANT–Y–PRIDD
9. FIVE PATHS
10. NEWCHURCH
11. BLUEBELL
12. THE BIRCHES
13. THE LODGE
14. BICCA

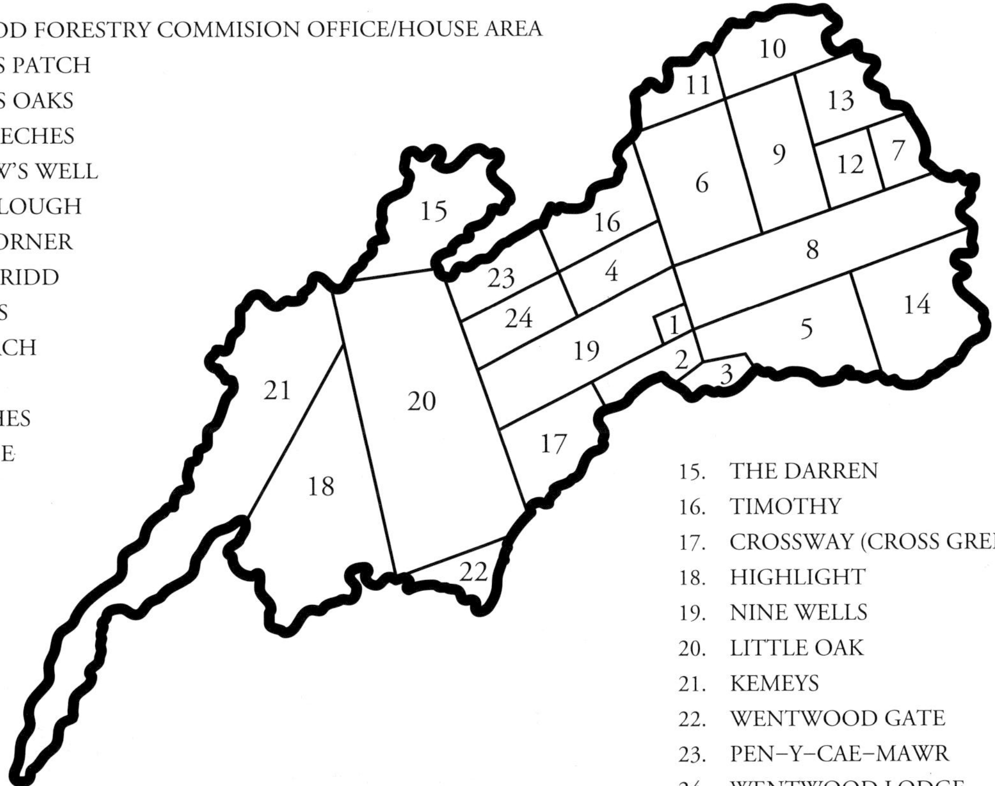

15. THE DARREN
16. TIMOTHY
17. CROSSWAY (CROSS GREEN)
18. HIGHLIGHT
19. NINE WELLS
20. LITTLE OAK
21. KEMEYS
22. WENTWOOD GATE
23. PEN–Y–CAE–MAWR
24. WENTWOOD LODGE

THE MINNETTS FORESTRY AREA
(IDENTIFYING COMPARTMENTS AND FEATURES)

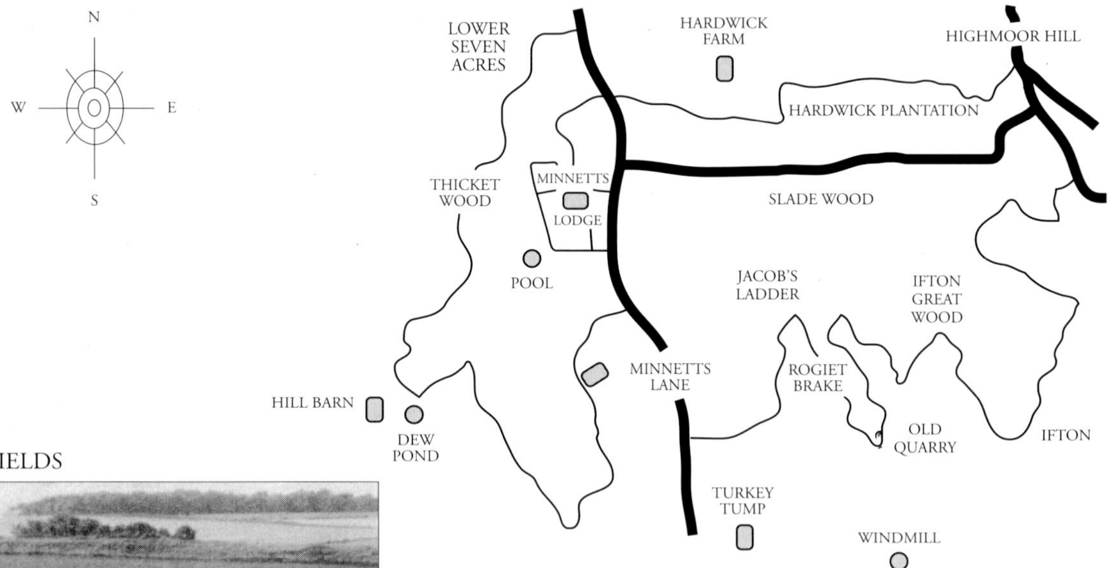

STORE FIELDS

THE DEVIL'S QUOIT, STORE FIELDS AND WESTERN END MINNETTS FORESTRY AREA. (PHOTOGRAPH TAKEN BEFORE THE CONSTRUCTION OF THE SECOND SEVERN CROSSING LINK-ROAD).

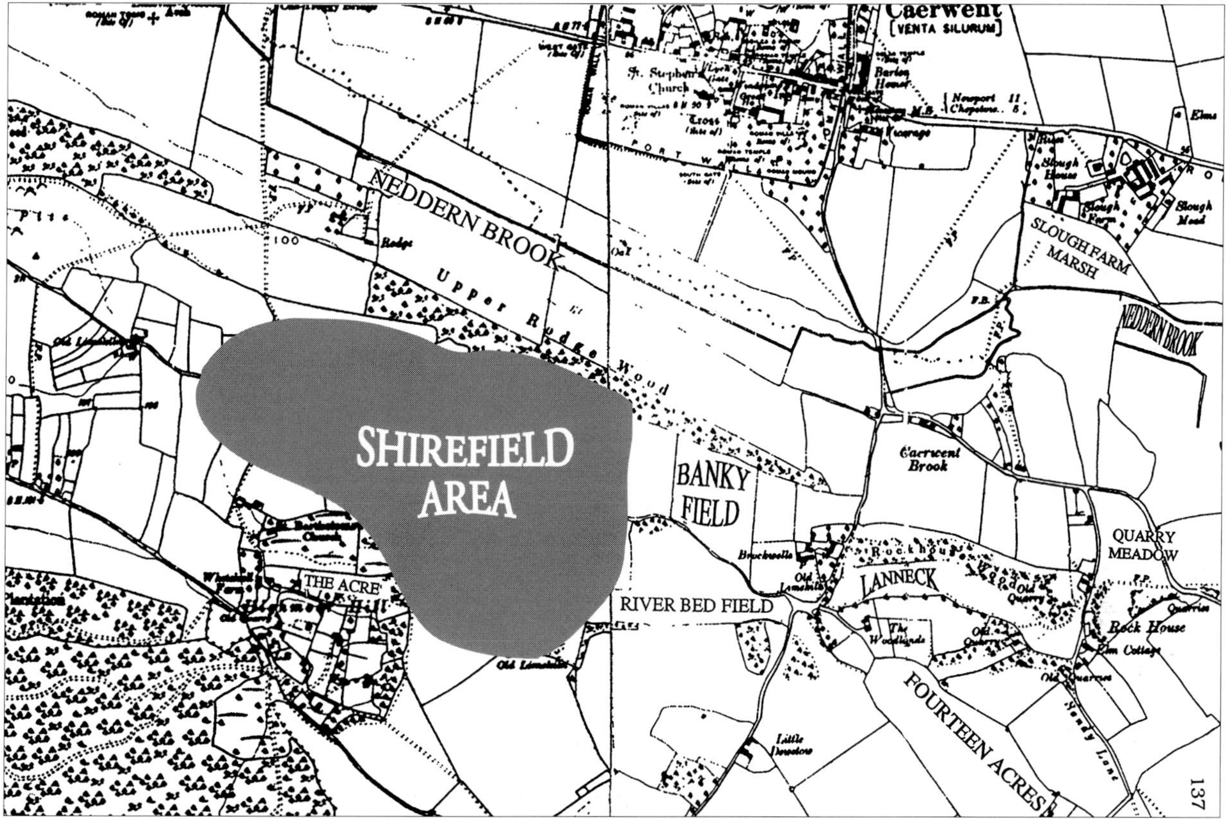

BROCKWELLS AREA IN THE EARLY 1950's

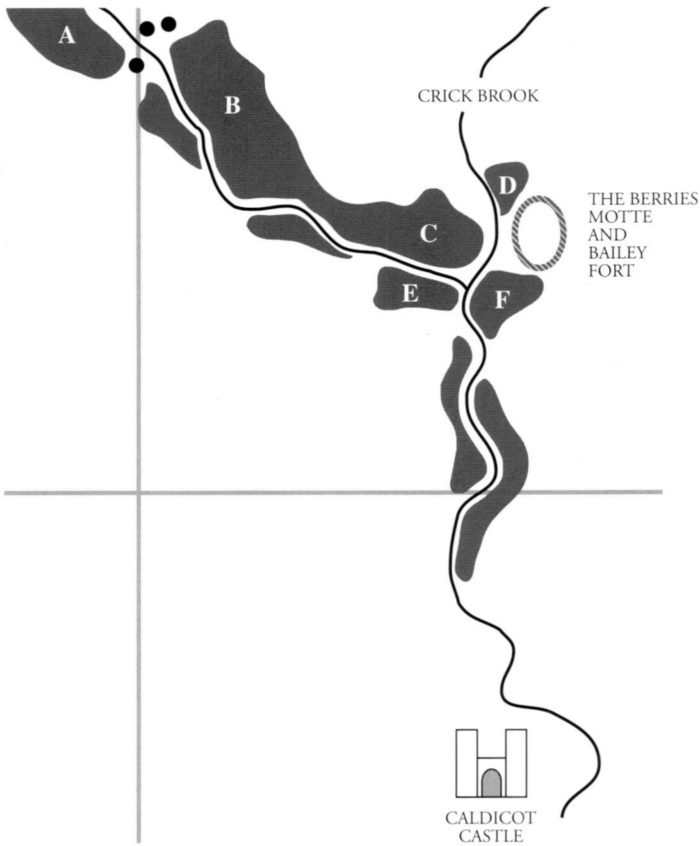

THE NEDDERN VALLEY FLOODS
(IDENTIFICATION OF MAJOR POOLS)

A	FIRST POOL	**D**	BOTTOM MARSH
B	BASTIN'S POOL	**E**	CHURCH FARM POOL
C	CHIVER'S POOL	**F**	BALLAN POOL

Bibliography

(By Chapter)

~

PREHISTORY

The Flora of Monmouthshire, A. E. Wade. National Museum of Wales, 1970.

The Rivers of Monmouthshire, Elsa J. Searle. Christopher Davies, Wales, 1970.

Geology of the Country Around Monmouth and Chepstow, F. B. A. Welch and F. M. Trotter, H.M.S.O., 1961.

Geology of the South Wales Coalfield, Part 1, The Country Around Newport (Mon.), H. C. Squirrel and R. A. Downing. (Third Edition), H.M.S.O., 1969.

Geology Explained in the Severn Vale and Cotswolds, William Dreghorn. David & Charles, Newton Abbot, 1967.

Geology Explained in the Forest of Dean and Wye Valley, William Dreghorn. David & Charles, Newton Abbot, 1968.

B.C.R.A. Bulletin 9 – British Cave Research Association, May 1975.

B.C.R.A. Bulletin 12 – British Cave Research Association, May 1976.

B.C.R.A. Transactions, British Cave Research Association, Vol. 6, No. 4, December 1979.

'Caves and Cave Life', Philip Chapman, *The New Naturalist*. Harper Collins, 1993.

FUNGI

Collins Field Guide, Mushrooms and Toadstools of Britain and Europe, R. Courtecuisse and B. Duhem. Harper Collins, 1995.

Collins Guide to Mushrooms and Toadstools, Morten Lange and F. Bayard Hora. Collins, 1963.

Mushrooms and Other Fungi of Britain and Europe, Roger Phillips. Ward Lock Ltd., 1981.

British Fungi (Book 2), E. A. Ellis. Jarrold & Sons Ltd., Norwich, 1976.

Kingfisher Field Guide to the Mushrooms and Toadstools of Britain and Europe, David Pegler, 1990.

PLANTS

New Flora of the British Isles, Clive Stace. Cambridge University Press, 1991.

The Flora of Monmouthshire, A. E. Wade. National Museum of Wales, 1970.

Welsh Ferns (Clubmosses, Quillworts and Horsetails), H. A. Hyde and A. E. Wade. National Museum of Wales, 1969.

INVERTREBRATES

The Oxford Book of Invertebrates, David Nichols, John Cooke, Derek Whiteley. Oxford University Press, 1971.

Collins Guide to the Insects of Britain and Western Europe, Michael Chinery. Collins, 1986.

Colour Identification Guide to Moths of the British Isles, Bernard Skinner. Viking, 1984.

Monmouthshire Lepidoptera (The Moths and Butterflies of Gwent), G. A. Neil Horton. Comma International Biological Systems, 1994.

The Intertidal Invertebrate Fauna of the Severn Estuary, C. R. Boyden, J. H. Crothers, C. Little and C. Metham. (Reprinted from *Field Studies*, 1977.

A Guide to Snails of Britain and Europe, Dr. V. Pfleger and Dr. June Chatfield. Hamlyn, 1988.

The Freshwater Life of the British Isles, John Clegg. Frederick Warne & Co. Ltd. (Third Edition), 1965.

Flies of the British Isles, Colyer and Hammond. Frederick Warne & Co. Ltd., 1951.

Beetles of the British Isles, E. F. Linssen. (Vols. 1 & 2). Frederick Warne & Co. Ltd., 1959.

The Countrylife Guide to Spiders of Britain and Northern Europe, Dick Jones, 1983.

The Hunting Wasp, John Crompton. Collins, 1948.

'Caves and Cave Life', Philip Chapman. *The New Naturalist*. Harper Collins, 1993.

FISH

Collins Guide to the Sea Fishes of Britain and North-western Europe, Bent J. Muus and Preben Dahlstrom. Collins, 1971.

Collins Guide to the Freshwater Fishes of Britain and Europe, Bent J. Muus and Preben Dahlstrom. Collins, 1971.

'Freshwater Fishes', *The New Naturalist*, Peter S. Maitland and R. Niall Campbell. Harper Collins, 1992.

AMPHIBIANS AND REPTILES

'Reptiles and Amphibians in Britain', *The New Naturalist*, Deryk Frazer. Collins, 1983.

BIRDS

Handbook of the Birds of Europe and Middle East and North Africa (The Birds of the Western Palearctic), Cramp and Simmons, *et. al.*, R.S.P.B./Oxford University Press (Vols. 1-7), 1977, 1980, 1983, 1985, 1988, 1992, 1993.

The Birds of Monmouthshire, G. C. S. Ingram and H. Morrey Salmon. (Revised by P. N. Humphreys). A Newport Museum Publication, 1963.

The Birds of Gwent, P. N. Ferns, H. W. Hamar, P. N. Humphreys, F. D. Kelsey, E. T. Sarson, W. A. Venables, I. R. Walker. Gwent Ornithological Society, 1977.

The Gwent Atlas of Breeding Birds, Stephanie Tyler, Jerry Lewis, Al Venables, John Walton. Gwent Ornithological Society, 1987.

Gwent Levels: The Evolution of a Wetland Landscape, Stephen Rippon. Council for British Archaeology Report 105, 1996.

MAMMALS

Collins Field Guide, Mammals of Britain and Europe, David Macdonald and Priscilla Barret. Harper Collins, 1993.

'The Cardiff Region: A Survey'. Cardiff University of Wales, 1960.

Atlas of Mammals in Britain, H. R. Arnold. I.T.E. Research Publication, No. 6, 1993.

THE NATURAL HISTORY OF CHURCH AND CHURCHYARD IN GWENT

Ancient Gwent Churches, John R. Guy and Ewart B. Smith. Starling Press, 1979.

Wildlife in the Churchyard (The Plants and Animals of God's Acre), Francesca Greenoak. Little, Brown & Company (UK) Limited, 1993.

Wildlife in Church and Churchyard (Plants, Animals and their Management), Nigel Cooper. Church House Publishing, 1995.

The Churchyard Yews of Gwent, J. Daryll Evans. Archangel Press, 1988.

GLOSSARY OF TERMS

The Local Historian's Encyclopaedia, John Richardson. Historical Publications Ltd., 1974.

'British Plant Life', *The New Naturalist*, W. B. Turrill. Collins (Third Edition), 1962.

Chambers Twentieth Century Dictionary, A. M. Macdonald. Chambers, 1972.

Acknowledgements

~

I am unaware of my initial interest in natural history but it developed very early in life. Certainly it was encouraged by my mother who always managed to produce the appropriate presents at Christmas and on birthdays.

This interest was stimulated further by my uncle, Beric Jones, and further still by Trevor Evans who was initially my science master in secondary school days, but later a friend and companion on many forays into the 'wilds' of Gwent.

With regard to the production of this book I am grateful to staff of H.M.P. Service (Usk and Prescoed), and also to Mrs Anne Jackson who gave much essential guidance, not to mention copious amounts of time, hard work and encouragement.

Over the years many people have passed to me their reports and information regarding aspects of wildlife and countryside matters in general – in some cases I never even knew their names. It is also the case that, over virtually half a century, many contributors have been erased from the memory, but their efforts are much appreciated nonetheless.

In the following list (given in alphabetical order of christian names) are named those people who have provided specifically such information as has been used in the pages of this book. To them I extend my sincere gratitude.

(*Note* – some people have been mentioned in the text, and may not, therefore, be mentioned here also).

Mr Adrian Amsden.
Dr. Alasdair Jacks.
Mr Alun Price.
Mrs Anne Jackson.
Mr Brian Whittaker.
Mr Bruce Campbell.
Mr Cecil Morgan.
Mr Chris Hatch.
Mr Colin Elliot.
Mrs Connie Harris.
Ms Cynthia Merrett.
Mr David Jones.

Mr David Lewis.
Mr Derek Edwards.
Mr Derek Upton.
Mr Des Tucker.
Mr Eric Loveys.
Mrs Florence Loveys.
Ms Gillian Davies.
Mr Graham Harris.
Mrs Helen Sheppard.
Mr Howard Slatter.
Mrs Jan Jenkins.
Mrs Jean Roberts.
Mr Jim Pitcher.
Mr John Davies.
Mr. John Elliot.
Mr John Hines.
Mr John Kennett.
Mrs Joyce Pollard.
Mr Keith Jones.
Mr Ken Davis.
Mrs Linda Bellamy.
Ms Linda Joyce.
Dr Martin Anthoney.
Mrs Mary Kennett.
Mr Mike Sayce.
Mr Neil Harrhy.
Dr Neil Horton.
Mr Nigel Phillips.
Mr Noel Bellamy.
Mr Norman Lacy.
Mr Norman Lawrence.
Mrs Pat Johns.
Mr Paul Sheppard.
Mrs Pen Lewis.
Dr Peter Andrews.
Mr Pete Boddington.
Mr Peter Hedges.
Mr Phil Morgan.
Mr Ray Harris.
Mr Rhys Jenkins.
Mr Robin Sellers.
Mr Ron Herbert.
Mrs Rosetta Lawrence.
Mr Stephen Farrar.
Mr Stephen Locke.
Mr Steve Jones.
Mr Terry Ryan.
Mr Tim Pollard.
Mr Tom Locke.
Mr Tony Jenkins.
Mr Trevor Evans.
Capt.W. K. Marshall.
Mr Wally Trigg.
Mr Walter Daniel.

Produced by: Multi-Tech Workshop
Hussein Akpinar
J. P. Bevans
David W. Bunce
Edward Richard Hall

Prescoed

Scientific Index of Species

(By Chapter)

~

PREHISTORY

Apodemus sylvaticus	Wood Mouse (Long-tailed Field Mouse)	15
Bison bonasus	Bison	15
Calamites sp.	(fossil horse-tail)	14
Canis lupus	Wolf	15
Cervus elephas	Red Deer	15
Clethrionomys glareolus	Bank Vole	15
Coelodonta antiquitatis	Woolly Rhinoceros	15
Crocuta crocuta	Spotted Hyena	15, 16
Equus sp.	horse	16
Favosites sp.	(fossil coral)	14
Felis leo	Lion	15
Gryphaea incurva	(fossil oyster)	15
Halycites sp.	Chain Coral	14
Ichthyosaurus sp.	(fossil 'fish-reptile')	15
Lepidodendron sp.	(fossil club-moss tree)	14
Lepus timidus	Mountain Hare	15
Lithostrotion sp.	(fossil coral)	14
Mammuthus primigenius	Mammoth	15
Meles meles	Badger	15
Plagiostoma giganteum	(fossil Liassic bivalve)	15
Plesiosaurus sp.	(fossil marine reptile)	15
Sus scrofa	Wild Pig	15
Tarandus rangifer	Reindeer	15
Ursus arctos	Brown Bear	15

FUNGI

Agaricus arvensis	Horse Mushroom	22
Agaricus campestris	Field Mushroom	22
Agaricus essettei		22
Agaricus langei		22

Agaricus macrosporus		22
Agaricus praeclaresquamosus		22
Agaricus silvaticus	Wood Mushroom	22
Agaricus silvicola	Wood Mushroom	22
Agaricus xanthoderma	Yellow Stainer	22
Agrocybe aegerita		23
Agrocybe praecox		23
Aleuria aurantia	Orange Peel Fungus	20
Amanita ceciliae		22
Amanita citrina	False Death Cap	22
Amanita fulva	Tawny Grissette	23
Amanita muscaria	Fly Agaric	23
Amanita pantherina	Panther Cap	23
Amanita phalloides	Death Cap	23
Amanita porphyria		23
Amanita rubescens	The Blusher	23
Amanita spissa		23
Amanita vaginata	Grisette	23
Anellaria semiovata		23
Armillaria mellea	Honey Fungus	21
Auricularia auricula-judae	Jew's Ear	20
Auricularia mesenterica	Tripe Fungus	20
Auriscalpium vulgare	Ear-pick Fungus	20
Baeospora myosura		22
Bolbitius vitellinus	Yellow Dung-cap	23
Boletus edulis	Penny Bun	24
Boletus luridus		24
Bulgaria inquinans	Black Bulgar	20
Calocera cornea		20
Calocera viscosa	Jelly Antler	20
Calocybe gambosa	St. George's Mushroom	21
Calvatia exipuliformis		24
Calvatia utriformis		24
Cantharellus cibarius	Chanterelle	20
Chalciporus piperatus	Peppery Bolete	24
Chlorocibaria aeruginascens	Green Cup Fungus	19
Claviceps purpurea	Ergot	19
Clavulina cinerea		21
Clavaria vermicularis	(White Spindles)	21
Clavaria muscoides		21
Clavaria inaequalis		21
Clavariadelphus pistillaris	(Dryads Club)	21
Clitocybe geotropa		21
Clitocybe langei		21
Clitocybe nebularis	Clouded Clitocybe	21
Clitocybe rivulosa		21
Clitocybe vibecina		21

Clitopilus prunulus	The Miller	23
Collybia butyracea	Butter Cap	21
Collybia confluens	Clustered Tough-shank	22
Collybia dryophila	Russet Tough-shank	22
Collybia fusipes	Spindle Shank	21
Collybia kuehnerioma		22
Collybia maculata	Spotted Tough-Shank	21
Collybia peronata	Wood Woolly-foot	21
Coltrichia perennis		20
Conocybe tenera	Brown Cone-cap	23
Coprinus atramentarius	Common Ink-cap	22
Coprinus cinereus	Dung-heap Ink-cap	22
Coprinus comatus	Shaggy Ink-cap	22
Coprinus disseminatus	Trooping Crumble-cap	22
Coprinus domesticus		22
Coprinus lagopus		22
Coprinus micaceus	Glistening Ink-cap	22
Coprinus niveus	Snowy Ink-cap	22
Coprinus picaceus	Magpie Ink-cap	22
Coprinus plicatilis	Little Japanese Umbrella	22
Coprinus radians		22
Cordyceps militaris	Caterpillar Fungus	19
Corticium quercinum		20
Cortinarius sanguineus		23
Coryne sarcoides		20
Craterellus cornucopoides	Horn of Plenty	20
Crepidotus mollis	Soft Slipper Toadstool	23
Crepidotus variabilis		23
Crucibulum laeve	Bird's-nest Fungus	24
Cyathus olla	Bird's-nest Fungus	24
Cyathus striatus	Bird's-nest Fungus	24
Cystoderma amianthinum	Saffron Parasol	22
Cystoderma granulosum		22
Dacrymyces deliquescens		20
Daedalea quercina	Maze Fungus	20
Daedaleopsis confragosa	Blushing Bracket	20
Daldinia concentrica	Cramp Ball	19
Dendropolyporus umbellatus		20
Entoloma clypeatum	Roman Shield Entoloma	23
Entoloma incanum		23
Entoloma porphyrophaeum		23
Entoloma sericeum		23
Exidia albida		20
Exidia glandulosa	Witches Butter	20
Fistulina hepatica	Beefsteak Fungus	20
Flammulina velutipes	Velvet Shank	22
Ganoderma adspersum		20

Ganoderma applanatum	Artist's Fungus	20
Ganoderma lucidum	Shining Ganoderma	20
Geastrum sessile		24
Geastrum triplex	Earth Star	24
Geoglossum fallax		20
Geopyxis carbonaria		20
Grifola frondosa		20
Gymnopilus junonius	Orange Pholiota	23
Gymnopilus penetrans		23
Hebeloma crustuliniforme	Poison Pie	23
Helvella crispa	Common Helvel	20
Helvella sulcata	Elfin's Saddle	20
Hericium flagellum	Coral Fungus	20
Hydnum repandum	Wood Hedgehog	20
Hygrocybe calyptriformis	Pink Meadow-cap	21
Hygrocybe coccinea	Scarlet Waxcap	21
Hygrocybe conica	Conical Waxcap	21
Hygrocybe glutinipes		21
Hygrocybe nivea	Snowy Waxcap	21
Hygrocybe psittacina	Parrot Waxcap	21
Hygrocybe punicea	Large Crimson Waxcap	21
Hygrophoropsis aurantiaca	False Chanterelle	24
Hygrophorus hypothejus	Herald of Winter	21
Hymenoscyphus fructigenus	Nut Cup Fungus	19
Hypholoma fasiculare	Sulphur Tuft	23
Hypholoma sublateritium	Brick Cap	23
Hypoxilon fragiforme		19
Inocybe geophylla var. lilacina		23
Inonotus dryadaeus		20
Inonotus hispidus	Shaggy Polypore	20
Kuehneromyces mutabilis	Brown-stew Fungus	23
Laccaria amethystina	Amethyst Deceiver	21
Laccaria laccata	The Deceiver	21
Lactarius acerrimus		23
Lactarius blennius		23
Lactarius deliciosus	Saffron Milk-cap	23
Lactarius deterrimus		23
Lactarius glyciosmus	Coconut-scented Milk-cap	23
Lactarius mitissimus		24
Lactarius necator		23
Lactarius pyrogalus		23
Lactarius quietus	Oak Milk-cap	24
Lactarius rufus	Rufous Milk-cap	23
Lactarius subdulcis	Sweet Milk-cap	24
Lactarius torminosus	Woolly Milk-cap	23
Lactarius uvidus		23
Laetiporus sulphureus	Sulphur Polypore	20

Langermannia gigantea	Giant Puffball	24
Leccinum scabrum	Birch Bolete	24
Leccinum versipelle	Orange Birch Bolete	24
Lepiota cristata	Stinking Parasol	22
Lepista nuda	Wood Blewit	21
Lepista personata	Field Blewit	21
Leucoagaricus leucothites		22
Leucopaxillus giganteus	Giant Clitocybe	21
Lycoperdon echinatum	Spiny Puffball	24
Lycoperdon foetidum		24
Lycoperdon perlatum	Common Puffball	24
Lycoperdon pyriforme	Stump Puffball	24
Lyophyllum connatum		21
Lyophyllum decastes		21
Macrocystidia cucumis		23
Macrolepiota gracilenta	Slender Parasol	22
Macrolepiota procera	Parasol Mushroom	22
Macrolepiota rhacodes	Shaggy Parasol	22
Marasmius androsacaceus	Horse-hair Fungus	21
Marasmius calopus		21
Marasmius oreades	Fairy-ring Champignon	21
Marasmius ramealis	Twig Marasmius	21
Marasmius rotula	Little Wheel Toadstool	21
Megacollybia platyphylla		22
Melanoleuca melaleuca	Changeable Melanoleuca	21
Meripilus giganteus	Giant Grifola	20
Micromphale foetidum		21
Morchella esculenta	Common Morel	20
Mutinus caninus	Dog Stinkhorn	24
Mycena epipterygia	Yellow-stemmed Mycena	22
Mycena galericulata	Bonnet Mycena	22
Mycena galopus	Milk-drop Mycena	22
Mycena haematopus	Bleeding Mycena	22
Mycena polygramma	Steely-stemmed Mycena	22
Mycena pura	Lilac mycena	22
Mycena sanguinolenta	Small Bleeding Mycena	22
Mycena vitilis		22
Nectria cinnabarina	Coral Spot Fungus	19
Neobulgaria pura		19
Nyctalis parasitica	Pick-a-back Toadstool	21
Oudemansiella mucida	Porcelain Fungus	22
Oudemansiella radicata	Rooting Shank	22
Panaeolina foenisecii		23
Panaeolus rickenii		23
Panaeolus sphinctrinus		23
Panellus stipticus		21
Paxillus involutus	Brown Roll Rim	24

Peziza badia	Pig's Ears	20
Peziza vesiculosa	Early Cup Fungus	20
Phaeolus sweinitzii	Sweinitz's Polypore	20
Phallus impudicus	Common Stinkhorn	24
Phellinus pomaceus		20
Pholiota aurivellus		23
Pholiota squarrosa	Shaggy Pholiota	23
Piptoporus betulinus	Birch Bracket	20
Pleurotus cornucopiae	Branched Oyster Mushroom	21
Pleurotus ostreatus	Oyster Mushroom	21
Pluteus cervinus	Deer Toadstool	23
Pluteus salicinus		23
Polyporus brumalis	Winter Polypore	20
Polyporus leptocephalus		20
Polyporus squamosus	Dryad's Saddle	20
Psathyrella candolleana	Fringed Crumble-cap	22
Psathyrella conopilus		22
Psathyrella hydrophilum	Watery Psathyrella	22
Psathyrella lacrymabunda	Weeping Widow	22
Pseudoclitocybe cyathiformis	The Goblet	21
Pseudohydnum gelatinosum	Jelly Tongue	20
Psilocybe semilanceata	Liberty Caps	23
Pycnoporus cinnabarinus		20
Ramaria invallii		21
Ramaria stricta	Straight-branched Coral	21
Reticularia lycoperdon	Bark Puffball	19
Rhizina undulata	Pine Fire Fungus	20
Rigidiporus ulmarius		20
Russula cyanoxantha	Charcoal Burner	23
Russula drimeia		23
Russula emetica var.	Silvestris	23
Russula krombholzii		23
Russula nigricans	Blackening Russula	23
Russula ochroleuca	Common Yellow Russula	23
Russula virescens	Sea-green Russula	23
Rutstroemia firma		19
Sarcoscypha coccinea	Scarlet Elf Cup	20
Scleroderma citrinum	Earth Ball	24
Scutellinia scutellata	Eye-lash Fungus	20
Sparassis crispa	Cauliflower Fungus	21
Sphaerobalus stellatus		24
Stereum hirsutum	Yellow Stereum	20
Stereum sanguinolentum		20
Strobilurus esculentus		22
Stropharia aeruginosa	Verdigris Agaric	23
Stropharia semiglobata		23
Suillus grevillei	Larch Bolete	24

Suillus luteus	Slippery Jack	24
Thelephora terrestris	Earth Fan	20
Trametes versicolor	Zoned Bracket	20
Tremella foliacea	Jelly Leaf	20
Tremella mesenterica	Yellow Brain Fungus	20
Tricholoma album		21
Tricholoma columbetta	Dove-colour Tricholoma	21
Tricholoma sulphureum	Sulphur Tricholoma	21
Tricholoma ustaloides		21
Tricholomopsis rutilans	Plums and Custard	21
Tylopilus felleus	Bitter Bolete	24
Vibrissia truncorum		19
Volvariella gloiocephala	Rose-gilled Grisette	23
Xerocomus badius	Bay Bolete	24
Xerocomus chrysenteron	Red-cracked Bolete	24
Xerocomus subtomentosus	Yellow-cracked Bolete	24
Xylaria hypoxilon	Candle-snuff Fungus	19
Xylaria polymorpha	Dead Man's Fingers	19

PLANTS

Achillea ptarmica	Sneezewort	28
Althaea officinalis	Marsh-mallow	31
Amaranthus sp.	Amaranth	34
Anas penelope	Wigeon	31
Anacamptis pyramidalis	Pyramidal Orchid	32, 33
Anagallis tenella	Bog Pimpernel	26
Anchusa arvensis	Bugloss	28
Apium graveolens	Wild Celery	31
Apium nodiflorum	Fool's Water-cress	29
Arctium lappa	Greater Burdock	29
Armeria maritima	Thrift	31
Ascophyllum nodosum	Knotted Wrack	31
Asplenium trichomanes-ramosum	Green Spleenwort	27
Aster tripolium	Sea Aster	31
Atropa belladonna	Deadly Nightshade	28
Azolla filiculoides	Water Fern	29
Beta vulgaris Ssp. maritima	Sea Beet	30
Blechnum spicant	Hard-fern	26
Branta bernicula	Brent Goose	31
Bupleurum tenuissimum	Slender Hare's-ear	31
Butomus umbellatus	Flowering-rush	29
Caluna vulgaris	Heather	26, 27, 28
Campanula latifolia	Giant Bellflower	28
Campanula patula	Spreading Bellflower	28
Campanula rotundifolia	Harebell	26

Carex digitata	Fingered Sedge	28
Carex disticha	Brown Sedge	30
Carex pseudocyperus	Cyperus Sedge	29
Carpinus betulus	Hornbeam	28
Catabrosa aquatica	Whorl-grass	29
Ceratocapnos claviculata	Climbing Corydalis	28
Chenopodium bonus-henricus	Good-King-Henry	34
Chrysoplenium alternifolium	Alternate-leaved Golden-saxifrage	26
Chrysanthemum segetum	Corn Marigold	34
Cirsium acaule	Dwarf Thistle	32
Cirsium dissectum	Meadow Thistle	30
Cirsium eriophorum	Woolly Thistle	27
Cirsium tenuiflorus	Slender Thistle	30
Claytonia sibirica	Pink Purslane	28
Cochlearia anglica	English Scurvygrass	31
Convallaria majalis	Lily-of-the-valley	32
Conyza canadensis	Canadian Fleabane	33
Crataegus monogyna	Hawthorn	29, 30
Cygnus bewickii	Bewick's Swan	31
Datura stramonium	Thorn-apple	33
Dipsacus pilosus	Small Teasel	28
Drosera rotundifolia	Round-leaved Sundew	27
Echium vulgare	Viper's-bugloss	33
Eleogiton fluitans	Floating Club-rush	29
Elytrigia atherica	Sea Couch	31
Empetrum nigrum	Crowberry	26, 27
Epilobium brunnescens	New Zealand Willowherb	33
Erica cinerea	Bell Heather	26, 28
Erica tetralix	Cross-leaved Heath	26, 28
Eriophorum vaginatum	Hare's-tail Cottongrass	27
Erodium maritimum	Sea Stork's-bill	33
Euphorbia amygdaloides	Wood Spurge	31
Euphorbia exigua	Dwarf Spurge	34
Euphorbia serrulata	Upright Spurge	32
Fatsia japonica		29
Festuca altissima	Wood Fescue	28
Fucus serratus	Saw Wrack	31
Fucus vesiculosus	Bladder Wrack	31
Galium Verum	Ladies Bedstraw	32
Genista anglica	Petty Whin	26
Geum rivale	Water Avens	27
Glaux maritima	Sea-milkwort	31
Gnaphalium sylvaticum	Heath Cudweed	28
Hedra helix	Ivy	29
Helianthemum nummularium	Common Rock-rose	33
Helleborus foetidus	Stinking Hellebore	32
Helleborus viridis	Green Hellebore	32

Heracleum mantegazzianum	Giant Hogweed	28
Hesperis matronalis	Dame's-violet	28
Hordelymus europaeus	Wood Barley	31
Hordeum marinum	Sea Barley	31
Hordeum secalinum	Meadow Barley	31
Hydrocharis morsus-ranae	Frogbit	29
Hypericum androsaemum	Tutsan	32
Hypericum elodes	Marsh St.John's-wort	26
Hypericum humifusum	Trailing St.John's-wort	28
Hypericum montanum	Pale St.John's-wort	32
Hypericum pulchrum	Slender St.Johns-wort	28
Iris pseudacorus	Yellow Iris	29
Jasione montana	Sheep's-bit	26, 28
Juncus gerardii	Saltmarsh Rush	30
Juncus maritimus	Sea Rush	31
Juncus squarrosus	Heath Rush	27
Kicksia elatime	Sharp-leaved Fluellen	34
Kicksia spuria	Round-leaved Fluellen	34
Lathyrus linifolius	Bitter Vetch	26
Lavatera arborea	Tree-mallow	31
Lepidium latifolium	Dittander	31
Limonium vulgare	Common Sea-lavender	31
Linaria repens	Pale Toadflax	33
Lotus glaber	Narrow-leaved Bird's-foot-trefoil	30
Luscinia megarynchos	Nightingale	33
Malva neglecta	Dwarf Mallow	34
Matricaria discoidea	Pineapple-weed	34
Melampyrum pratense	Common Cow-wheat	33
Melica nutans	Moutain Melick	28
Mercurialis annua	Annual Mercury	33
Milium effusum	Wood Millet	31
Miltochrista miniata	Rosy Footman Moth	33
Mimulus guttatus	Monkeyflower	28
Misopates orontium	Weasel's-snout	34
Molinia caerulea	Purple Moor-grass	27
Myrrhis odorata	Sweet Cicely	27
Narcissus pseudo-narcissus Ssp.pseudonarcissus	Daffodil	28
Nardus stricta	Mat-grass	27
Neottia nidus-avis	Bird's-nest Orchid	32
Oenothera glazoviana	Large-flowered Evening-primrose	33
Ophrys apifera	Bee Orchid	32
Orchis mascula	Early-purple Orchid	32
Orchis morio	Green-winged Orchid	32
Orobanche hederae	Ivy Broomrape	29
Paris quadrifolia	Herb Paris	32
Pastinaca sativa var. sylvestris	Wild Parsnip	29

Petasites japonicus	Giant Butterbur	28
Phragmites australis	Common Reed	29
Picris echioides	Bristly Ox-tongue	29
Pinguicula vulgaris	Common Butterwort	27
Plantago maritima	Sea Plantain	31
Plantanthera bifolia	Lesser Butterfly-orchid	32
Plantanthera chlorantha	Greater Butterfly-orchid	32
Populus nigra Ssp. betulifolia	Black Popular	28
Potamogeton crispus	Curled Pondweed	29
Primula veris	Cowslip	32
Prunus padus	Bird Cherry	27
Prunus spinosa	Blackthorn	29
Puccinellia maritima	Common Saltmarsh-grass	30
Puccinellia rupestris	Stiff Saltmarsh-grass	30
Ranunculus baudotii	Brackish Water-crowfoot	30
Raphanus raphanistrum Ssp. maritimus	Sea Radish	30
Reseda lutea	Wild Migonette	33
Rhinanthus minor	Yellow-rattle	32
Rubia peregrina	Wild Madder	33
Rumex hydrolapathum	Water Dock	29
Sagittaria sagittifolia	Arrowhead	29
Salix triandra	Almond Willow	29
Salvia pratensis	Meadow Clary	32
Sambucus ebulus	Dwarf Elder	26
Samous valerandi	Brookweed	30
Sanguisorba officinalis	Great Burnet	26
Saponaria officinalis	Soapwort	28
Saxifraga granulata	Meadow Saxifrage	28
Schoenoplectus tabernaemontanii	Grey Club-rush	30
Scutellaria minor	Lesser Skullcap	26
Senecio erucifolius	Hoary Ragwort	29
Senecio squalidus	Oxford Ragwort	33
Senecio viscosus	Sticky Groundsel	33
Serratula tinctoria	Saw-wort	32, 33
Sison ammomum	Stone Parsley	30
Sparganium emersum	Unbranched Bur-reed	28
Sparganium erectum	Branched Bur-reed	29
Spartina anglica	Common Cord-grass	31
Spergula arvensis	Corn Spurrey	34
Spergularia marina	Lesser Sea-spurrey	31
Spergularia media	Greater Sea-spurrey	31
Spiranthes spiralis	Autumn Lady's-tresses	32
Stachys arvensis	Field Woundwort	28
Suaeda maritima	Annual Sea-blite	31
Teucrium scorodonia	Wood Sage	26
Thalictrum flavum	Common Meadow-rue	28

Torilis nodosa	Knotted Hedge-parsley	30
Tragopogon porrifolius	Salsify	29
Trichophorum cespitosum	Deergrass	27
Trifolium arvense	Hare's-foot Clover	33
Trifolium fragiferum	Strawberry Clover	31
Trifolium ornithopodioides	Bird's-foot Clover	30
Trifolium squamosum	Sea Clover	30
Triglochin maritimum	Sea Arrowgrass	31
Tyto alba	Barn Owl	33
Urtica urens	Small Nettle	34
Vaccinium myrtillus	Bilberry	26, 27, 28
Vaccinium vitis-idaea	Cowberry	27
Veronica montana	Wood Speedwell	31
Vicia orobus	Wood Bitter-vetch	26
Vicia sylvatica	Wood Vetch	31
Viola palustris	Marsh Violet	32
Vipera berus	Adder	33
Wahlenbergia hederacea	Ivy-leaved Bellflower	26
Zostera sp.	Eelgrass	31

INVERTEBRATES

Abraxas sylvata	Clouded Magpie Moth	47
Acheta domesticus	House Cricket	43
Acronicta alni	Alder Moth	46
Adela reaumurella		45
Adscita statices	Common Forester	45
Allolobophora sp.		40
Aloconota subgrandis		50
Alucita hexadactyla		45
Amphimallon solstitialis	Summer (July) Chafer	51
Amphipyra pyramidea	Copper Underwing	46
Anatis ocellata	Eyed Ladybird	52
Anax imperator	Emperor Dragonfly	42
Ancylus fluviatilis	River Limpet	38
Anodonta anatina	Duck Mussel	39
Anodonta cygnea	Swan Mussel	39
Apanteles glomeratus		49
Aphodius fimetarius		51, 58
Apion miniatum		53
Apis mellifera	Honeybee	50, 57
Araneus diadematus	Garden Spider	55
Araneus quadratus		55
Araniella cucurbitina		55
Archieris parthenias	Orange Underwing	46
Arctosa cinerea	Shingle Spider	54

Arenicloa marina	Lug-worm	40
Aricia agestis	Brown Argus	44
Armadillidium vulgare	Pill Woodlouse	41
Asellus aquaticus	Water Louse	41
Asilus crabroniformis	Hornet Robber-fly	47, 57, 58
Astacus pallipes	Common Crayfish	41
Attagenus pellio		52
Aurelia aurita	Common Jellyfish	37
Balanus balanoides	acorn-barnacle	41
Bithynia tentaculata		38
Blatta orientalis	Common Cockroach	43
Bombus terrestris	bumble-bee	50
Bombylius major	bee-fly	47
Buccinium umdatum	Whelk	38
Callophrys rubi	Green Hairstreak	44
Carabus violaceus	Violet Ground Beetle	50
Carcinas maenas	Shore Crab	41
Cassida rubiginosa	Tortoise Beetle	53
Cataclysta lemnata		45
Ceramica pisi	Broom Moth	46
Cerastoderma edule	Common Cockle	39
Cercopis vulnerata		44
Chirocephala diaphanus	Fairy Shrimp	41
Chorthippus parallelelus	Meadow Grasshopper	58
Chrysis sp.	ruby-tail wasp	49
Chrysolina fastuosa		53
Cicadella viridis		44
Cicindela campestris	Green Tiger Beetle	50
Cinara piceae		44
Clausilia bidentata		38
Clossinana euphrosyne	Small Pearl-bordered Fritillary	44
Clubiona sp.	grass-twist spider	54
Clytra quadripunctata		52
Clytus arietis	Wasp Beetle	52
Coleophora caespitiella		45
Coleophora laricella	Larch-leaf Miner	45
Conocephalus dorsalis	Short-winged Cone-head	42
Crangon crangon	Common Shrimp	41
Ctenicera cuprea	Upland Click-beetle	51
Ctenicera pectinicornis		51
Daphnia sp.	water flea	40
Deraecoris ruber		43
Dolichovespula norvegica	Norwegian Wasp	49
Dolichovespula sylvestris	Tree Wasp	49
Dorcus parallelipipedus	Lesser Stag Beetle	51
Drepana binaria		46

Dysdera crocata		54
Dytiscus marginalis	Great Diving Beetle	53
Eisenia foetida	Brandling Worm	40
Endomychus coccineus		52
Endrosis sarcitrella	White-shouldered House-moth	45
Ephemera danica	May-fly	42
Eriogaster lanestris	Small Eggar	46
Eriopygodes imbecilla	Silurian	46
Erynnis tages	Dingy Skipper	45
Euclidia glyphica	Burnet Companion	46
Formica rufa	Wood Ant	49
Geometra papilionaria		47
Geophilus sp.		53
Geotrupes sp.	dor beetle	51
Glomeris sp.	Pill Millipede	53
Goniodiscus rotundatus		39
Haemopis sanguisuga	Horse Leech	40
Helicigona lapicida	Lapidary Snail	39
Hipparchis semele	Grayling Butterfly	44
Hirudo medicinalis	Medicinal Leech	40
Hofmannophila pseudospretella	Brown House Moth	45
Hydra sp.		37
Hydrobia ulvae	Laver Spire Snail	38
Hydrophilus piceus	Great Silver Beetle	53
Hylobius abietis	Pine Weevil	53
Hypoderma bovis	Warble Fly	48
Hypsopygia costalis		45
Idotea sp.		41
Ilyocaris cimicoides	Saucer Bug	43
Lamprochernes	false scorpion	53
Lampyris noctiluca	Glow-worm	51, 56
Lasiocampa quercus	Oak Eggar	45
Lasius flavus	Yellow Meadow Ant	49
Lasius fuliginosus	Jet-black Ant	49
Lasius niger	Black Garden Ant	49
Lepidochitona cinerea		37
Lepisma saccharina	Silverfish	42
Leptophyes punctatissima	Speckled Bush-cricket	42
Ligia oceanica	Sea Slater	41
Limenitis camilla	White Admiral	44
Limnaea auricularia	Ear Snail	38
Limnaea peregra	Wandering Snail	38
Limnaea stagnalis	Great Pond Snail	38
Linyphia sp.	money spider	55
Lipara lucens		48
Littorina littoralis	Flat Winkle	37
Littorina littorea	Common Periwinkle	37

Littorina saxatilis	Rough Winkle	38
Lucanus cervus	Stag Beetle	51
Lumbrius terrestris		40
Macoma balthica	Baltic Tellin	39
Marpessa laminata		39
Meconema thalassinum	Oak Bush-cricket	42
Megachile sp.		50
Mellinus arvensis		49
Meloe sp.	oil beetle	52
Mesembrina meridiana		48, 58
Mesoacidalia aglaja	Dark Green Fritillary	44
Meta menardi	Cave Spider	54
Micrommata virescens		54
Misumena vatia	Crab Spider	54
Molanna angustata		47
Mycetophagus quadripustulatus		52
Mytilus edulis	Common Mussel	39
Neanthes diversicolor	Estuarine Ragworm	40
Neanthes virens		40
Necrophorus sp.		50
Nemophora degeerella		45
Neoamphitrite figulus		40
Nepa cinerea	Water Scorpion	43
Noctua fimbriata	Broad-bordered Yellow Underwing	46
Nuctenea cornuta		55
Nymphalis antipoa	Camberwell Beauty	44
Nymphula nymphaeata		45
Odezia atrata	Chimney Sweeper	47
Odynerus spinipes		49
Oniscus asellus		41
Ornithomyia avicularia	Common Louse-fly	48
Ourapteryx sambucaria	Swallow-tail Moth	47
Pagurus bernhardus	Hermit Crab	41
Palaemonetes varians	Estuarine Prawn	41
Palomena prasina		43
Panorpa communis	Scorpion-fly	44
Patella vulgata	Common Limpet	37
Petrobius brevistylis		41
Philoscia muscorum		41
Pholcus phalangioides	Cobweb Spider	53
Pholidoptera griseoaptera	Dark Bush-cricket	42
Phryganea grandis	Large Red Caddis-fly	47
Physa fontinalis		38
Phytomyza ilicis		48
Planorbis corneus	Great Ramshorn Snail	38
Planorbis planorbis	Ramshorn Snail	38
Platycnemis pennipes	White-legged Damselfly	42

Podura aquatica		42
Poecilobothrus nobilitatus		47
Polydesmus sp.		53
Pomatias elegans	Round-mouthed Snail	38
Pontania proxima		49
Porcellio scaber		41
Potamanthus luteus		42
Prionus coriarius	Tanner Beetle	52
Proasellus cavaticus		41
Pseudoips fagana	Green Silver-lines	46
Pupilla sp.		39
Pyralis farinalis	Meal moth	45
Pyrgus malvae	Grizzled Skipper	45
Pyrochroa coccinea	Cardinal Beetle	52
Quercusia quercus	Purple Hairstreak	44
Ranatra linearis	Long-bodied Water-scorpion	43
Reduvius personatus		43
Rhagio scolopacea	Down-looker Fly	47
Rhagium bifasciatum	Double-banded Rhagium	52
Rhodogaster viridis		48
Salticus scenicus	Zebra Spider (Zebra Wall Spider)	54
Sarcophaga sp.	fleshfly	58
Scoliopteryx libatrix	Herald Moth	46
Scrobicularia plana	Peppery Furrow-shell	39
Scytodes thoracica	Spitting Spider	54
Sepia officinalis	Cuttlefish	39
Sepsis fulgens		48
Sertularia cupressina	Whiteweed	37
Sinodendron cylindricum	Black Rhinoceros Beetle	50
Sirex noctilio	Steel-blue Wood-wasp	48
Sphaereum corneum		39
Staphylinus olens	Devil's Coach-horse	50
Stomoxys calcitrans	Stable Fly	48
Strangalia maculata		52
Strangalia punctata		52
Strangalia quadrifasciata		52
Strymonidia w-album	White-letter Hairstreak	44
Succinea sp.	amber snail	38
Sympetrum pedemontanum		42
Sympetrum scoticum	Black Sympetrum	42
Tabanus sudeticus		47
Tachina fera		48
Tealia felina	Dahlia Anemone	37
Tegenaria sp.	house spider	54
Tetrix subulata	Slender Ground-hopper	42
Tetrix undulata	Common Ground-hopper	42
Tettigonia viridissima	Great Green Bush-cricket	42

Theridion pallens		54
Thyratira batis		46
Timarcha tenebricosa	Bloody-nosed Beetle	53
Tipula sp.	crane-fly	58
Tortrix viridana	Oak-leaf Roller-moth	45
Trichia sp.		39
Trichiosoma tibiale	Hawthorn Saw-fly	48
Trichius fasciatus	Bee Beetle	51
Triphosa dubitata	Tissue Moth	46
Tubularia indivisa		37
Typhaeus typhoeus	Minotaur Beetle	51
Uroceras gigas	Giant Wood-wasp	48
Urophora cardui		47
Velia caprai	Water Cricket	43
Vespa crabro	Hornet	49, 56, 57
Vespula germanica	German Wasp	49
Vespula rufa	Red Wasp	49
Vespula vulgaris	Common Wasp	49
Vitrina pelucida		39
Viviparus viviparus	River Snail	38
Volucella bombylans		47
Xestobium rufovillosum	Death-watch Beetle	52
Yponomeuta cagnatella	Spindle Ermine	56
Yponomeuta evonymella	Bird-cherry Ermine	55
Zeuzera pyrina	Wood Leopard Moth	45

FISH

Abramis brama	Common Bream	66
Acipenser sturio	Sturgeon	64
Alosa fallax	Twaite Shad	64
Anguilla anguilla	Common Eel	64
Aspitrigia cuculus	Red Gurnard	63
Conger conger	Conger Eel	62
Cottus gobio	Bullhead	66
Cyprinus carpio	Carp	66
Dicentrarchus labrax	Bass	63
Esox lucius	Pike	65
Gadus morrhua	Cod	63
Gaidropsarus vulgaris	Three-bearded Rockling	63
Gasterosteus aculeatus	Three-spined Stickleback	64
Gobio gobio	Gudgeon	66
Lampetra planeri	Brook Lamprey	65
Leuciscus cephalus	Chub	66
Leuciscus leuciscus	Dace	65
Liparis liparis	Sea Snail	63

Liza ramada	Thin-lipped Grey Mullet	63
Lophius piscatorius	Angler Fish	63
Merlangius merlangus	Whiting	63
Merluccius merluccius	Hake	63
Mola mola	Sunfish	63
Noemacheilus barbatulus	Stone Loach	66
Perca fluviatilis	Perch	66
Petromyzon marinus	Sea Lamprey	64
Phoxinus phoxinus	Minnow	66
Platichthys flesus	Flounder	65
Pomatoschistus microps	Common Goby	63
Pugnitius pugnitius	Ten-spined Stickleback	65
Raja batis	Skate	62
Raja clavata	Thorn-back Ray	62
Rutilus rutilus	Roach	65
Salmo gairdneri	Rainbow Trout	65
Salmo salar	Salmon	64
Salmo trutta	Trout	64, 65
Scardinius erythrophthalmus	Rudd	66
Solea solea	Sole	63
Sygnathus acus	Great Pipefish	62
Thymallus thymallus	Grayling	65
Tinca tinca	Tench	66
Trisopterus luscus	Bib	63
Xiphias gladius	Swordfish	63

AMPHIBIANS AND REPTILES

Anguis fragilis	Slow-worm	68, 70, 71
Bufo bufo	Common Toad	68, 69
Lacerta vivipara	Common Lizard	68, 71
Lasius flavus	Yellow Meadow Ant	69
Natrix natrix	Grass Snake	68, 71
Rana temporia	Common Frog	68, 70
Senecio jacobaeae	Ragwort	70
Triturus cristatus	Great Crested Newt	68, 68, 70
Triturus helveticus	Palmate Newt	68, 69
Triturus vulgaris	Smooth Newt	68, 69, 70
Vipera berus	Adder	68, 71, 72

BIRDS

Accipiter gentilis	Goshawk	79
Alauda arvensis	Skylark	92
Anas acuta	Pintail	92, 93
Anas clypeata	Shoveler	92, 93

Anas crecca	Teal	92
Anas penelope	Wigeon	92
Anas platyrhynchos	Mallard	92
Anas querquedula	Garganey	75, 76, 92
Anthus pratensis	Meadow Popit	92
Ardea cinerea	Grey Heron (Heron)	74
Arenaria interpres	Turnstone	93
Asio flammeus	Short-eared Owl	85
Athene noctua	Little Owl	85, 86, 92
Aythya fuligula	Tufted Duck	92
Botaurus lentiginosus	American Bittern	80
Branta Canadensis	Canada Goose	78
Calidris alpina	Dunlin	86, 92, 93
Calidris canutus	Knot	86, 93
Carduelis cannabina	Linnet	91
Carduelis carduelis	Goldfinch	91
Carduelis chloris	Greenfinch	91
Carduelis flammea	Redpoll	91
Carduelis spinus	Siskin	91
Charadrius hiaticula	Ringed Plover	93
Chenopodium album	Fat-hen	91
Columba palumbus	Woodpigeon	83
Corvus corax	Raven	79
Corvus corone	Carrion Crow	88, 89
Corvus frugilegus	Rook	88
Cuculus canorus	Cuckoo	84
Cygnus bewickii	Bewick's Swan	78, 92, 93
Cygnus cygnus	Whooper Swan	78
Cygnus olor	Mute Swan	78
Falco tinnuculus	Kestrel	85
Fringilla coelebs	Chaffinch	87, 88, 91
Fringilla montifringilla	Brambling	91
Fulica atra	Coot	75
Gallinago gallinago	Snipe	82, 92, 93
Haematopus ostralegus	Oystercatcher	81
Hedera helix	Ivy	88
Limosa limosa	Black-tailed Godwit	92, 93
Locustella naevia	Grasshopper Warbler	87
Luscinia megarhynchos	Nightingale	89, 90
Meles meles	Badger	77
Microtus agrestis	Short-tailed Vole	85, 86
Motacilla flava	Yellow Wagtail	92, 93
Mustela erminea	Stoat	85
Mustela nivalis	Weasel	85
Passer montanus	Tree Sparrow	89, 91, 92
Perdix perdix	Partridge	79, 80, 92

Phalacrocorax carbo	Cormorant	74
Pinus sylvestris	Scot's Pine	88
Rallus aquaticus	Water Rail	80
Regulus ignicapillus	Firecrest	87, 88
Saxicola torquata	Stonechat	92
Scolopax rusticola	Woodcock	82
Streptopelia decaocto	Collared Dove	82, 83
Stretopelia turtur	Turtle Dove	83, 84
Strix aluco	Tawny Owl	86
Sylvia curruca	Lesser Whitethroat	93
Tadorna ferruginea	Ruddy Shelduck	77
Tadorna tadorna	Shelduck	76, 92, 93
Tringa totanus	Redshank	81, 92, 93
Tyto alba	Barn Owl	85, 86
Vanellus vanellus	Lapwing	81, 82, 92
Vulpes vulpes	Fox	77

MAMMALS

Abies grandis	Grand Fir	101
Allium ursinum	Wild Garlic (Ramsons)	102
Amphimallon solstitialis	July Chafer	98
Anguilla anguilla	Common (Green) Eel	104
Apodemus flavicollis	Yellow-necked Mouse	100 107
Apodemus sylvaticus	Wood Mouse	100, 107
Ardea cinerea	Grey Heron	100
Arvicola terrestris	Water Vole	99, 100
Balaenoptera acutorostrata	Lesser Rorqual (Minke Whale)	107
Balaenoptera borealis	Sei Whale	107
Barbastellus barbastellus	Barbastelle Bat	106
Chamaecyparis lawsoniana	Lawson Cypress	101
Clematis vitalba	Clematis (Traveller's Joy)	101
Clethrionomys glareolus	Bank Vole	106
Dama dama	Fallow Deer	105
Delphinus delphis	Common Dolphin	97
Eptesicus serotinus	Serotine Bat	106
Erinaceus europaeus	Hedgehog	106
Halichoerus grypus	Grey Seal	97
Larix sp.	larch	101
Lepus europaeus	Brown Hare	98, 99
Lonicera periclymenum	Honeysuckle	101
Lutra lutra	Otter	108
Meles meles	Badger	107
Micromys minutus	Harvest Mouse	107
Microtus agrestis	Field Vole (Short-tailed Vole)	107
Muntiacus reevsi	Muntjac	108

Mus musculus	House Mouse	107
Muscardinus avellanarius		100, 101, 102
Mustela erminea	Stoat	102, 103
Mustela eversmanni	Steppe Polecat	103
Mustela furo	Ferret	103
Mustela nivalis	Weasel	102, 103
Mustela putorius	Polecat	103, 104
Mustela vison	Mink	100, 104, 105, 107
Myotis brandtii	Brandt's Bat	106
Myotis daubentonii	Daubenton's Bat	106
Myotis mystacinus	Whiskered Bat	106
Myotis nattereri	Natterer's Bat	106
Neomys fodiens	Water Shrew	106
Nyctalus noctula	Noctule	98
Oryctolagus cuniculus	Rabbit	98, 99, 103
Passer domesticus	House sparrow	103
Picea abies	Norway Spruce	101
Pinus sylvestris	Scot's Pine	101
Pipistrellus pipistrellus	Pipistrelle	106
Phoca vitulina	Common seal	108
Phocoena phocoena	Porpoise	97
Plecotus auritus	Common Long-eared Bat	106
Rattus norvegicus	Brown Rat (Common Rat)	107
Rhinolophus ferrumequinum	Greater Horseshoe Bat	97, 98
Rhinolophus hipposideros	Lesser Horseshoe Bat	97, 98
Sciurus carolinensis	Grey Squirrel	106
Sciurus vulgaris	Red Squirrel	97
Sorex araneus	Common Shrew	106
Sorex minutus	Pygmy Shrew	106
Talpa europaea	Mole	106
Vulpes vulpes	Red Fox (Fox)	107

DIARY FOR WINTER 1962/1963

Accipiter nisus	Sparrow Hawk	114
Aegithalos caudatus	Long-tailed Tit	112
Alauda arvensis	Skylark	114
Anser albifrons	White-fronted Goose	113, 115, 116, 118
Arvicola terrestris	Water Vole	119
Carduelis chloris	Greenfinch	113
Columba oenas	Stock Dove	114, 115
Columba palumbus	Woodpigeon	113, 114, 116
Cygnus olor	Mute Swan	115
Dendrocopos major	Great Spotted Woodpecker	115, 116
Emberiza citrinella	Yellow Bunting	113
Fringilla coelebs	Chaffinch	113, 114, 118

Gallinago gallinago	Snipe	115
Lepus europaeus	Brown Hare	113
Parus ater	Coal Tit	112
Parus caeruleus	Blue Tit	112
Parus major	Great Tit	112
Passer montanus	Tree Sparrow	113, 114
Picus viridis	Green Woodpecker	114
Prunella modularis	Dunnock (Hedge Accentor)	118
Talpa europaea	Mole	119
Turdus iliacus	Redwing	112, 114
Turdus pilaris	Fieldfare	112, 119
Turdus philomenos	Song Thrush	118
Tyto alba	Barn Owl	115, 116
Vanellus vanellus	Lapwing	119

SELECTED NOTES FROM THE DIARIES

Acrocephalus palustris	Marsh Warbler	125
Agrius convolvuli	Convolvulus Hawkmoth	130
Anguilla anguilla	Elver (Common Eel)	129
Anodonta cygnea	Swan Mussel	124
Anthopleura thallia		128
Argynnis adippe	High Brown Fritillary	120
Argynnis paphia	Silver-washed Fritillary	120
Aricia agestis	Brown Argus	127
Asilus crabroniformis	Hornet Robberfly	127
Aurelia aurita	Common Jellyfish	121
Balaenoptera borealis	Rudolphi's Rorqual (Sei Whale)	122
Blatta orientalis	Common Cockroach	125
Botaurus stellaris	Bittern	130
Bufo bufo	Toad (Common Toad)	123
Certhia familiaris	Tree Creeper	129
Cervus elephas	Red Deer	121
Chrysolophus pictus	Golden Pheasant	121
Clematis vitalba	Clematis (Traveller's Joy)	129
Coleophora laricella	Larch-leaf Miner-moth	127
Coleus croceus	Clouded Yellow	120
Corvus corax	Raven	123
Crataegus monogyna	Hawthorn	120
Crex crex	Corn Crake	125
Datura stramonium	Thorn-apple	125
Esox lucius	Pike	125
Fagus syvatica	Beech	131
Garrulus glandarius	Jay	129
Gobio gobio	Gudgeon	131
Gymnocarpium dryopteris	Oak Fern	125

Helarctos malayanus	Sun Bear	121
Hirundo rustica	Swallow	128
Lama peruana	Llama	121
Larus ridibundus	Black-headed Gull	124
Lepus europaeus	Brown Hare	120
Limnodromus sp.	Dowitcher	123, 124
Liparis sp.	Sea Snail	128
Loxia curvirostra	Crossbill (Common Crossbill)	120
Lutra lutra	Otter	131
Meta menardi	Cave Spider	124
Micromys minutus	Harvest Mouse	126
Motacilla flava	Yellow Wagtail	128
Muscardinus avellanarius	Dormouse	120, 129
Mustela nivalis	Weasel	128
Myxosoma corebralis		131
Numenius phaeopus	Whimbrel	130
Oceanodroma leucorhoa	Leach's Petrel	130
Oryctolagus cuniculus	Rabbit	120
Parus ater	Coal Tit	129
Pavo cristatus	Peacock (Blue Peafowl)	121
Phalaropus fulicarius	Grey Phalarope	126
Philudoria potatoria	Drinker Moth	128
Phoxinus phoxinus	Minnow	131
Picea abies	Norway Spruce	126
Platalea leucorodia	Spoonbill	125
Procyon lotor	Raccoon	121
Prunella laciniata	Cut-leaved selfheal	123
Prunus avium	Wild Cherry	129
Quercus robur	Pedunculate Oak	131
Rana temporia	Frog (Common Frog)	123
Rattus norvegicus	Brown Rat	125
Riparia riparia	Sand Martin	122
Rissa tridactyla	Kittiwake	129
Sagartia troglodytes		128
Salmo trutta	Trout	131
Scoliopteryx libatrix	Herald Moth	124
Sepia officinalis	Cuttlefish (Common Cuttlefish)	127
Sequoiadendron giganteum	Giant Redwood	129
Sertularia cupressina	Whiteweed	128
Strix aluco	Tawny Owl	120
Strymonidia w-album	White-letter Hairstreak	120
Sturnus vulgaris	Starling	123, 127, 128
Sula bassana	Gannet	126
Syrmaticus reevesii	Reeve's Pheasant	121
Tadorna tadorna	Shelduck	127
Tealia felina	Dahlia anemone	128
Trifolium subterraneum	Subterranean Clover	123

Tringa totanus	Redshank	123, 124
Troglodytes troglodytes	Wren	129
Tubularia indivisa		128
Viscum album	Mistletoe	131
Vulpes vulpes	Fox	121, 129

WILDLIFE IN GWENT'S CHURCHES AND CHURCHYARDS

Aglais urticae	Small Tortoiseshell	135
Apis mellifera	Honey Bee	133
Certhyia familiaris	Treecreeper	134
Hedera helix	Ivy	135
Hirundo rustica	Swallow	132
Lasius flavus	Yellow Meadow Ant	134
Orobanche hederae	Ivy Broomrape	135
Parus ater	Coal Tit	134
Quercus X pseudosuber	Lucombe Oak	134
Rhizocarpon geographicum	Map Lichen	134
Scolyopteryx libatrix	Herald Moth	135
Sequoiadendron giganteum	Giant Redwood	134
Sequioa sempervirens	Coast Redwood	134
Taxis baccata	Yew	133
Tilia sp.	lime	133, 134
Troglodytes troglodytes	Wren	134
Tyto alba	Barn Owl	132
Umbilicus rupestris	Navelwort	134
Vespa crabro	Hornet	135

Common Name Index of Species

(By Chapter)

~

PREHISTORY

Badger	Meles meles	15
Bank Vole	Clethrionomys glareolus	15
Bison	Bison bonasus	15
Brown Bear	Ursus arctos	15
Chain Coral	Halycites sp.	14
fossil oyster	Gryphaea incurva	15
fossil 'fish-reptile'	Ichthyosaurus sp.	15
fossil club-moss tree	Lepidodendron sp.	14
fossil coral	Favosites sp.	14
fossil coral	Lithostrotion sp.	14
fossil horse-tail	Calamites sp.	14
fossil Liassic bivalve	Plagiostoma giganteum	15
fossil marine reptile	Plesiosaurus sp.	15
horse	Equus sp.	16
Lion	Felis leo	15
Mammoth	Mammuthus primigenius	15
Mountain Hare	Lepus timidus	15
Red Deer	Cervus elephas	15
Reindeer	Tarandus rangifer	15
Spotted Hyena	Crocuta crocuta	15, 16
Wild Pig	Sus scrofa	15
Wolf	Canis lupus	15
Wood Mouse (Long-tailed Field Mouse)	Apodemus sylvaticus	15
Woolly Rhinoceros	Coelodonta antiquitatis	15

FUNGI

Amethyst Deceiver	Laccaria amethystina	21
Artist's Fungus	Ganoderma applanatum	20
Bark Puffball	Reticularia lycoperdon	19
Bay Bolete	Xerocomus badius	24

Beefsteak Fungus	Fistulina hepatica	20
Birch Bolete	Leccinum scabrum	24
Birch Bracket	Piptoporus betulinus	20
Bird's-nest Fungus	Crucibulum laeve	24
Bird's-nest Fungus	Cyathus olla	24
Bird's-nest Fungus	Cyathus striatus	24
Bitter Bolete	Tylopilus felleus	24
Black Bulgar	Bulgaria inquinans	20
Blackening Russula	Russula nigricans	23
Bleeding Mycena	Mycena haematopus	22
Blushing Bracket	Daedaleopsis confragosa	20
Bonnet Mycena	Mycena galericulata	22
Branched Oyster Mushroom	Pleurotus cornucopiae	21
Brick Cap	Hypholoma sublateritium	23
Brown Cone-cap	Conocybe tenera	23
Brown Roll Rim	Paxillus involutus	24
Brown-stew Fungus	Kuehneromyces mutabilis	23
Butter Cap	Collybia butyracea	21
Candle-snuff Fungus	Xylaria hypoxilon	19
Caterpillar Fungus	Cordyceps militaris	19
Cauliflower Fungus	Sparassis crispa	21
Changeable Melanoleuca	Melanoleuca melaleuca	21
Chanterelle	Cantharellus cibarius	20
Charcoal Burner	Russula cyanoxantha	23
Clouded Clitocybe	Clitocybe nebularis	21
Clustered Tough-shank	Collybia confluens	22
Coconut-scented Milk-cap	Lactarius glyciosmus	23
Common Helvel	Helvella crispa	20
Common Ink-cap	Coprinus atramentarius	22
Common Morel	Morchella esculenta	20
Common Puffball	Lycoperdon perlatum	24
Common Stinkhorn	Phallus impudicus	24
Common Yellow Russula	Russula ochroleuca	23
Conical Waxcap	Hygrocybe conica	21
Coral Fungus	Hericium flagellum	20
Coral Spot Fungus	Nectria cinnabarina	19
Cramp Ball	Daldinia concentrica	19
Dead Man's Fingers	Xylaria polymorpha	19
Death Cap	Amanita phalloides	23
Deer Toadstool	Pluteus cervinus	23
Dog Stinkhorn	Mutinus caninus	24
Dove-colour Tricholoma	Tricholoma columbetta	21
Dryad's Saddle	Polyporus squamosus	20
Dryads Club	Clavariadelphus pistillaris	21
Dung-heap Ink-cap	Coprinus cinereus	22
Ear-pick Fungus	Auriscalpium vulgare	20
Early Cup Fungus	Peziza vesiculosa	20

Earth Ball	Scleroderma citrinum	24
Earth Fan	Thelephora terrestris	20
Earth Star	Geastrum triplex	24
Elfin's Saddle	Helvella sulcata	20
Ergot	Claviceps purpurea	19
Eye-lash Fungus	Scutellinia scutellata	20
Fairy-ring Champignon	Marasmius oreades	21
False Chanterelle	Hygrophoropsis aurantiaca	24
False Death Cap	Amanita citrina	22
Field Blewit	Lepista personata	21
Field Mushroom	Agaricus campestris	22
Fly Agaric	Amanita muscaria	23
Fringed Crumble-cap	Psathyrella candolleana	22
Giant Clitocybe	Leucopaxillus giganteus	21
Giant Grifola	Meripilus giganteus	20
Giant Puffball	Langermannia gigantea	24
Glistening Ink-cap	Coprinus micaceus	22
Green Cup Fungus	Chlorocibaria aeruginascens	19
Grisette	Amanita vaginata	23
Herald of Winter	Hygrophorus hypothejus	21
Honey Fungus	Armillaria mellea	21
Horn of Plenty	Craterellus cornucopoides	20
Horse Mushroom	Agaricus arvensis	22
Horse-hair Fungus	Marasmius androsacaceus	21
Jelly Antler	Calocera viscosa	20
Jelly Leaf	Tremella foliacea	20
Jelly Tongue	Pseudohydnum gelatinosum	20
Jew's Ear	Auricularia auricula-judae	20
Larch Bolete	Suillus grevillei	24
Large Crimson Waxcap	Hygrocybe punicea	21
Liberty Caps	Psilocybe semilanceata	23
Lilac mycena	Mycena pura	22
Little Japanese Umbrella	Coprinus plicatilis	22
Little Wheel Toadstool	Marasmius rotula	21
Magpie Ink-cap	Coprinus picaceus	22
Maze Fungus	Daedalea quercina	20
Milk-drop Mycena	Mycena galopus	22
Nut Cup Fungus	Hymenoscyphus fructigenus	19
Oak Milk-cap	Lactarius quietus	24
Orange Birch Bolete	Leccinum versipelle	24
Orange Peel Fungus	Aleuria aurantia	20
Orange Pholiota	Gymnopilus junonius	23
Oyster Mushroom	Pleurotus ostreatus	21
Panther Cap	Amanita pantherina	23
Parasol Mushroom	Macrolepiota procera	22
Parrot Waxcap	Hygrocybe psittacina	21
Penny Bun	Boletus edulis	24

Peppery Bolete	Chalciporus piperatus	24
Pick-a-back Toadstool	Nyctalis parasitica	21
Pig's Ears	Peziza badia	20
Pine Fire Fungus	Rhizina undulata	20
Pink Meadow-cap	Hygrocybe calyptriformis	21
Plums and Custard	Tricholomopsis rutilans	21
Poison Pie	Hebeloma crustuliniforme	23
Porcelain Fungus	Oudemansiella mucida	22
Red-cracked Bolete	Xerocomus chrysenteron	24
Roman Shield Entoloma	Entoloma clypeatum	23
Rooting Shank	Oudemansiella radicata	22
Rose-gilled Grisette	Volvariella gloiocephala	23
Rufous Milk-cap	Lactarius rufus	23
Russet Tough-shank	Collybia dryophila	22
Saffron Milk-cap	Lactarius deliciosus	23
Saffron Parasol	Cystoderma amianthinum	22
Scarlet Elf Cup	Sarcoscypha coccinea	20
Scarlet Waxcap	Hygrocybe coccinea	21
Sea-green Russula	Russula virescens	23
Shaggy Ink-cap	Coprinus comatus	22
Shaggy Parasol	Macrolepiota rhacodes	22
Shaggy Pholiota	Pholiota squarrosa	23
Shaggy Polypore	Inonotus hispidus	20
Shining Ganoderma	Ganoderma lucidum	20
Slender Parasol	Macrolepiota gracilenta	22
Slippery Jack	Suillus luteus	24
Small Bleeding Mycena	Mycena sanguinolenta	22
Snowy Ink-cap	Coprinus niveus	22
Snowy Waxcap	Hygrocybe nivea	21
Soft Slipper Toadstool	Crepidotus mollis	23
Spindle Shank	Collybia fusipes	21
Spiny Puffball	Lycoperdon echinatum	24
Spotted Tough-Shank	Collybia maculata	21
St. George's Mushroom	Calocybe gambosa	21
Steely-stemmed Mycena	Mycena polygramma	22
Stinking Parasol	Lepiota cristata	22
Straight-branched Coral	Ramaria stricta	21
Stump Puffball	Lycoperdon pyriforme	24
Sulphur Polypore	Laetiporus sulphureus	20
Sulphur Tricholoma	Tricholoma sulphureum	21
Sulphur Tuft	Hypholoma fasiculare	23
Sweet Milk-cap	Lactarius subdulcis	24
Sweinitz's Polypore	Phaeolus sweinitzii	20
Tawny Grissette	Amanita fulva	23
The Blusher	Amanita rubescens	23
The Deceiver	Laccaria laccata	21
The Goblet	Pseudoclitocybe cyathiformis	21

The Miller	Clitopilus prunulus	23
Tripe Fungus	Auricularia mesenterica	20
Trooping Crumble-cap	Coprinus disseminatus	22
Twig Marasmius	Marasmius ramealis	21
Velvet Shank	Flammulina velutipes	22
Verdigris Agaric	Stropharia aeruginosa	23
Watery Psathyrella	Psathyrella hydrophilum	22
Weeping Widow	Psathyrella lacrymabunda	22
White Spindles	Clavaria vermicularis	21
Winter Polypore	Polyporus brumalis	20
Witches Butter	Exidia glandulosa	20
Wood Blewit	Lepista nuda	21
Wood Hedgehog	Hydnum repandum	20
Wood Mushroom	Agaricus silvaticus	22
Wood Mushroom	Agaricus silvicola	22
Wood Woolly-foot	Collybia peronata	21
Woolly Milk-cap	Lactarius torminosus	23
Yellow Brain Fungus	Tremella mesenterica	20
Yellow Dung-cap	Bolbitius vitellinus	23
Yellow Stainer	Agaricus xanthoderma	22
Yellow Stereum	Stereum hirsutum	20
Yellow-cracked Bolete	Xerocomus subtomentosus	24
Yellow-stemmed Mycena	Mycena epipterygia	22
Zoned Bracket	Trametes versicolor	20

PLANTS

Adder	Vipera berus	33
Almond Willow	Salix triandra	29
Alternate-leaved Golden-saxifrage	Chrysoplenium alternifolium	26
Amaranth	Amaranthus sp.	34
Annual Mercury	Mercurialis annua	33
Annual Sea-blite	Suaeda maritima	31
Arrowhead	Sagittaria sagittifolia	29
Autumn Lady's-tresses	Spiranthes spiralis	32
Barn Owl	Tyto alba	33
Bee Orchid	Ophrys apifera	32
Bell Heather	Erica cinerea	26, 28
Bewick's Swan	Cygnus bewickii	31
Bilberry	Vaccinium myrtillus	26, 27, 28
Bird Cherry	Prunus padus	27
Bird's-foot Clover	Trifolium ornithopodioides	30
Bird's-nest Orchid	Neottia nidus-avis	32
Bitter Vetch	Lathyrus linifolius	26
Black Poplar	Populus nigra Ssp. betulifolia	28
Blackthorn	Prunus spinosa	29

Bladder Wrack	Fucus vesiculosus	31
Bog Pimpernel	Anagallis tenella	26
Brackish Water-crowfoot	Ranunculus baudotii	30
Branched Bur-reed	Sparganium erectum	29
Brent Goose	Branta bernicula	31
Bristly Ox-tongue	Picris echioides	29
Brookweed	Samous valerandi	30
Brown Sedge	Carex disticha	30
Bugloss	Anchusa arvensis	28
Canadian Fleabane	Conyza canadensis	33
Climbing Corydalis	Ceratocapnos claviculata	28
Common Butterwort	Pinguicula vulgaris	27
Common Cord-grass	Spartina anglica	31
Common Cow-wheat	Melampyrum pratense	33
Common Meadow-rue	Thalictrum flavum	28
Common Reed	Phragmites australis	29
Common Rock-rose	Helianthemum nummularium	33
Common Saltmarsh-grass	Puccinellia maritima	30
Common Sea-lavender	Limonium vulgare	31
Corn Marigold	Chrysanthemum segetum	34
Corn Spurrey	Spergula arvensis	34
Cowberry	Vaccinium vitis-idaea	27
Cowslip	Primula veris	32
Cross-leaved Heath	Erica tetralix	26, 28
Crowberry	Empetrum nigrum	26, 27
Curled Pondweed	Potamogeton crispus	29
Cyperus Sedge	Carex pseudocyperus	29
Daffodil	Narcissus pseudo-narcissus Ssp.pseudonarcissus	28
Dame's-violet	Hesperis matronalis	28
Deadly Nightshade	Atropa belladonna	28
Deergrass	Trichophorum cespitosum	27
Dittander	Lepidium latifolium	31
Dwarf Elder	Sambucus ebulus	26
Dwarf Mallow	Malva neglecta	34
Dwarf Spurge	Euphorbia exigua	34
Dwarf Thistle	Cirsium acaule	32
Early-purple Orchid	Orchis mascula	32
Eelgrass	Zostera sp.	31
English Scurvygrass	Cochlearia anglica	31
Field Woundwort	Stachys arvensis	28
Fingered Sedge	Carex digitata	28
Floating Club-rush	Eleogiton fluitans	29
Flowering-rush	Butomus umbellatus	29
Fool's Water-cress	Apium nodiflorum	29
Frogbit	Hydrocharis morsus-ranae	29
Giant Bellflower	Campanula latifolia	28

Giant Butterbur	Petasites japonicus	28
Giant Hogweed	Heracleum mantegazzianum	28
Good-King-Henry	Chenopodium bonus-henricus	34
Great Burnet	Sanguisorba officinalis	26
Greater Burdock	Arctium lappa	29
Greater Butterfly-orchid	Plantanthera chlorantha	32
Greater Sea-spurrey	Spergularia media	31
Green Hellebore	Helleborus viridis	32
Green Spleenwort	Asplenium trichomanes-ramosum	27
Green-winged Orchid	Orchis morio	32
Grey Club-rush	Schoenoplectus tabernaemontanii	30
Hard-fern	Blechnum spicant	26
Hare's-foot Clover	Trifolium arvense	33
Hare's-tail Cottongrass	Eriophorum vaginatum	27
Harebell	Campanula rotundifolia	26
Hawthorn	Crataegus monogyna	29, 30
Heath Cudweed	Gnaphalium sylvaticum	28
Heath Rush	Juncus squarrosus	27
Heather	Caluna vulgaris	26, 27, 28
Herb Paris	Paris quadrifolia	32
Hoary Ragwort	Senecio erucifolius	29
Hornbeam	Carpinus betulus	28
Ivy	Hedra helix	29
Ivy Broomrape	Orobanche hederae	29
Ivy-leaved Bellflower	Wahlenbergia hederacea	26
Knotted Hedge-parsley	Torilis nodosa	30
Knotted Wrack	Ascophyllum nodosum	31
Ladies Bedstraw	Galium Verum	32
Large-flowered Evening-primrose	Oenothera glazoviana	33
Lesser Butterfly-orchid	Plantanthera bifolia	32
Lesser Sea-spurrey	Spergularia marina	31
Lesser Skullcap	Scutellaria minor	26
Lily-of-the-valley	Convallaria majalis	32
Marsh St.John's-wort	Hypericum elodes	26
Marsh Violet	Viola palustris	32
Marsh-mallow	Althaea officinalis	31
Mat-grass	Nardus stricta	27
Meadow Barley	Hordeum secalinum	31
Meadow Clary	Salvia pratensis	32
Meadow Saxifrage	Saxifraga granulata	28
Meadow Thistle	Cirsium dissectum	30
Monkeyflower	Mimulus guttatus	28
Moutain Melick	Melica nutans	28
Narrow-leaved Bird's-foot-trefoil	Lotus glaber	30
New Zealand Willowherb	Epilobium brunnescens	33
Nightingale	Luscinia megarynchos	33
Oxford Ragwort	Senecio squalidus	33

Pale St.John's-wort	Hypericum montanum	32
Pale Toadflax	Linaria repens	33
Petty Whin	Genista anglica	26
Pineapple-weed	Matricaria discoidea	34
Pink Purslane	Claytonia sibirica	28
Purple Moor-grass	Molinia caerulea	27
Pyramidal Orchid	Anacamptis pyramidalis	32, 33
Rosy Footman Moth	Miltochrista miniata	33
Round-leaved Fluellen	Kicksia spuria	34
Round-leaved Sundew	Drosera rotundifolia	27
Salsify	Tragopogon porrifolius	29
Saltmarsh Rush	Juncus gerardii	30
Saw Wrack	Fucus serratus	31
Saw-wort	Serratula tinctoria	32, 33
Sea Arrowgrass	Triglochin maritimum	31
Sea Aster	Aster tripolium	31
Sea Barley	Hordeum marinum	31
Sea Beet	Beta vulgaris Ssp. maritima	30
Sea Clover	Trifolium squamosum	30
Sea Couch	Elytrigia atherica	31
Sea Plantain	Plantago maritima	31
Sea Radish	Raphanus raphanistrum Ssp. maritimus	30
Sea Rush	Juncus maritimus	31
Sea Stork's-bill	Erodium maritimum	33
Sea Wormwood	Seriphidium maritimum	30
Sea-milkwort	Glaux maritima	31
Sharp-leaved Fluellen	Kicksia elatime	34
Sheep's-bit	Jasione montana	26, 28
Slender Hare's-ear	Bupleurum tenuissimum	31
Slender St.Johns-wort	Hypericum pulchrum	28
Slender Thistle	Cirsium tenuiflorus	30
Small Nettle	Urtica urens	34
Small Teasel	Dipsacus pilosus	28
Sneezewort	Achillea ptarmica	28
Soapwort	Saponaria officinalis	28
Spreading Bellflower	Campanula patula	28
Sticky Groundsel	Senecio viscosus	33
Stiff Saltmarsh-grass	Puccinellia rupestris	30
Stinking Hellebore	Helleborus foetidus	32
Stone Parsley	Sison ammomum	30
Strawberry Clover	Trifolium fragiferum	31
Sweet Cicely	Myrrhis odorata	27
Thorn-apple	Datura stramonium	33
Thrift	Armeria maritima	31
Trailing St.John's-wort	Hypericum humifusum	28
Tree-mallow	Lavatera arborea	31
Tutsan	Hypericum androsaemum	32

Unbranched Bur-reed	Sparganium emersum	28
Upright Spurge	Euphorbia serrulata	32
Viper's-bugloss	Echium vulgare	33
Water Avens	Geum rivale	27
Water Dock	Rumex hydrolapathum	29
Water Fern	Azolla filiculoides	29
Weasel's-snout	Misopates orontium	34
Whorl-grass	Catabrosa aquatica	29
Wigeon	Anas penelope	31
Wild Celery	Apium graveolens	31
Wild Madder	Rubia peregrina	33
Wild Migonette	Reseda lutea	33
Wild Parsnip	Pastinaca sativa var. sylvestris	29
Wood Barley	Hordelymus europaeus	31
Wood Bitter-vetch	Vicia orobus	26
Wood Fescue	Festuca altissima	28
Wood Millet	Milium effusum	31
Wood Sage	Teucrium scorodonia	26
Wood Speedwell	Veronica montana	31
Wood Spurge	Euphorbia amygdaloides	31
Wood Vetch	Vicia sylvatica	31
Woolly Thistle	Cirsium eriophorum	27
Yellow Iris	Iris pseudacorus	29
Yellow-rattle	Rhinanthus minor	32

INVERTEBRATES

acorn-barnacle	Balanus balanoides	41
Alder Moth	Acronicta alni	46
amber snail	Succinea sp.	38
Baltic Tellin	Macoma balthica	39
Bee Beetle	Trichius fasciatus	51
bee-fly	Bombylius major	47
Bird-cherry Ermine	Yponomeuta evonymella	55
Black Garden Ant	Lasius niger	49
Black Rhinoceros Beetle	Sinodendron cylindricum	50
Black Sympetrum	Sympetrum scoticum	42
Bloody-nosed Beetle	Timarcha tenebricosa	53
Brandling Worm	Eisenia foetida	40
Broad-bordered Yellow Underwing	Noctua fimbriata	46
Broom Moth	Ceramica pisi	46
Brown Argus	Aricia agestis	44
Brown House Moth	Hofmannophila pseudospretella	45
bumble-bee	Bombus terrestris	50
Burnet Companion	Euclidia glyphica	46
Camberwell Beauty	Nymphalis antipoa	44

Cardinal Beetle	Pyrochroa coccinea	52
Cave Spider	Meta menardi	54
Chimney Sweeper	Odezia atrata	47
Clouded Magpie Moth	Abraxas sylvata	47
Cobweb Spider	Pholcus phalangioides	53
Common Cockle	Cerastoderma edule	39
Common Cockroach	Blatta orientalis	43
Common Crayfish	Astacus pallipes	41
Common Forester	Adscita statices	45
Common Ground-hopper	Tetrix undulata	42
Common Jellyfish	Aurelia aurita	37
Common Limpet	Patella vulgata	37
Common Louse-fly	Ornithomyia avicularia	48
Common Mussel	Mytilus edulis	39
Common Periwinkle	Littorina littorea	37
Common Shrimp	Crangon crangon	41
Common Wasp	Vespula vulgaris	49
Copper Underwing	Amphipyra pyramidea	46
Crab Spider	Misumena vatia	54
crane-fly	Tipula sp.	58
Cuttlefish	Sepia officinalis	39
Dahlia Anemone	Tealia felina	37
Dark Bush-cricket	Pholidoptera griseoaptera	42
Dark Green Fritillary	Mesoacidalia aglaja	44
Death-watch Beetle	Xestobium rufovillosum	52
Devil's Coach-horse	Staphylinus olens	50
Dingy Skipper	Erynnis tages	45
dor beetle	Geotrupes sp.	51
Double-banded Rhagium	Rhagium bifasciatum	52
Down-looker Fly	Rhagio scolopacea	47
Duck Mussel	Anodonta anatina	39
Ear Snail	Limnaea auricularia	38
Emperor Dragonfly	Anax imperator	42
Estuarine Prawn	Palaemonetes varians	41
Estuarine Ragworm	Neanthes diversicolor	40
Eyed Ladybird	Anatis ocellata	52
Fairy Shrimp	Chirocephala diaphanus	41
false scorpion	Lamprochernes	53
Flat Winkle	Littorina littoralis	37
fleshfly	Sarcophaga sp.	58
Garden Spider	Araneus diadematus	55
German Wasp	Vespula germanica	49
Giant Wood-wasp	Uroceras gigas	48
Glow-worm	Lampyris noctiluca	51, 56
grass-twist spider	Clubiona sp.	54
Grayling Butterfly	Hipparchis semele	44
Great Diving Beetle	Dytiscus marginalis	53

Great Green Bush-cricket	Tettigonia viridissima	42
Great Pond Snail	Limnaea stagnalis	38
Great Ramshorn Snail	Planorbis corneus	38
Great Silver Beetle	Hydrophilus piceus	53
Green Hairstreak	Callophrys rubi	44
Green Silver-lines	Pseudoips fagana	46
Green Tiger Beetle	Cicindela campestris	50
Grizzled Skipper	Pyrgus malvae	45
Hawthorn Saw-fly	Trichiosoma tibiale	48
Herald Moth	Scoliopteryx libatrix	46
Hermit Crab	Pagurus bernhardus	41
Honeybee	Apis mellifera	50, 57
Hornet	Vespa crabro	49, 56, 57
Hornet Robber-fly	Asilus crabroniformis	47, 57, 58
Horse Leech	Haemopis sanguisuga	40
House Cricket	Acheta domesticus	43
house spider	Tegenaria sp.	54
Jet-black Ant	Lasius fuliginosus	49
Lapidary Snail	Helicigona lapicida	39
Larch-leaf Miner	Coleophora laricella	45
Large Red Caddis-fly	Phryganea grandis	47
Laver Spire Snail	Hydrobia ulvae	38
Lesser Stag Beetle	Dorcus parallelipipedus	51
Long-bodied Water-scorpion	Ranatra linearis	43
Lug-worm	Arenicloa marina	40
May-fly	Ephemera danica	42
Meadow Grasshopper	Chorthippus parallelelus	58
Meal moth	Pyralis farinalis	45
Medicinal Leech	Hirudo medicinalis	40
Minotaur Beetle	Typhaeus typhoeus	51
money spider	Linyphia sp.	55
Norwegian Wasp	Dolichovespula norvegica	49
Oak Bush-cricket	Meconema thalassinum	42
Oak Eggar	Lasiocampa quercus	45
Oak-leaf Roller-moth	Tortrix viridana	45
oil beetle	Meloe sp.	52
Orange Underwing	Archieris parthenias	46
Peppery Furrow-shell	Scrobicularia plana	39
Pill Millipede	Glomeris sp.	53
Pill Woodlouse	Armadillidium vulgare	41
Pine Weevil	Hylobius abietis	53
Purple Hairstreak	Quercusia quercus	44
Ramshorn Snail	Planorbis planorbis	38
Red Wasp	Vespula rufa	49
River Limpet	Ancylus fluviatilis	38
River Snail	Viviparus viviparus	38
Rough Winkle	Littorina saxatilis	38

Round-mouthed Snail	Pomatias elegans	38
ruby-tail wasp	Chrysis sp.	49
Saucer Bug	Ilyocaris cimicoides	43
Scorpion-fly	Panorpa communis	44
Sea Slater	Ligia oceanica	41
Shingle Spider	Arctosa cinerea	54
Shore Crab	Carcinas maenas	41
Short-winged Cone-head	Conocephalus dorsalis	42
Silurian	Eriopygodes imbecilla	46
Silverfish	Lepisma saccharina	42
Slender Ground-hopper	Tetrix subulata	42
Small Eggar	Eriogaster lanestris	46
Small Pearl-bordered Fritillary	Clossinana euphrosyne	44
Speckled Bush-cricket	Leptophyes punctatissima	42
Spindle Ermine	Yponomeuta cagnatella	56
Spitting Spider	Scytodes thoracica	54
Stable Fly	Stomoxys calcitrans	48
Stag Beetle	Lucanus cervus	51
Steel-blue Wood-wasp	Sirex noctilio	48
Summer (July) Chafer	Amphimallon solstitialis	51
Swallow-tail Moth	Ourapteryx sambucaria	47
Swan Mussel	Anodonta cygnea	39
Tanner Beetle	Prionus coriarius	52
Tissue Moth	Triphosa dubitata	46
Tortoise Beetle	Cassida rubiginosa	53
Tree Wasp	Dolichovespula sylvestris	49
Upland Click-beetle	Ctenicera cuprea	51
Violet Ground Beetle	Carabus violaceus	50
Wandering Snail	Limnaea peregra	38
Warble Fly	Hypoderma bovis	48
Wasp Beetle	Clytus arietis	52
Water Cricket	Velia caprai	43
water flea	Daphnia sp.	40
Water Louse	Asellus aquaticus	41
Water Scorpion	Nepa cinerea	43
Whelk	Buccinium undatum	38
White Admiral	Limenitis camilla	44
White-legged Damselfly	Platycnemis pennipes	42
White-letter Hairstreak	Strymonidia w-album	44
White-shouldered House-moth	Endrosis sarcitrella	45
Whiteweed	Sertularia cupressina	37
Wood Ant	Formica rufa	49
Wood Leopard Moth	Zeuzera pyrina	45
Yellow Meadow Ant	Lasius flavus	49
Zebra Spider (Zebra Wall Spider)	Salticus scenicus	54

FISH

Angler Fish	Lophius piscatorius	63
Bass	Dicentrarchus labrax	63
Bib	Trisopterus luscus	63
Brook Lamprey	Lampetra planeri	65
Bullhead	Cottus gobio	66
Carp	Cyprinus carpio	66
Chub	Leuciscus cephalus	66
Cod	Gadus morrhua	63
Common Bream	Abramis brama	66
Common Eel	Anguilla anguilla	64
Common Goby	Pomatoschistus microps	63
Conger Eel	Conger conger	62
Dace	Leuciscus leuciscus	65
Flounder	Platichthys flesus	65
Grayling	Thymallus thymallus	65
Great Pipefish	Sygnathus acus	62
Gudgeon	Gobio gobio	66
Hake	Merluccius merluccius	63
Minnow	Phoxinus phoxinus	66
Perch	Perca fluviatilis	66
Pike	Esox lucius	65
Rainbow Trout	Salmo gairdneri	65
Red Gurnard	Aspitrigia cuculus	63
Roach	Rutilus rutilus	65
Rudd	Scardinius erythrophthalmus	66
Salmon	Salmo salar	64
Sea Lamprey	Petromyzon marinus	64
Sea Snail	Liparis liparis	63
Skate	Raja batis	62
Sole	Solea solea	63
Stone Loach	Noemacheilus barbatulus	66
Sturgeon	Acipenser sturio	64
Sunfish	Mola mola	63
Swordfish	Xiphias gladius	63
Ten-spined Stickleback	Pugnitius pugnitius	65
Tench	Tinca tinca	66
Thin-lipped Grey Mullet	Liza ramada	63
Thorn-back Ray	Raja clavata	62
Three-bearded Rockling	Gaidropsarus vulgaris	63
Three-spined Stickleback	Gasterosteus aculeatus	64
Trout	Salmo trutta	64, 65
Twaite Shad	Alosa fallax	64
Whiting	Merlangius merlangus	63

AMPHIBIANS AND REPTILES

Adder	Vipera berus	68, 71, 72
Common Frog	Rana temporia	68, 70
Common Lizard	Lacerta vivipara	68, 71
Common Toad	Bufo bufo	68, 79
Grass Snake	Natrix natrix	68, 71
Great Crested Newt	Triturus cristatus	68, 69, 70
Palmate Newt	Triturus helveticus	68, 69
Ragwort	Senecio jacobaeae	70
Slow-worm	Anguis fragilis	68, 70, 71
Smooth Newt	Triturus vulgaris	68, 69, 70
Yellow Meadow Ant	Lasius flavus	69

BIRDS

American Bittern	Botaurus lentiginosus	80
Badger	Meles meles	77
Barn Owl	Tyto alba	85, 86
Bewick's Swan	Cygnus bewickii	78, 92, 93
Black-tailed Godwit	Limosa limosa	92, 93
Brambling	Fringilla montifringilla	91
Canada Goose	Branta Canadensis	78
Carrion Crow	Corvus corone	88, 89
Chaffinch	Fringilla coelebs	87, 88, 91
Collared Dove	Streptopelia decaocto	82, 83
Coot	Fulica atra	75
Cormorant	Phalacrocorax carbo	74
Cuckoo	Cuculus canorus	84
Dunlin	Calidris alpina	86, 92, 93
Fat-hen	Chenopodium album	91
Firecrest	Regulus ignicapillus	87, 88
Fox	Vulpes vulpes	77
Garganey	Anas querquedula	75, 76, 92
Goldfinch	Carduelis carduelis	91
Goshawk	Accipiter gentilis	79
Grasshopper Warbler	Locustella naevia	87
Greenfinch	Carduelis chloris	91
Grey Heron (Heron)	Ardea cinerea	74
Ivy	Hedera helix	88
Kestrel	Falco tinnuculus	85
Knot	Calidris canutus	86, 93
Lapwing	Vanellus vanellus	81, 82, 92
Lesser Whitethroat	Sylvia curruca	93
Linnet	Carduelis cannabina	91
Little Owl	Athene noctua	85, 86, 92

Mallard	Anas platyrhynchos	92
Meadow Popit	Anthus pratensis	92
Mute Swan	Cygnus olor	78
Nightingale	Luscinia megarhynchos	89, 90
Oystercatcher	Haematopus ostralegus	81
Partridge	Perdix perdix	79, 80, 92
Pintail	Anas acuta	92, 93
Raven	Corvus corax	79
Redpoll	Carduelis flammea	91
Redshank	Tringa totanus	81, 92, 93
Ringed Plover	Charadrius hiaticula	93
Rook	Corvus frugilegus	88
Ruddy Shelduck	Tadorna ferruginea	77
Scot's Pine	Pinus sylvestris	88
Shelduck	Tadorna tadorna	76, 92, 93
Short-eared Owl	Asio flammeus	85
Short-tailed Vole	Microtus agrestis	85, 86
Shoveler	Anas clypeata	92, 93
Siskin	Carduelis spinus	91
Skylark	Alauda arvensis	92
Snipe	Gallinago gallinago	82, 92, 93
Stoat	Mustela erminea	85
Stonechat	Saxicola torquata	92
Tawny Owl	Strix aluco	86
Teal	Anas crecca	92
Tree Sparrow	Passer montanus	89, 91, 92
Tufted Duck	Aythya fuligula	92
Turnstone	Arenaria interpres	93
Turtle Dove	Stretopelia turtur	83, 84
Water Rail	Rallus aquaticus	80
Weasel	Mustela nivalis	85
Whooper Swan	Cygnus cygnus	78
Widgeon	Anas penelope	92
Woodcock	Scolopax rusticola	82
Woodpigeon	Columba palumbus	83
Yellow Wagtail	Motacilla flava	92, 93

MAMMALS

Badger	Meles meles	107
Bank Vole	Clethrionomys glareolus	106
Barbastelle Bat	Barbastellus barbastellus	106
Brandt's Bat	Myotis brandtii	106
Brown Hare	Lepus europaeus	98, 99
Brown Rat	Rattus norvegicus	107
Clematis (Traveller's Joy)	Clematis vitalba	101

Common (Green) Eel	Anguilla anguilla	104
Common Dolphin	Delphinus delphis	97
Common Long-eared Bat	Plecotus auritus	106
Common seal	Phoca vitulina	108
Common Shrew	Sorex araneus	106
Daubenton's Bat	Myotis daubentonii	106
Dormouse	Muscardinus avellanarius	100, 101, 102
Fallow Deer	Dama dama	105
Ferret	Mustela furo	103
Field Vole (Short-tailed Vole)	Microtus agrestis	107
Grand Fir	Abies grandis	101
Greater Horseshoe Bat	Rhinolophus ferrumequinum	97, 98
Grey Heron	Ardea cinerea	100
Grey Seal	Halichoerus grypus	97
Grey Squirrel	Sciurus carolinensis	106
Harvest Mouse	Micromys minutus	107
Hedgehog	Erinaceus europaeus	106
Honeysuckle	Lonicera periclymenum	101
House Mouse	Mus musculus	107
House sparrow	Passer domesticus	103
July Chafer	Amphimallon solstitialis	98
larch	Larix sp.	101
Lawson Cypress	Chamaecyparis lawsoniana	101
Lesser Horseshoe Bat	Rhinolophus hipposideros	97, 98
Lesser Rorqual (Minke Whale)	Balaenoptera acutorostrata	107
Mink	Mustela vison	100, 104, 105, 107
Mole	Talpa europaea	106
Muntjac	Muntiacus reevsi	108
Natterer's Bat	Myotis nattereri	106
Noctule	Nyctalus noctula	98
Norway Spruce	Picea abies	101
Otter	Lutra lutra	108
Pipistrelle	Pipistrellus pipistrellus	106
Polecat	Mustela putorius	103, 104
Porpoise	Phocoena phocoena	97
Pygmy Shrew	Sorex minutus	106
Rabbit	Oryctolagus cuniculus	98, 99, 103
Red Fox (Fox)	Vulpes vulpes	107
Red Squirrel	Sciurus vulgaris	97
Scot's Pine	Pinus sylvestris	101
Sei Whale	Balaenoptera borealis	107
Serotine Bat	Eptesicus serotinus	106
Steppe Polecat	Mustela eversmanni	103
Stoat	Mustela erminea	102, 103
Water Shrew	Neomys fodiens	106
Water Vole	Arvicola terrestris	99, 100
Weasel	Mustela nivalis	102, 103

Whiskered Bat	Myotis mystacinus	106
Wild Garlic (Ramsons)	Allium ursinum	102
Wood Mouse	Apodemus sylvaticus	100, 107
Yellow-necked Mouse	Apodemus flavicollis	100, 107

DIARY FOR WINTER 1962/1963

Barn Owl	Tyto alba	115, 116
Blue Tit	Parus caeruleus	112
Brown Hare	Lepus europaeus	113
Chaffinch	Fringilla coelebs	113, 114, 118
Coal Tit	Parus ater	112
Dunnock (Hedge Accentor)	Prunella modularis	118
Fieldfare	Turdus pilaris	112, 119
Great Spotted Woodpecker	Dendrocopos major	115, 116
Great Tit	Parus major	112
Green Woodpecker	Picus viridis	114
Greenfinch	Carduelis chloris	113
Lapwing	Vanellus vanellus	119
Long-tailed Tit	Aegithalos caudatus	112
Mole	Talpa europaea	119
Mute Swan	Cygnus olor	115
Redwing	Turdus iliacus	112, 114
Skylark	Alauda arvensis	114
Snipe	Gallinago gallinago	115
Song Thrush	Turdus philomenos	118
Sparrow Hawk	Accipiter nisus	114
Stock Dove	Columba oenas	114, 115
Tree Sparrow	Passer montanus	113, 114
Water Vole	Arvicola terrestris	119
White-fronted Goose	Anser albifrons	113, 115, 116, 118
Woodpigeon	Columba palumbus	113, 114, 116
Yellow Bunting	Emberiza citrinella	113

SELECTED NOTES FROM THE DIARIES

Beech	Fagus syvatica	131
Bittern	Botaurus stellaris	130
Black-headed Gull	Larus ridibundus	124
Brown Argus	Aricia agestis	127
Brown Hare	Lepus europaeus	120
Brown Rat	Rattus norvegicus	125
Cave Spider	Meta menardi	124
Clematis (Traveller's Joy)	Clematis vitalba	129
Clouded Yellow	Coleus croceus	120

Coal Tit	Parus ater	129
Common Cockroach	Blatta orientalis	125
Common Jellyfish	Aurelia aurita	121
Convolvulus Hawkmoth	Agrius convolvuli	130
Corn Crake	Crex crex	125
Crossbill (Common Crossbill)	Loxia curvirostra	120
Cut-leaved selfheal	Prunella laciniata	123
Cuttlefish (Common Cuttlefish)	Sepia officinalis	127
Dahlia anemone	Tealia felina	128
Dormouse	Muscardinus avellanarius	120, 129
Dowitcher	Limnodromus sp.	123, 124
Drinker Moth	Philudoria potatoria	128
Elver (Common Eel)	Anguilla anguilla	129
Fox	Vulpes vulpes	121, 129
Frog (Common Frog)	Rana temporia	123
Gannet	Sula bassana	126
Giant Redwood	Sequoiadendron giganteum	129
Golden Pheasant	Chrysolophus pictus	121
Grey Phalarope	Phalaropus fulicarius	126
Gudgeon	Gobio gobio	131
Harvest Mouse	Micromys minutus	126
Hawthorn	Crataegus monogyna	120
Herald Moth	Scoliopteryx libatrix	124
High Brown Fritillary	Argynnis adippe	120
Hornet Robberfly	Asilus crabroniformis	127
Jay	Garrulus glandarius	129
Kittiwake	Rissa tridactyla	129
Larch-leaf Miner-moth	Coleophora laricella	127
Leach's Petrel	Oceanodroma leucorhoa	130
Llama	Lama peruana	121
Marsh Warbler	Acrocephalus palustris	125
Minnow	Phoxinus phoxinus	131
Mistletoe	Viscum album	131
Norway Spruce	Picea abies	126
Oak Fern	Gymnocarpium dryopteris	125
Otter	Lutra lutra	131
Peacock (Blue Peafowl)	Pavo cristatus	121
Pedunculate Oak	Quercus robur	131
Pike	Esox lucius	125
Rabbit	Oryctolagus cuniculus	120
Raccoon	Procyon lotor	121
Raven	Corvus corax	123
Red Deer	Cervus elephas	121
Redshank	Tringa totanus	123, 124
Reeve's Pheasant	Syrmaticus reevesii	121
Rudolphi's Rorqual (Sei Whale)	Balaenoptera borealis	122
Sand Martin	Riparia riparia	122

Sea Snail	Liparis sp.	128
Shelduck	Tadorna tadorna	127
Silver-washed Fritillary	Argynnis paphia	120
Spoonbill	Platalea leucorodia	125
Starling	Sturnus vulgaris	123, 127, 128
Subterranean Clover	Trifolium subterraneum	123
Sun Bear	Helarctos malayanus	121
Swallow	Hirundo rustica	128
Swan Mussel	Anodonta cygnea	124
Tawny Owl	Strix aluco	120
Thorn-apple	Datura stramonium	125
Toad (Common Toad)	Bufo bufo	123
Tree Creeper	Certhia familiaris	129
Trout	Salmo trutta	131
Weasel	Mustela nivalis	128
Whimbrel	Numenius phaeopus	130
White-letter Hairstreak	Strymonidia w-album	120
Whiteweed	Sertularia cupressina	128
Wild Cherry	Prunus avium	129
Wren	Troglodytes troglodytes	129
Yellow Wagtail	Motacilla flava	128

WILDLIFE IN GWENT'S CHURCHES AND CHURCHYARDS

Barn Owl	Tyto alba	132
Coal Tit	Parus ater	134
Coast Redwood	Sequioa sempervirens	134
Lucombe Oak	Quercus x pseudosuber	134
Giant Redwood	Sequoiadendron giganteum	134
Herald Moth	Scolyopteryx libatrix	135
Honey Bee	Apis mellifera	133
Hornet	Vespa crabro	135
Ivy	Hedera helix	135
Ivy Broomrape	Orobanche hederae	135
lime	Tilia sp.	133, 134
Map Lichen	Rhizocarpon geographicum	134
Navelwort	Umbilicus rupestris	134
Small Tortoiseshell	Aglais urticae	135
Swallow	Hirundo rustica	132
Treecreeper	Certhyia familiaris	134
Wren	Troglodytes troglodytes	134
Yellow Meadow Ant	Lasius flavus	134
Yew	Taxis baccata	133